Student Support and Benefits Handbook: England, Wales and Northern Ireland

6th edition

David Malcolm

Child Poverty Action Group

CPAG promotes action for the prevention and relief of poverty among children and families with children. To achieve this, CPAG aims to raise awareness of the causes, extent, nature and impact of poverty, and strategies for its eradication and prevention; bring about positive policy changes for families with children in poverty; and enable those eligible for income maintenance to have access to their full entitlement. If you are not already supporting us, please consider making a donation, or ask for details of our membership schemes, training courses and publications.

Published by Child Poverty Action Group
94 White Lion Street, London N1 9PF
Tel: 020 7837 7979
staff@cpag.org.uk
www.cpag.org.uk

A CIP record for this book is available from the British Library

ISBN: 978 1 906076 18 4

Child Poverty Action Group is a charity registered in England and Wales (registration number 294841) and in Scotland (registration number SC039339), and is a company limited by guarantee, registered in England (registration number 1993854). VAT number: 690 808117

Cover design by Devious Designs
Typeset by David Lewis XML Associates Ltd
Printed in the UK by CPI William Clowes Beccles NR34 7TL
Cover photo by Steve Eason/Photofusion

The author

David Malcolm is the Head of Social Policy at NUS, responsible for its work on student finance, student welfare and equalities. He has worked in student welfare for 12 years, including a year as the sabbatical Vice President Welfare at the University of Strathclyde Students' Association.

Acknowledgements

The author would particularly like to thank Lindsey Fidler, Jayne Aldridge, Jeanette Jones and Carolyn George for their work on previous editions of this *Handbook*.

Grateful thanks are due to Keith Houghton, John Caldwell, Jayne Aldridge, Kelly Hayworth, Elaine Robinson, Gareth Davies, Sarah Wayman, Angela Toal and Barry Hansford for lending their time and expertise in checking and advising on this *Handbook*.

Many thanks also go to Judith Paterson for providing a framework for developing this *Handbook* in England, Wales and Northern Ireland.

For her swift and efficient editing and production management, thanks go to Alison Key. Thanks also to Paulette Storey for producing the index and Paula McDiarmid for proofreading the text.

Finally, thanks to the staff at the Department for Innovation, Universities and Skills, the Department for Work and Pensions, the Department of Health, and the Low Incomes Tax Reform Group for their assistance in verifying information.

The law covered in this book was correct on 1 October 2008 and includes Regulations laid up to this date.

Contents

Foreword

As this, the sixth edition of the *Student Support and Benefits Handbook*, is published, the fight continues to end child poverty and to enable access to a fairly funded education system across the UK.

In 2006, top-up fees were introduced for full-time undergraduate students in England and Northern Ireland, with Wales now following this year. Average graduate debt is set to increase, with students from the lowest socio-economic groups – those that research suggests are most debt averse – likely to leave their studies with debts of up to £20,000 or more. At the same time, funding for adult learners in further education in England has been cut, and many postgraduates struggle to find any funding whatsoever.

Despite the fact that we are a rich country, one in three children in the UK still lives in poverty. Rightly, politicians see education and work as crucial routes out of poverty, and vital to the economic health of the nation. Yet students from the poorest backgrounds are still hugely under-represented in further and higher education, even more so in the elite institutions.

And, although we know that over the last decade there has been a significant improvement – for the first time, the majority of school leavers now continue in education – this expansion does not extend in anywhere near the same proportion to families living in poverty.

Many policies introduced to try and bridge the gap are welcomed: the New Deal; the minimum wage; investment in childcare; increases in child benefit and income support for families; a new tax credits system; and education maintenance allowances. These are the kind of social policies that improve the living standards of poorer families and act as a first step in helping them make the difficult transition into education.

However, low-income students still face formidable barriers to their participation and to their achievement. Students from low-income families tend to have to work more during term time, are able to rely less on family support (both financial and otherwise), and must navigate the ever-changing and quite bewildering student support and social security benefits systems, often with little or no guidance. Recent changes to income support entitlement for lone parents are likely to make matters worse.

Furthermore, when people on low incomes do enter education they tend to follow a more complicated path, taking more breaks, deferring enrolment, and switching, repeating or restarting their courses for non-academic reasons. We know these people are also more likely to drop out or forego opportunities to progress to more advanced courses. All this complicates even further their financial support and adds to the pressures they face in determining their entitlements.

'How will study affect my benefits?' is a key question for anyone who is living on benefits and thinking about going into education. No one can make a decision to start or continue studying without knowing they can support themselves and their family. Good advice is critical. Student support across England, Wales, Northern Ireland and Scotland differs and, as a devolved issue, we can expect differences to remain. Advisers, therefore, need information that relates specifically to the different nations across the UK.

Fair access to education – indeed, education itself – is about much more than money, but clear, relevant information on financial support for students is vital. This is why the NUS is proud to collaborate with CPAG in producing this *Handbook*.

This book covers students in England, Wales and Northern Ireland, complementing CPAG's *Benefits for Students in Scotland Handbook*. It is free to students' unions that affiliate to the NUS, and available to purchase by other interested services. We hope it will aid advisers, act as a tool to help break down barriers and, in the process, help people from disadvantaged backgrounds enter and complete further and higher education courses.

Of course, this *Handbook* is no silver bullet. If the Government is serious about its pledge to eradicate child poverty through education, it must commit seriously on a number of levels: fairer access to student support; increased capacity in the student advice sector; further development in childcare services; a wholesale change in attitude in some of our older and larger educational institutions; a raising of aspirations and achievement in schools in disadvantaged areas; and more resources channeled into our community support services. All remain substantial challenges. The spectre of still higher tuition fees looms, and an increase could have serious consequences for participation in the future.

When we see an entirely equal proportion of people from poor and rich backgrounds entering the higher and further education system we will know that poverty is on its way to being eradicated. Until then, NUS is fully committed to supporting our members, breaking down financial barriers and fighting injustice throughout the education funding system.

NUS would like to thank the author and checkers for their hard work and dedication throughout this project.

Wes Streeting, NUS President
Ama Uzowuru, NUS Vice President Welfare

How to use this *Handbook*

This *Handbook* is intended for those who advise students in England, Wales and Northern Ireland about their entitlement to student support, benefits, tax credits and other financial issues, such as tax and health benefits. It covers both further and higher education.

The *Handbook* covers rules affecting students studying in England, Wales and Northern Ireland who are eligible for support through English, Welsh and Northern Irish funding bodies such as the Department for Innovation, Universities and Skills and the National Assembly for Wales. It does not cover the rules for students getting support from Scotland or elsewhere outside England, Wales or Northern Ireland.

CPAG publishes a companion volume entitled *Benefits for Students in Scotland Handbook*. Details can be found in Appendix 1.

Rates of government support

The *Handbook* is up to date at 1 October 2008 and is intended to be used for the academic year 2008/09.

Rates of student support, benefits and tax credits used are those for the 2008/09 academic year, and where these were available, the 2009/10 academic year. Please note that benefit and tax credit rates are uprated in April 2009 (these rates are usually available from January or February), whereas student support rates are uprated in September 2009.

Definitions

Most full-time students are excluded from benefits – mainly those benefits for which entitlement relies on a means test. There is one set of definitions of 'full-time student' used for means-tested benefits: income support, jobseeker's allowance, housing benefit and council tax benefit. But other definitions are used for council tax, carer's allowance, employment and support allowance and incapacity benefit. And even for the means-tested benefits, some students can claim despite being classed as full time. It is best not to assume that because a student is excluded from one benefit, s/he is excluded from them all. Who counts as a 'full-time student' is explained in detail in the relevant chapters.

Means-testing students

Government support systems do not necessarily treat student income in the same way. Different means tests apply to means-tested benefits, tax credits, health benefits and student support. It is always worth checking across these systems when calculating a student's total entitlement to government support. To help students and their advisers do this, these systems are addressed separately in their respective chapters covering treatment of income.

Structure of the *Handbook*

Part 1 looks at students' entitlement to student support. **Part 2** covers students' entitlement to benefits and tax credits. **Part 3** considers how income affects the amount of benefits or tax credits, with a particular focus on how student support is treated. **Part 4** covers other matters, such as tax and taking time out from studying.

Chapters are footnoted with references to the legal authorities. Where an abbreviation is used in the footnotes or in the text this is explained in Appendix 3 and on pxiv. If you are appealing against a benefit or tax credit decision, you may want to refer to the law. Appendix 1 suggests where you can obtain copies of Acts, Regulations and caselaw.

Your feedback counts

NUS and CPAG hope that this publication will serve as a useful resource for students and their advisers to help them deal with the complexity of financial support. We are aiming for a publication that is clear and that responds to the needs of its audience. The sixth edition of the book is set to be the largest yet, and we would appreciate any comments on how it may be improved for future years. Please contact CPAG's publications department or David Malcolm at NUS: david.malcolm@nus.org.uk.

Abbreviations

AA	attendance allowance	HND	Higher National Diploma
AHP	allied health professions	IB	incapacity benefit
AHRC	Arts and Humanities Research Council	ILA	individual learning account
		IS	income support
BBSRC	Biotechnology and Biological Sciences Research Council	ITT	initial teacher training
		JSA	jobseeker's allowance
BEd	Bachelor of Education	LSC	Learning and Skills Council
BSA	Business Services Authority	MA	maternity allowance
CA	carer's allowance	MRC	Medical Research Council
CCW	Care Council for Wales	NC	National Certificate
CTB	council tax benefit	NERC	National Environment Research Council
CTC	child tax credit		
DCSF	Department for Children, Schools and Families	ND	National Diploma
		NHS	National Health Service
DELLS	Department for Education, Lifelong Learning and Skills	NI	national insurance
		NICO	National Insurance Contributions Office
DELNI	Department for Employment and Learning Northern Ireland	NVQ	National Vocational Qualification
DHSSPS	Department for Health, Social Services and Public Safety	PAYE	pay as you earn
		PC	pension credit
DIUS	Department for Innovation, Universities and Skills	PGCE	Postgraduate Certificate in Education
DLA	disability living allowance	PLP	Programme-led Pathways
DSDNI	Department for Social Development Northern Ireland	SAP	statutory adoption pay
		SCITT	school-centred initial teacher training
DWP	Department for Work and Pensions		
E2E	Entry to Employment	SERPS	state earnings-related pension scheme
EEA	European Economic Area		
ELB	education and library board	SFE	Student Finance England
ELWa	Education and Learning Wales	SMP	statutory maternity pay
ESA	employment and support allowance	SPP	statutory paternity pay
		SSI	Social Services Inspectorate
ESRC	Economic and Social Research Council	SSP	statutory sick pay
		SSSS	Secondary Shortage Subject Scheme
EU	European Union		
FE	further education	STFC	Science and Technology Facilities Council
HB	housing benefit		
HE	higher education	TTA	Teacher Training Agency
The Revenue	Her Majesty's Revenue and Customs	UKCISA	UK Council for International Student Affairs
HNC	Higher National Certificate	WTC	working tax credit

Means-tested benefit rates 2008/09

Income support and income-based jobseeker's allowance

Personal allowances

		£pw
Single	Under 25	47.95
	25 or over	60.50
Lone parent	Under 18	47.95
	18 or over	60.50
Couple	Both under 18 (maximum)	72.35
	One 18 or over (maximum)	94.95
	Both 18 or over	94.95

Premiums

Carer		27.75
Pensioner	Single (JSA only)	63.55
	Couple	94.40
Disability	Single	25.85
	Couple	36.85
Enhanced disability	Single	12.60
	Couple	18.15
Severe disability	Single	50.35
	Couple – one qualifies	50.35
	Couple – both qualify	100.70

Children (pre-6 April 2004 claims with no child tax credit)

Dependent children	Under 20	52.59
Family premium		16.75
Disabled child premium		48.72
Enhanced disability premium		19.60

Pension credit

		£pw
Standard minimum guarantee	Single	124.05
	Couple	189.35
Severe disability addition	One qualifies	50.35
	Two qualify	100.70
Carer's addition		27.75
Savings credit threshold	Single	91.20
	Couple	145.80

Employment and support allowance

Personal allowances

		Assessment phase	Main phase
Single	Under 25	47.95	60.50
	25 or over	60.50	60.50
Lone parent	Under 18	47.95	60.50
	18 or over	60.50	60.50
Couple	Both under 18 (maximum)	72.35	94.95
	Both 18 or over	94.95	94.95

Premiums

		Assessment phase	Main phase
Carer		27.75	27.75
Severe disability		50.35	50.35
Enhanced disability	Single	12.60	12.60
	Couple	18.15	18.15
Pensioner	Single, usual rate	63.55	39.55
	Single, support group	63.55	34.55
	Couple, usual rate	94.40	70.40
	Couple, support group	94.40	65.40

Components

	Assessment phase	Main phase
Work-related activity	-	24.00
Support	-	29.00

Housing benefit and council tax benefit

Personal allowances

		£pw
Single	Under 25	47.95
	25 or over	60.50
Lone parent	Under 18	47.95
	18 or over	60.50
Couple	Both under 18	72.35
	One or both 18 or over	94.95

		£pw
Children	Under 20	52.59
Pensioner 60 or over (not on	Single under 65	124.05
IS or income-based JSA)	Single 65 or over	143.80
	Couple both under 65	189.35
	Couple one or both 65 or over	215.50

Premiums

Family	Ordinary rate	16.75
	Some lone parents	22.20
	Baby addition	10.50
Carer		27.75
Disability	Single	25.85
	Couple	36.85
Disabled child		48.72
Severe disability	One qualifies	50.35
	Two qualify	100.70
Enhanced disability	Single	12.60
	Couple	18.15
	Child	19.60

Components

Work-related activity		24.00
Support		29.00

Non-means-tested benefit rates 2008/09

	Claimant £pw	Adult dependant £pw
Attendance allowance		
Higher rate	67.00	
Lower rate	44.85	
Bereavement benefits		
Bereavement payment (lump sum)	2,000.00	
Bereavement allowance (maximum)	90.70	
Carer's allowance	50.55	30.20
Child benefit		
Only/eldest child	18.80	
Other child(ren)	12.55	
Disability living allowance		
Care component		
Highest	67.00	
Middle	44.85	
Lowest	17.75	
Mobility component		
Higher	46.75	
Lower	17.75	
Contributory employment and support allowance		
Assessment phase		
Basic allowance (under 25)	47.95	
Basic allowance (25 or over)	60.50	
Main phase		
Basic allowance (16 or over)	60.50	
Support component	29.00	
Work-related activity component	24.00	
Short-term incapacity benefit		
Lower rate	63.75	39.40
Higher rate	75.40	39.40

	Claimant £pw	Adult dependant £pw
Long-term incapacity benefit	84.50	50.55
Age-related additions:		
Under 35	17.75	
35–44	8.90	
Contribution-based jobseeker's allowance		
Under 25	47.95	
25 or over	60.50	
Maternity allowance		
Standard rate	117.18	39.40
Variable rate	90% of earnings	
Retirement pension	90.70	54.35
Severe disablement allowance	51.05	30.40
Age-related additions:		
Under 40	17.75	
40–49	11.40	
50–59	5.70	
Statutory adoption pay	117.18	
Statutory maternity pay		
Lower rate	117.18	
Higher rate	90% of earnings	
Statutory paternity pay	117.18	
Statutory sick pay	75.40	

Tax credit rates 2008/09

		£ per day	£ per year
Child tax credit			
Family element	Basic	1.50	545
	Including baby element	3.00	1,090
Child element		5.72	2,085
Disability element		6.96	2,540
Severe disability element		2.80	1,020
Working tax credit			
Basic element		4.94	1,800
Couple element		4.85	1,770
Lone parent element		4.85	1,770
30-hour element		2.02	735
Disability element		6.59	2,405
Severe disability element		2.80	1,020
50-plus element	Working 16–29 hours	3.39	1,235
	Working 30 hours or more	5.05	1,840
Childcare element	Eligible childcare costs to a maximum of:		
	One child (weekly rate)		80% of 175
	Two or more children (weekly rate)		80% of 300
Income thresholds			
First income threshold	WTC alone or with CTC		6,420
	CTC alone		15,575
Second income threshold			50,000

Student support rates 2008/09

	per year
Further education	
Adult learning grant (England)	up to £30 per week
Care to Learn childcare bursary	
England (London)	up to £175 per child per week
England (outside London)	up to £160 per child per week
Northern Ireland	up to £165 per child per week
DARD awards (Northern Ireland)	
Parental home	up to £2,362
Outside parental home	up to £1,659
Education maintenance allowance	
England	up to £30 per week
Wales	up to £60 per fortnight
Northern Ireland	up to £60 per fortnight
Further education awards (Northern Ireland)	
Tuition fee grant	up to £890
Tuition fee grant (advanced courses)	up to £1,165
Maintenance bursary	up to £2,000
Individual learning accounts (Wales)	up to £200
Welsh Assembly learning grant	up to £1,500
Higher education	
Full-time undergraduates	
Adult dependants' grant	up to £2,575
Childcare grant	
One child	up to £148.75 per week
Two or more children	up to £255 per week
Disabled students' allowance	
Non-medical personal helper	up to £20,000 per academic year
Major items of specialist equipment	up to £5,030 for duration of course
Other expenditure	up to £1,680 per academic year
Additional expenditure on travel	full reimbursement
Higher education bursary (Northern Ireland)	up to £2,000

	per year
Higher education grant (England and Wales)	up to £1,000
Maintenance grant	up to £2,835
Parents' learning allowance	up to £1,470
Special support grant	up to £2,835

Student loan	*Full year*	*Final year*
Living away from home, studying in London	£6,475	£5,895
Living away from home, studying outside London	£4,625	£4,280
Living at home	£3,580	£3,235

Note: 25% of the student loan is means tested. The rate of loan may be reduced if you are eligible for a maintenance grant, Welsh Assembly learning grant or Northern Ireland higher education bursary.

	per year
Tuition fee grant (old system students)	up to £1,255
Tuition fee grant (new system Welsh-domiciled students in Wales)	up to £1,890
Tuition fee loan	up to £3,145
Welsh Assembly learning grant (Wales)	
Pre-2006 starters	up to £1,500
2006 or later starters	up to £2,835

Part-time undergraduates

	per year
Course costs grant (England and Northern Ireland)	up to £255
Tuition fee grant (England and Northern Ireland)	
Course intensity equivalent to:	
50–59% of a full-time course	up to £785
60–74%	up to £945
75%+	up to £1,180
Tuition fee grant (Wales)	
Course intensity equivalent to:	
50–59% of a full-time course	up to £620
60–74%	up to £745
75%+	up to £930
Welsh Assembly Learning Grant	up to £1050

Healthcare students

Means-tested bursary (England and Wales)	*Old system*	*New system*
Studying in London	up to £3,050	up to £3,306
Studying elsewhere	up to £2,483	up to £2,739
Living in parental home (London or elsewhere)	up to £2,031	up to £2,287

	per year
Means-tested bursary (Northern Ireland)	
Living away from parental home	up to £2,300
Living in parental home	up to £1,875

Non-means-tested bursary (England and Wales)	Old system	New system
Studying in London	£7,374	£7,629
Studying elsewhere	£6,275	£6,531
Living in parental home (London or elsewhere)	£6,275	£6,531

Non-means-tested bursary (Northern Ireland)	
Old system – aged under 26 at start of course	£5,910
Old system – aged over 26 at start of course	£6,655
New system	£5,910

Student loan (England and Wales)	Full year	Final year
Studying in London	£3,185	£2,435
Studying outside London	£2,265	£1,765
Living in parental home (London or elsewhere)	£1,700	£1,290

Student loan (Northern Ireland)	Full year	Final year
Living away from parental home	£2,300	£1,765
Living in parental home	£1,875	£1,290

Note: there are a range of supplementary grants for healthcare students not listed here. See Chapter 6 for further details.

Social work students

NHS BSA social work bursary (England)	
Studying in London	up to £4,975
Studying elsewhere	up to £4,575
CCW social work bursary (Wales)	£2,500
SSI social work bursary (Northern Ireland)	£4,000

Teacher training students

Graduate teacher programme (England)	
Salary	minimum £15,113
Training grant (to school)	up to £4,920
Registered teacher programme (England)	
Salary	minimum £15,113
Training grant (to school)	£9,100
Secondary undergraduate placement grants (Wales)	
Shortage subjects	£1,000
Non-shortage subjects	£600
Teacher training bursary (England)	
Primary	£4,000 per year
Secondary shortage subjects	£9,000
Other secondary subjects	£6,000

	per year
Teacher training grant (Wales)	
Primary	£2,200
Secondary shortage subjects	£7,200
Other secondary subjects	£4,200
Welsh medium incentive supplement (Wales)	
Science and maths	£1,800
Other subjects	£1,500

Postgraduates

See p52 for a table of research council and research board stipend rates.

Other sources

Career development loans (England and Wales)   £300 to £8,000
for duration of course

Part 1

Student support

Chapter 1

Further education student support

This chapter covers:
1. Student support in England (below)
2. Student support in Wales (p12)
3. Student support in Northern Ireland (p13)

Financial support available for further education students is generally split between those aged 16 to 19 and those aged 19 and over. Most of the statutory funding available is for the former group; a range of discretionary support is available for both.

1. Student support in England

Support for 16–19-year-olds

Tuition fees

Subject to certain residency conditions, if you are under 19 on 31 August prior to your enrolment and beginning either a full- or part-time further education (FE) course funded by the Learning and Skills Council (LSC), you do not have to pay tuition fees. Some private colleges, however, may ask for a fee.

Schools' access funds

Local authorities administer a needs-based fund for school pupils aged 16 or over but under 19. The funds are aimed at groups with low staying-on rates, but high achievers should not be excluded. Payments are in the form of grants and each local authority has its own eligibility criteria.

Education maintenance allowances[1]

An education maintenance allowance is a statutory financial award, aimed at supporting young people from low-income households who undertake a full-time FE course in college, school or certain work-based learning programmes, such as apprenticeships, Programme-led Pathways (PLP) and Entry to Employment (E2E) courses.

It consists of:

- a weekly payment of £10, £20 or £30 (income dependent) during term time only;
- up to four £100 bonuses for college or school-based learners (based on a two-year programme);
- intermittent bonuses for E2E, PLP or apprenticeship learners.

The education maintenance allowance is paid for two years, although a third year may be possible depending on your circumstances.

Who is eligible

In order to apply for an education maintenance allowance you must meet the course and personal eligibility criteria.

You must be participating in a programme of full-time education (at least 12 guided learning hours (16 for E2E) for at least 12 weeks) at a recognised school, sixth form, FE college or work-based learning provider. You must not be receiving any Department for Children, Schools and Families (DCSF), Department for Innovation, Universities and Skills (DIUS) or other government funding that would prevent you from receiving an education maintenance allowance – eg, a dance and drama award, jobseeker's allowance (JSA) or NHS bursary.

You must also fulfil certain residency requirements. You must be:

- a UK citizen or a person who is 'settled' in the UK within the meaning of the Immigration Act 1971 (ie, you have the right of abode or indefinite leave to enter or remain in the UK), and ordinarily resident in the UK for the three years prior to the start of the course; *or*
- a citizen of the European Union (EU) (or the spouse, civil partner or child of an EU citizen), and ordinarily resident in the European Economic Area (EEA – ie, the countries of the EU plus Norway, Liechtenstein and Iceland) for three years prior to the start of the course; *or*
- an EEA or Turkish migrant worker (or the spouse, civil partner or child of such a person) ordinarily resident in the UK at the start of the course and ordinarily resident in the EEA for the three years prior to the start of the course; *or*
- an officially recognised refugee or her/his spouse, civil partner or child, or have been granted humanitarian protection, or have EU temporary protection.

Note: some temporary absences abroad may be disregarded when assessing your entitlement. Rules on residency are complicated, so if you are in doubt, speak to an adviser in the student services department in your college or contact the National Union of Students (NUS – see Appendix 2).

You are eligible to apply for an education maintenance allowance if you turn 17, 18 or 19 between 1 September 2008 and 31 August 2009. An allowance may be available if you turn 20 between 1 September 2008 and 31 August 2009 and have a letter from a Connexions personal adviser stating that you should be eligible.

Payments

Payments are available for up to three full academic years and are dependent on you fulfilling the conditions laid out in your contract (see p6). How much you receive depends on your household income, which is assessed at the start of the year.

The income assessed is usually that of your parents, guardians or other main carers. If you live with only one parent, your other parent will not be assessed and any maintenance s/he pays is not be counted as income. The income assessed is that earned in the preceding full tax year – eg, for applications made for autumn 2008, this is the 2007/08 tax year. Any income you have (eg, from a part-time job) is not included. If you are a parent and you care for a child yourself, you are assessed on your own income.

If you enrol on an E2E programme you automatically receive an education maintenance allowance, irrespective of your household income.

If you live with foster parents or are in the care of the local authority, you automatically receive the full allowance (£30 a week), although you will have to provide proof of your status, such as a letter from the local authority. If you do not live with your parents or other carers and receive income support (IS), you will also automatically receive the full allowance.

If your household has applied for tax credits, all you need to submit is the tax credit award notice, otherwise you, or your parents or carers, must send appropriate evidence, such as a P60 form from an employer. Social security benefits, including child benefit, are disregarded when calculating your household income. The education maintenance allowance payments are disregarded for the purpose of calculating your family's entitlement to means-tested benefits. Therefore, if you or your family are claiming benefits, you can receive an education maintenance allowance in addition to them.

You are eligible for the full payment of £30 a week if your gross (before tax) annual household income is £20,817 or less. A payment of £20 a week is made if your gross household income is between £20,818 and £25,521. A payment of £10 a week is made if your gross household income is between £25,522 and £30,810. If your gross household income is over £30,810 a year, you are not eligible for an allowance.

Bonuses

In January and July of each year, a £100 bonus is available for learners in schools and colleges, if you have met the goals set by the school or college in your education maintenance allowance contract (see p6). Bonuses for a two-year programme are worth up to £400 in total.

Bonuses for learners on E2E or PLP schemes are structured differently and come in smaller, but more frequent, amounts, so that the total bonus money available throughout a programme of learning is the same amount as for learners in schools or colleges. As with other learners, bonuses are dependent on you meeting goals set out in a learning agreement. Speak to your learning provider about the structure in your learning programme.

Education maintenance allowance contract

In order to receive your weekly payments and any bonuses, you are required to sign an education maintenance allowance contract. This is provided by your school, college or learning provider and sets out what you are expected to achieve in terms of attendance and academic work. This document is signed by you, your parents (or another responsible adult) and the learning provider. No bonuses are payable unless a contract is signed. If you fail to meet part of the contract in any week (eg, fail to attend classes or hand in homework) you will not be paid your allowance for that week and it may be taken into account when deciding if you should receive your next bonus.

Although weekly payments are dependent on 100 per cent attendance, some types of absence are permitted or 'authorised'. However, it is advisable to notify the college of any absences if you want to be considered for your payment and any bonuses, particularly if you know in advance that you will be absent.

These authorised absences can include such events as sickness, unavoidable medical appointments, religious holidays, emergency caring duties, a driving test, a family funeral, representative duties such as a college governors' meeting and official business of the NUS. Colleges make the final decision on authorised absences and you should discuss with your own institution any absence you may have to take.

Applications

To apply for the scheme, contact your school, college, learning provider or local authority and request an education maintenance allowance application pack. Further details can also be found at ema.direct.gov.uk or telephone 0800 121 8989.

Care to Learn

Care to Learn is a scheme funded by the LSC to help young parents in England pay for childcare costs while in full-time or part-time further education, E2E, or other non-employed work-based learning schemes. If you are eligible, the scheme will pay for the costs of registered childcare while you are at school, college or on placement, including fees that must be paid during holidays, plus the cost of transport to and from the childcare provider. You can claim up to a maximum of £175 a week per child if you live in any of the 31 London boroughs or the City of

London, or £160 a week per child if you live elsewhere. It does not affect, nor is it affected by, social security benefits.

You can apply if you are aged under 20 on 1 August 2008, living in England and caring for your own child(ren). You must want to start or continue a publicly funded course at school or sixth-form college, or to start a course at an FE college. If you are already studying at an FE college and were not previously claiming childcare through Care to Learn or are a student in Wales, you are not eligible for this scheme and should apply to the college's Learner Support Fund (see p8) or Financial Contingency Fund (see p13).

The scheme only funds registered or approved childcare. If you have informal childcare arrangements you may still apply for support through the Learner Support Fund (see p8).

Further information (including how to apply) can be found at www.direct.gov.uk/caretolearn or by phoning the helpline on 0800 121 8989.

Transport

Local authorities continue to have responsibility for ensuring adequate provision of home to school or college transport for those aged 16 to 18,[2] although this might not be free of charge. Contact your college or local authority for further information, or go to www.moneytolearn.direct.gov.uk for details of local policies. Many colleges and sixth-form colleges provide subsidised transport and you should also ask them for details.

Residential bursaries

If a course you want to do is not available locally, you may be able to get help with accommodation for a course further afield. Some specialist colleges which concentrate on agriculture, horticulture or art and design offer residential bursaries through the Learner Support Fund. There are 51 of these colleges and a list is available at www.moneytolearn.direct.gov.uk – see p8 for more details of Learner Support Fund assistance. The bursaries are available for full-time study and are also available for travel costs if you have to live at home but travel significant distances to college.

If you wish to study a course not on the list mentioned above, but which is not available locally, you may be able to receive help under the Residential Support Scheme. This offers up to £3,458 per year (£4,079 in London) for accommodation costs if the course you want to do requires 15 hours' attendance a week, is at least 10 weeks long and is not available within 15 miles or a two-hour return journey from your home. What you receive will depend on your family income, and you must be ordinarily resident in England. More information and an application pack is available from www.moneytolearn.direct.gov.uk, telephone 0800 121 8989.

Asylum seekers

Although most public funds are not available, if you are an asylum seeker aged under 19 you can apply to the college's Learner Support Fund (see below) for financial assistance. You may also wish to contact the Education Grants Advisory Service at www.egas-online.org.uk for sources of funding or contact the Ruth Hayman Trust at www.ruthhaymantrust.com.

Learner Support Fund

If you are studying at a college, including sixth-form colleges, you may be able to get additional help for your living or course costs through the discretionary Learner Support Fund. This is an amount of money given to colleges by the LSC for students in need and is administered differently from higher education funds. There are three types of payments:
- hardship funds;
- residential bursaries (these are different to the residential bursaries mentioned above);
- childcare support.

Hardship funds

These are open to all students studying at a college who meet the personal, residential and course conditions (see pp19–21). The funds are used to 'anticipate need', to act as a safety net for students and for innovative initiatives. Examples of payments include:
- means-tested bursaries;
- purchasing 'benefits' or support, or offering equipment or services at low cost;
- small payments to meet the costs of equipment;
- childcare costs for over 19-year-olds only (under-19-year-olds must use the Care to Learn scheme) – see below;
- tuition fees for ESOL courses or otherwise in exceptional circumstances.

Local colleges have the discretion to decide how to prioritise spending and to stipulate their assessment criteria, which means the exact nature and levels of support available to you will depend on your college. The college must, nevertheless, have an appeals procedure to challenge decisions.

If you are receiving an education maintenance allowance you can still receive payments from the hardship funds if you can demonstrate you have additional costs not provided for by your payment. If you are in exceptional need, a loan may be provided from the funds.

Childcare support

Support can be used to meet the costs of any registered childcare for learners aged 20 or over. The support available is not likely to be more than that available through the Care to Learn scheme (approximately £5,000 per child), but this may differ from college to college. Funds can be paid directly to the childcare provider or directly to you. Again, this depends on college policy. If you are aged under 20 and starting a new course, you should apply to the Care to Learn scheme (see p6) for help with registered childcare.

Support for students aged 19 and over

Tuition fees

In order to improve the literacy and numeracy of the adult population in England, the Government will pay the tuition fees for all adults who wish to undertake training that will lead to their first Level 2 qualification (the equivalent of five GCSEs at grades A*-C), or for those aged under 35, their first Level 3 qualification. Check with your college that you and your course are both eligible. There are residency conditions.

Otherwise, colleges can opt into a voluntary system of fee remission for anyone who is aged 19 and over and who is:

- on means-tested benefits or contribution-based JSA;
- an unwaged dependant of anyone in receipt of means-tested benefits, pension credit or contribution-based JSA;
- in receipt of working tax credit and with a gross (before tax) income of £15,050;
- taking a programme where the primary learning objective is adult basic education;
- undertaking an English course because s/he is not currently fluent in that language.

When a college opts into this system, you are exempt from fee payment and the LSC compensates the college for 100 per cent of your fees. Check whether your college offers fee remission through this system.

If you are not in any of the above groups, you may have to pay tuition fees. If you are having problems meeting the costs of fees, you should approach the college's student services to inquire about help through the Learner Support Fund (see p8).

Adult learning grants[3]

Adult learning grants are available across England. These are grants of up to £30 a week for full-time learners aged over 19 who are studying for their first full Level 2 or Level 3 qualification.

Course requirements

Your course must lead to either your first Level 2 or Level 3 qualification. Your college will be able to tell you if this is the case. It must involve at least 450 hours of guiding learning in the year, or at least 12 hours a week. It also has to be approved by the LSC – again, your college can tell you if this is the case.

Residence requirements

You must fulfil certain residency requirements. You must be either:

- a UK citizen or a person who is 'settled' in the UK within the meaning of the Immigration Act 1971 (ie, you have the right of abode or indefinite leave to enter or remain in the UK), and ordinarily resident in the UK for the three years prior to the start of the course; *or*
- a citizen of the EU or Switzerland (or her/his spouse, civil partner or child), and ordinarily resident in the EEA (the countries of the EU plus Norway, Liechtenstein and Iceland) or Switzerland for three years prior to the start of the course; *or*
- an EEA or Swiss migrant worker (or the spouse, civil partner or child of such a person) ordinarily resident in the UK at the start of the course and ordinarily resident in the EEA or Switzerland for the three years prior to the start of the course; *or*
- an officially recognised refugee or her/his spouse, civil partner or child, or have been granted humanitarian protection, or have EU temporary protection.

Note: some temporary absences abroad may be disregarded when assessing your entitlement. Rules on residency are complicated, so if you are in doubt, speak to an adviser in your college's student services department or contact the NUS.

Applications

You can get an application form from the student services department at your college, or by calling 0800 121 8989.

Income assessment

The grants are means tested and if you are in receipt of any out-of-work benefits, such as IS, incapacity benefit or JSA, you cannot claim an additional adult learning grant. However, other benefits such as housing benefit, child benefit and disability benefits do not affect your entitlement to a grant.

The income of any cohabiting partner (of the same or opposite sex, whether or not you are married or in a civil partnership) will also be taken into account when assessing your entitlement. Grants are available to single students with an income in the 2007/08 tax year of less than £19,513 and to students with cohabiting partners with a joint income of less than £30,810.

Sixth-form childcare

If you are aged 20 or over and are studying at a school sixth form or sixth-form college, you can apply for help with your childcare costs. Your study can be full time or part time, but the childcare must be approved by Ofsted. You can claim up to £160 of actual weekly costs per child (£175 in London) if your child(ren) is under age 15 (or under 16 if s/he has special educational needs).

The maximum level you can claim also depends on your household income in the previous full tax year (for the 2008/09 academic year, this is the 2007/08 tax year). You can claim maximum help if your household income is below £30,152 a year and a partial amount if your household income is below £50,502 a year. If your income is higher than this, you cannot claim. Part-time learners will have the maximum support they can claim reduced *pro rata*.

This help is not available to learners in general colleges.

More information is available at www.direct.gov.uk/adultlearning.

Learner Support Fund

If you are studying at a college, you may be able to get additional help for your living or course costs, including childcare, through the Learner Support Fund. See p8 for more details.

Other grants

City and Guilds bursaries

For students on qualifying City and Guilds, Hospitality Awarding Body or National Proficiency Test Certificate courses, a small number of bursaries are available to help with the costs of study.

Applicants must be living in the UK and intend to study in the UK to qualify. Applications are considered twice a year, in June and December. For more information, see www.cityandguilds.com/bursaries.

New Deal education and training option

If you are placed on the New Deal scheme by your Jobcentre Plus office, it may be possible for you to take advantage of the education and training option to gain qualifications which will enhance your employability while still receiving an allowance equivalent to the benefits you would otherwise receive. The maximum permitted length of the course is one year. Those aged 18 to 24 can study up to NVQ Level 2, while those aged 24 and over may study up to NVQ Level 3. There is some discretion on the part of your New Deal adviser to allow you to study a more advanced qualification if you already possess these levels at the 'maximum' level. The option is not available to those on the 50-plus scheme.

National traineeships and modern apprenticeships

Both these schemes are designed to allow 16–24-year-olds to enter work-based education and gain an NVQ while earning. More information is available from the LSC website at www.apprenticeships.org.uk and the Jobcentre Plus site at www.jobcentreplus.gov.uk/customers/helpwithtraining.

2. **Student support in Wales**

Support for 16–19-year-olds

Tuition fees

Subject to certain residency conditions, if you are under 19 on 31 August prior to your enrolment and beginning either a full- or part-time further education (FE) course funded by Welsh Assembly, you do not have to pay tuition fees. Some private colleges, however, may ask for a fee.

Education maintenance allowances

In Wales, the education maintenance allowance scheme is identical to that in England (see p3), except that you are paid fortnightly instead of weekly and it is not available to learners on apprenticeships or other work-based training.

More information can be found at www.studentfinancewales.co.uk/ema.

Passport to Study grants

Some local authorities in Wales offer extra funding for young people in further education whose parents are out of work, or receiving benefits because of having a low income or a disability. These are usually called Passport to Study grants and normally come in the form of assistance with travel costs. Contact your local authority to see if it offers any such funding, and what terms and conditions apply.

Financial Contingency Fund

If you are studying at a college, you may be able to get additional help for your living or course costs from the Financial Contingency Fund. This operates in a broadly similar manner to Learner Support Funds in England. See p41 for more details.

Support for students aged 19 and over

Tuition fees

There is no statutory fee remission if you are aged 19 or over. Some colleges may run schemes that provide full or partial remission if, for example, you are on a low income or in receipt of means-tested benefits. Ask your college what it provides.

Individual learning accounts

The Welsh Assembly has reintroduced individual learning accounts for students in Wales who have no or low qualifications.[4] If you do not hold a qualification above Level 2 (ie, above GCSE level, GNVQ intermediate or NVQ Level 2), you may be entitled to a grant of up to £200 to help pay tuition fees or for certain materials on courses that lead to qualifications up to Level 3 (ie, A level, GNVQ higher or NVQ Level 3). How much you receive depends on your personal circumstances. More information can be found at www.ilawales.co.uk or from Learndirect on 0800 100 900.

Welsh Assembly learning grants[5]

If you are aged 19 or over and on a low income, you may be eligible for a means-tested Welsh Assembly learning grant for further education of up to £1,500. A grant of at least £450 is available if you are on a full-time course (500 contact hours or more a year) and your family income is below £17,251. If your household income is below £11,491, £1,000 is available. The full £1,500 will be offered if your household income is less than £5,745. Part-time students (those who have between 275 and 499 contact hours a year) can receive a reduced grant of £300, £450 or £750 on the same salary bands.

The grants are administered through Welsh local authorities, but students may attend any institution in the UK. More information is available at www.studentfinancewales.co.uk/alg.

Financial Contingency Fund

If you are studying at a college, you may be able to get additional help for your living or course costs from the Financial Contingency Fund. This operates in a broadly similar manner to Learner Support Funds in England. See p41 for more details.

Other grants
New Deal education and training option

Welsh students may be able to receive the New Deal education and training option. See p11 for details.

Modern apprenticeships

Both these schemes are designed to allow 16–24-year-olds to enter work-based education and gain an NVQ while earning. More information is available from Careers Wales at www.careerswales.com.

3. **Student support in Northern Ireland**

Support for 16–19-year-olds
Tuition fees

If you are a full-time student you will have your tuition fees paid in full. If you are a part-time student, concessionary tuition fees may apply.

Education maintenance allowances

In Northern Ireland the education maintenance allowance scheme is almost identical to that in England (see p3). However, there are some small differences.

In Northern Ireland your course must consist of at least 15 guided learning hours per week rather than 12, and it is not available to students on apprenticeships or other work-based learning programmes. Students in Northern Ireland are entitled to an education maintenance allowance if they turn 16, 17, 18 or 19 between 2 July 2006 and I July 2007. Additionally, you are paid fortnightly instead of weekly.

The thresholds for payment are also slightly different. You are eligible for the full payment of £30 a week if your gross (before tax) annual household income is £21,330 or less. A payment of £20 a week is made if your gross household income is between £21,331 and £26,160. A payment of £10 a week is made if your gross household income is between £26,161 and £31,580. If your gross household income is over £31,580 a year, you are not eligible for an allowance.

More information can be found at www.emani.gov.uk.

Care to Learn

The Department for Employment and Learning's Care to Learn scheme is designed to help young parents in Northern Ireland pay for childcare costs while in full- or part-time further education. If you are eligible, the scheme will pay for the costs of registered childcare while you are at school, college or on placement, including fees that must be paid during holidays, plus the cost of transport to and from the childcare provider, up to a maximum of £165 per child per week. It does not affect, nor is it affected by, social security benefits.

You can apply if you are aged 16 or over but under 19 at the start of your course of study, live in Northern Ireland and fulfil certain residency requirements, and you care for your own child(ren). You must wish to start or continue a publicly-funded course at school or sixth-form college, or to start a course at a further education (FE) college. If you are already receiving childcare funding from other government sources, you are not eligible for this scheme and should apply to the college's support fund if that funding is inadequate.

The scheme will only fund childcare from a provider registered with the Health and Social Services Board. If you have informal childcare arrangements, you can still apply for support through your college's support fund.

Further information (including details of how to apply) should be available from your college.

Support for students aged 19 and over

Tuition fees

Tuition fee remission is provided if you are studying a full-time eligible vocational course up to Level 3 (ie, GNVQ higher or NVQ Level 3).

A **'full-time course'** is defined as a course lasting a minimum of 30 weeks and consisting of at least 15 hours and at least seven sessions per week, or 21 hours per week with no sessional requirement. GCSE, A level or AS level subjects are not eligible except when studied in combination with a relevant vocational qualification at a similar level. If your course does not qualify for tuition fee remission you may be able to receive help from your college support fund.

Further education awards

If you are on a full-time FE course, you can apply to the local education and library board (ELB) for a non-repayable maintenance grant called a further education award (previously known as discretionary awards). These awards can also provide additional help with tuition fees if required. There are two types of award: FE awards and advanced FE awards. Both pay extra allowances similar to those available for higher education students (see p48) to students with dependants, disabled students and care leavers. All parts of these grants (apart from the disabled students' allowances) are means tested.

Both grants have residency requirements, and you cannot be in receipt of another award such as an education maintenance allowance or Department for Agriculture and Rural Development grant (see p16) at the same time. Advanced awards are for courses requiring at least five GCSE passes at grade C or above, and other awards are for courses without this requirement. Although the awards are no longer being referred to as 'discretionary' they remain so – funds are insufficient to provide all applicants with grants and you should apply as soon as possible.

Note: the closing date for applications for each year is the end of June prior to the start of the course for full-time students and the end of October for part-time students.

In 2008/09, tuition fees of up to £1,165 will be paid for advanced FE courses, and up to £890 for other courses. Both attract means-tested bursaries for maintenance of up to £2,000. The maximum amount is available if your household income is less than £11,275, and a partial amount on incomes between £11,275 and £22,550. No maintenance grant is payable if your household income exceeds £22,550.

Extra support may be available if you have children or a disability.

Part-time courses

Part-time courses attract funding at lower levels.

For advanced courses you can receive tuition fee support of up to £583 a year, and for other courses up to £445 a year. A means-tested course costs grant of up to £255 is available for students with an income of less than £25,000.

For further information on FE awards, contact the Further Education Awards Section, 1 Hospital Road, Omagh, Co Tyrone BT79 0AW, Tel: 028 8225 4546 or email: feawards@welbni.org.

Support funds

There are two discretionary funds administered by colleges that offer additional help if you are a part-time or full-time FE student aged 19 or over. Support funds are aimed at those experiencing financial difficulties and may include help with living costs and/or fees (eligibility criteria apply). The additional support funds are aimed at students with learning difficulties who are not in receipt of other help for disabled students, such as a disabled students' allowance, and can be used to pay for additional human or technical support, such as IT hardware.

Other grants

Department for Agriculture and Rural Development grant

If you are attending an FE course at the Enniskillen, Greenmount or Loughry campuses of the College of Agriculture, Food and Rural Enterprise, you may be eligible for financial support from the Department for Agriculture and Rural Development.

To be eligible, you must be ordinarily resident in Northern Ireland and fulfill certain other residency requirements. You can be any age.

Support comes in the form of a means-tested living costs grant of up to £1,659 if you live in your parents' home or up to £2,362 if you do not. Further allowances may be available if you have children or adult dependants, or if you are a care leaver or have a disability which means you have extra costs associated with study.

Further information can be found at www.cafre.ac.uk. Applications should be made to Further Education Awards Section, 1 Hospital Road, Omagh, Co Tyrone BT79 0AW, Tel: 028 8225 4546, email: feawards@welbni.org.

Notes

1. **Student support in England**
   1 While the power to provide education maintenance allowances is in s14 Education Act 2002, the DCSF has chosen not to make detailed regulations for the national scheme for this academic year. However, the full guidance can be found in the providers section at ema.direct.gov.uk.
   2 s509 Education Act 1996
   3 Adult Learning Grant Guidance, DIUS, June 2008

2. **Student support in Wales**
   4 Individual Learning Accounts (Wales) Regulations 2003, No.918
   5 E(ALGS)(W) Regs

Chapter 2

Undergraduate student support: England

This chapter covers:
1. Full-time undergraduates (below)
2. Part-time undergraduates (p31)
3. Hardship funds (p33)

Basic facts
- Undergraduate students can apply for a mixture of grants and loans, depending on their personal circumstances.
- The support available in England differs to that available in Wales and Northern Ireland.
- Separate provisions apply to healthcare and initial teacher training students.
- Social work students may be eligible for a social work bursary.
- Access to Learning funds are available for those in financial difficulty.

The type of financial support you can receive when you are learning depends on several factors, including when you begin your course, the length of the course, the discipline you are studying, whether the course is full time or part time, and your age.

1. Full-time undergraduates

Full-time undergraduates in England on eligible courses (see p21) and who are personally eligible (see p19) can apply for financial assistance from the Department for Innovation, Universities and Skills (DIUS). Separate provision is available for part-time undergraduates (see p31) and those studying degree or higher diploma courses in healthcare (see p56).

Changes to student support in 2008/09 and 2009/10

There are a number of changes to student support in the 2008/09 academic year. These include an increase in the earnings thresholds for the maintenance and special support grants for new students in 2008, and an increase in the maximum amounts payable for non-medical help in the disabled students' allowance.

Changes to support in 2009/10 have been announced. The most significant of these is that the upper end of the thresholds for the maintenance and special support grants are again changing for new students, so that partial support will only be available for students whose income is £50,020 or less. Full details will be available in the seventh edition of this *Handbook*.

In addition, the Student Loans Company (SLC) will be responsible for assessing and processing student finance applications from all new students starting in the 2009/10 academic year, and applications for support can be made from the September preceding the year of entry. The new service is known as Student Finance England (SFE) and from January 2009, prospective students intending to enter higher education (HE) in September 2009 or later should apply to SFE for support. New and continuing students in the 2008/09 academic year should continue to apply to their local authority, except if the local authority is participating in a pilot scheme in which the SLC already carries out this function.

Rates of support for 2009/10 have also been confirmed and are listed in the relevant sections that follow.

Support in Wales, Northern Ireland and Scotland

Since 2006/07 student support in Wales has been separate from that in England, and funding for Welsh-domiciled students has begun to diverge. See Chapter 3 for more details.

Northern Irish and Scottish-domiciled students are also funded under separate systems. See Chapter 4 for details of the system in Northern Ireland and CPAG's *Benefits for Student in Scotland Handbook* for details in Scotland.

Students who entered higher education before September 1998

If you entered higher education before the 1998/99 academic year, you should be receiving your funding under the mandatory award system.[1] However, the DIUS believes that all students funded on this system have either graduated or otherwise left their courses. If you think you should be funded under this system, seek specialist advice from your students' union or institution.

Students who entered higher education between 1 September 1998 and 1 September 2006

If you began your course between 1 September 1998 and 1 September 2006 and do not fit into the gap year provision explained below, you will receive financial help for student support as an 'old system' student. Your university or college should charge you no more than £1,255 tuition fees in 2008/09 and you may be entitled to fee remission (see p19).

Gap year students

Some gap year students who began in the 2006/07 academic year are treated as 'old system' students if they deferred entry to higher education from the 2005/06 academic year and had confirmed their place at their institution by 1 August 2005. If you think you should qualify, speak to an adviser.

Students who entered higher education on or after 1 September 2006

You qualify for support as a 'current system' student if:[2]
- you are entering higher education for the first time in 2006 or later and do not fall under the gap year provisions outlined above;
- you started a Postgraduate Certificate in Education course on or after 1 September 2006;
- you have withdrawn from a previous course of study and did not arrange a transfer before leaving your previous course.

Some changes to student support made in 2008 affect only those students who started their course in the 2008/09 academic year or later. Such students are referred to as '2008 cohort' students in this *Handbook*.

Fees and student support

In 2008/09, colleges and universities can charge fees of up to £3,145 a year in certain circumstances.[3] These circumstances are not the same as those for student support, so it is important to check how much tuition fees you will be charged by your institution. If you began a course before 1 September 2006 and transfer to a similar course at the same institution, you will be charged no more than £1,255 tuition fees each year. If, however, you transfer to a similar course at a different institution or a different course at the same institution, you can be charged up to £3,145 each year. However, because you were receiving student support before 1 September 2006 and have not withdrawn from education, you will receive the student support package that you have always received – eg, an income-assessed tuition fee grant of a maximum of £1,255 and up to £1,000 HE grant, in addition to the maintenance loan and other supplementary grants for which you may be eligible.

Who is eligible for support

In order to receive help under any system you must be 'personally eligible' (see below) and studying an eligible course (see p21).

Personal eligibility

To be personally eligible for support you must meet the residence condition.[4] This usually means that you must:

- be settled in the UK within the meaning of the 1971 Immigration Act (this includes those with British citizenship, right of abode, and those with indefinite leave to enter/remain in the UK);
- be resident in England on the first day of the first academic year;
- have lived in the 'UK and Islands' for three years immediately before the start of the course;
- not have spent any of the three years in the 'UK and Islands' mainly for the purpose of receiving full-time education. If you were in full-time education during the three years, you can still receive support if you can prove this was not the main reason for you being in the UK.

Note: there are exceptions to this rule, many of which are complex. You may wish to speak to an adviser in your institution or students' union.

European Union nationals

Broadly, if you are a European Union (EU) national you can qualify for 'home student' status (see p21) if you have been resident in the UK for three years immediately before the start of the course and you are resident in England or Wales on the first day of the first academic year. If any of that time was spent mainly for the purpose of receiving full-time education, you must have been ordinarily resident in the UK, elsewhere in the European Economic Area (EEA) and/or Switzerland immediately before the three-year period. The EEA consists of the 27 member states of the EU plus Norway, Iceland and Liechtenstein.

Alternatively, if you have 'the right of permanent residence' after having become settled in the UK you may qualify for 'home' student status. This can also be granted if you are a 'relevant family member' of a person with the right of permanent residence and you have been resident in the UK for three years or more.[5] However, if any of that time was spent mainly for the purpose of full-time education, you must have been resident in the UK or elsewhere in the EEA and/or Switzerland immediately before the three-year period.

If you are a national of an EU member state, or a 'relevant family member' of such a national, and coming to the UK to undertake higher education, you may be eligible for help with fees only. You must have lived in the EEA and/or Switzerland for three years prior to the start of your course, and no part of the three years can have been mainly for the purposes of full-time education. If a new country joins the EU, it is considered to have always been in the EEA when determining the three years' residency. Consequently, as Bulgaria and Romania joined the EU on 1 January 2007, for the purposes of assessing support they are now regarded as having always been part of the EEA.

Migrant workers

If you are an EEA or Swiss migrant worker and are, or have been, working in the UK, or you are a 'relevant family member' of such a migrant worker, you may be eligible for support as a 'home student'. A **'home student'** is eligible for help with both tuition fees and living costs (subject to an income assessment). You must also have three years' residence in the EEA and/or Switzerland.

A 'relevant family member' includes children, a spouse or civil partner or, for EEA workers only, dependent direct ascendants such as parents or grandparents.

If you are a UK national and have been living in another EEA country or Switzerland and you return to the UK to study you may be eligible for support as a 'home student'. You must apply for support in the part of the UK in which you were living before you left the country.[6]

Children of Turkish migrant workers can also receive home fees and support if their parents have been ordinarily resident in the UK and lawfully employed, and if the child is ordinarily resident in the UK on the first day of the first academic year of the course and has been ordinarily resident in the EEA, Switzerland and/or Turkey for the three years prior to the start of the course.[7]

Refugees

If you are recognised as a refugee by the UK Government and have lived in the 'UK and Islands' since being granted this status, or you are a 'relevant family member' of such a person (defined in this case as the person's spouse, civil partner or child), you should be treated as a 'home student' (see above).

If you applied for asylum and have been granted humanitarian protection or discretionary leave (or exceptional leave), you may be treated as a 'home student' for support if you received this leave before the start of the first day of the first academic year of your course and you meet the three-year residency criteria (see above).

Course eligibility

Broadly, the course must be full time (as defined by the education provider) and be:[8]

- a first degree;
- a Diploma of Higher Education (DipHE);
- a BTEC higher national certificate (HNC) or higher national diploma (HND);
- a course of initial teacher training;
- a course for the further training of teachers, or youth or community workers;
- a course to prepare for certain professional examinations of a standard higher than A level, or BTEC HNC/HND where a first degree is not required for entry;
- a course not higher than a first degree, but higher than those described in the above bullet point.

Student support

Tuition fees and loans

Students who entered higher education between 1 September 1998 and 1 September 2006, and gap year students

If you entered higher education between 1 September 1998 and 1 September 2006, or if you were considered a gap year student in 2006/07 (see p19), you may be liable to pay a contribution towards your tuition fees, up to a maximum of £1,255 per academic year (rising each year with inflation – in 2009/10 this will be £1,285). However, students with a low household income can receive help with all or some of this contribution.[9] Any help you receive from your local authority towards your fees is subject to an assessment of your own and (where appropriate) your parents' or partner's income.

Any eligible continuing student who is liable for fees after the income assessment for the tuition fee grant has been carried out can take out a loan for the fees.[10] For example, if the local authority has agreed to pay £600 towards your fees, you can apply for a tuition fees loan for the remaining £655 (£685 in 2009/10).

If you have previously attended an HE course, you may be subject to the rules on 'previous study'.[11] Broadly, the support you can receive is equivalent to the length of your new course plus one year, less any year of study previously undertaken. If you have studied part of a year you will be treated as if you have undertaken a full year of study. The elements of support that are affected vary according to whether you have a previous honours degree and according to the course you are now studying. If you are transferring courses you will also fall under these previous study rules. Further information is available from www.dcsf.gov.uk/studentsupport.

Students who entered higher education on or after 1 September 2006

Any student commencing her/his studies on or after 1 September 2006 (except those who can benefit from the gap year provision – see p19) falls within the variable fees regime in England. You may be liable for fees of up to £3,145 per academic year (rising each year with inflation – in 2009/10 this will be £3,225) and are no longer eligible for a tuition fee grant. Providing you are a home or EU student, you can apply for a non-income-assessed tuition fee loan to cover the cost of the fees.[12] The repayment terms are the same as for an income-contingent maintenance loan (see p23). In addition, you may be eligible for a grant of up to £2,835 and, in some circumstances, a bursary from your institution (see p31).

Higher education grant

Students who started new courses between September 2004 and August 2006 (or who are treated as 'old system' students if they started their course in the 2006/07 academic year) are eligible for an HE grant of up to £1,000.[13] Students on full-time, sandwich and part-time initial teacher training courses are eligible to apply. However, if you started your course before September 2004 you are not eligible for this grant.

Student maintenance loans

Student maintenance loans are available to eligible students to help with living costs, such as food and rent. Two different types of loan exist.

Mortgage-style loans were available to those students who were eligible to receive mandatory awards. These are no longer available to current students, but see p24 for information on repayment.

Income-contingent loans form part of the help available to students under the present student support regulations. Twenty-five per cent of the loan is subject to an income assessment. The remaining 75 per cent is not income assessed.

Maximum amount of income-contingent loan 2008/09[14]

	Full year	Final year
London	£6,475	£5,895
Elsewhere	£4,625	£4,280
Parental home	£3,580	£3,235
Overseas rate	£5,510	£4,790

Maximum amount of income-contingent loan 2009/10[15]

	Full year	Final year
London	£6,643	£6,048
Elsewhere	£4,745	£4,391
Parental home	£3,673	£3,319
Overseas rate	£5,653	£4,915

Long courses loan

You may be entitled to additional amounts of loan for any extra weeks of attendance over the standard 30 weeks and three days.

For students who started before 1 September 2008, this will simply be added to the standard loan amount paid. For 2008 cohort students this additional amount is known specifically as the 'long courses loan', and is treated differently in the income assessment. In both cases, however, any additional amount is paid along with other forms of support at the start of each term, and is repaid along with other student loan debt.

The table below outlines the amount paid for each week your course exceeds the standard length. If your course year lasts 45 weeks or more you will be paid for a full 52 weeks of attendance.

Amount of long courses loan 2008/09[16]

	Weekly amount
London	£103
Elsewhere	£81
Parental home	£53
Overseas rate	£112

Amount of long courses loan 2009/10[17]

	Weekly amount
London	£106
Elsewhere	£83
Parental home	£54
Overseas rate	£115

Repayment

Both categories of loan are repayable at the end of your studies. The repayment method differs for each type of loan. Mortgage-style loans are normally paid over 60 fixed monthly instalments from the April following your graduation or the point you otherwise leave your course.[18] However, you can request that repayments are deferred if you earn less than 85 per cent of the national average wage. In 2008/09 repayments can be deferred if your gross earnings do not exceed £2,161 a month.

Liability to repay mortgage-style loans can be cancelled in certain circumstances. These are if:

- you die;
- you are permanently incapacitated from work because of a disability;
- you reach the age of 50 (or 60 if you were 40 or over when you last took out a loan);
- 25 years after the April following your graduation, whichever comes first.

The amount of money you pay back each month on an income-contingent loan depends on your earnings. From the April after you graduate or otherwise leave your course you will begin to make repayments once you earn above £15,000 a year. Repayments start at a rate of 9 per cent of all income above that threshold. For example, if you earn £16,000 a year, you will pay back 9 per cent of £1,000 (ie, £90 a year or £7.50 a month).

Liability to repay income-contingent loans can also be cancelled if you die or are permanently incapacitated from work because of a disability. If you are an 'old system' student they are also cancelled if you reach the age of 65. 'Current system' students have their liability cancelled 25 years after the April following their graduation.

Students who graduate in 2010 or later can take a repayment holiday of up to five years, so that even if you are earning over the repayment threshold you do not have to make any payments. Interest continues to accrue during this time.

Maintenance grant

The maintenance grant is available to students from low-income backgrounds who commenced their studies on or after 1 September 2006.[19] This grant is payable for maintenance costs and the maximum rate in 2008/09 is £2,835 (£2,906 in 2009/10). The first £1,260 (£1,292 in 2009/10) of the grant is paid to substitute for part of the maintenance loan – eg, if you receive £900 maintenance grant, the maximum rate of loan you can borrow is reduced by £900. Any maintenance grant in excess of £1,260 (or £1,292 in 2009/10) does not further reduce the loan.

Special support grant

The special support grant is available to students from low-income backgrounds who commenced their studies on or after 1 September 2006 and who are eligible to receive means-tested benefits, such as income support or housing benefit.[20] The maximum rate is £2,835 in 2008/09 (£2,906 in 2009/10). This grant is payable for course-related costs and is not taken into account as income when working out entitlement to means-tested benefits. This grant is payable in addition to the full maintenance loan.

Adult dependants' grant

If you have an adult dependant(s) 'wholly or mainly financially dependent' on you, you may be eligible for an adult dependants' grant.[21] Eligible adult dependants include your spouse or civil partner, or (if you are aged 25 and over) a cohabiting partner. The maximum grant is £2,575 (£2,642 in 2009/10), but the amount you receive depends on your situation and the income of your dependant(s). The amount you are eligible to receive is halved if your spouse/partner receives full-time student support from the DIUS.

Parents' learning allowance

If you are a parent with dependent children you may be eligible for a parents' learning allowance.[22] This is intended to help cover your course-related costs. How much you get depends on your income and that of your partner, spouse and any other dependants. It is not counted as income when assessing your social security benefit entitlement.

The maximum entitlement is £1,470 (£1,508 in 2009/10). If a couple are both full-time students, both can claim the full allowance, subject to their household income.

Childcare grant

If you have responsibility for a child under the age of 15 (or 17 if s/he has special educational needs) and you use registered or approved childcare, you can apply for a childcare grant.[23] You cannot receive the childcare grant if you receive the childcare element of working tax credit (WTC – see Chapter 19). You can choose to change your funding from WTC to the childcare grant if you wish.

A 'registered childcare provider' is a person who is registered under the Children Act[24] and who provides daycare. The person must care for one or more children aged under eight for more than two hours a day for payment. The care must be provided on domestic premises, used wholly or mainly as a private dwelling. A relative who provides childcare for your child would qualify as long as s/he is registered with the Office for Standards in Education (Ofsted) and s/he is also looking after other children who are unrelated to her/him. Nurseries, out-of-hours school clubs and holiday playschemes also count as registered childcare.

'Approved childcare' covers provision for children aged eight or over. The childcare must be approved by an accredited organisation under the Tax Credit (New Category of Childcare Provider) Regulations 1999. From September 2005, this definition was widened to include carers who are approved under the voluntary Childcare Approval Scheme. This scheme covers childcare in the parent's home for children of any age and childcare for children aged eight or over provided by a childminder in her/his own home or other domestic premises.

The grant can cover up to 85 per cent of your actual costs of childcare, with a maximum payment of £148.75 a week for one child or £255 a week for two or more children. The maximum amount of grant available annually is £7,735 for one child and £13,260 for two or more children. These rates remain unchanged in 2009/10.

The childcare grant is income-assessed; the amount you receive depends on your income and the income of any dependants.

Disabled students' allowance

If you incur additional course-related costs as a consequence of a disability, you can apply for a disabled students' allowance.[25] This is a needs-based allowance, and if you apply to your local authority or Student Finance England (SFE) for assistance under this scheme you will need to provide medical proof of your disability, such as a letter from your doctor, educational psychologist or other specialist. If the local authority accepts this proof, it will help you arrange a needs assessment with a recognised assessor, who will recommend what additional support or equipment you should be supplied with.

Maximum amounts approved by the local authority 2008/09[26]

Non-medical personal helper(s)	£20,000 per academic year
Major items of specialist equipment	£5,030 for duration of the course
Other expenditure	Up to £1,680 per academic year
Extra travel expenditure resulting from disability	Full reimbursement

Maximum amounts approved by the local authority or SFE 2009/10[27]

Non-medical personal helper(s)	£20,520 per academic year
Major items of specialist equipment	£5,161 for duration of the course
Other expenditure	Up to £1,724 per academic year
Extra travel expenditure resulting from disability	Full reimbursement

Assessment of income

Most elements of student support are subject to an income assessment.[28] You may be assessed as either a dependent (see below) or an independent student (see p28).
Your own income is always assessed, plus that of your:
* natural parent(s), if you do not have 'independent' status (see p28); *or*
* spouse, if you are married; *or*
* civil partner, if you have entered into a civil partnership; *or*
* cohabiting partner of the opposite sex, if you are aged 25 or over and started your course in September 2000 or later; *or*
* cohabiting partner of the same sex, if you are aged 25 or over and started your course in September 2005 or later.

If your parents are separated, divorced or widowed and you are not deemed independent, the income of the parent with whom you live is taken into account. If you do not live with either parent, SFE will decide which parent's income is most appropriate to use.

If you started your course after September 2004, the income of your parent's spouse, civil or cohabiting partner will also be assessed, even if that person is not your own parent.

If you are considered a dependent student, the local authority or SFE looks at your parents' gross taxable income over the last full tax year (for the academic year 2008/09, this is 6 April 2007 to 5 April 2008), then subtracts pension scheme and superannuation payments which attract tax relief. A further £1,100 is deducted for each additional dependent child or if your parent is a student her/himself.[29]

The remaining amount is added to any gross taxable income you have for the 2008/09 academic year (subject to various disregards, including all earnings from part-time or casual work) to form your household income figure.[30]

The household income figure is then used to determine how much the household is expected to contribute to your costs and, therefore, how much support you will receive from the Government.

Future changes

In 2009/10, the rules on income assessment will change so that your parents' income from the year before the preceding tax year will be used. This means that in 2009/10 the 2007/08 tax year will be used again.[31]

Note: if the level of your parents' income falls by at least 15 per cent during the academic year, you can request a reassessment from the local authority or SFE.[32]

Independent students

You are assessed as an '**independent student**' if:[33]

- you are either aged 25 before the beginning of the academic year in which your course begins or you become 25 during the academic year (in which case you will have independent status from the beginning of the following academic year); *or*
- you are married or in a civil partnership before the course begins or you marry or enter a civil partnership during the course (in which case you will become independent from the beginning of the following academic year); *or*
- you have been financially self-reliant for any three years before the academic year in which your course begins (this qualifying period can include periods of unemployment and participation in training schemes for the unemployed, such as modern apprenticeships or the New Deal); *or*
- you have responsibility for one or more children; *or*
- you have received a pension, allowance or other benefit as a result of your sickness, disability or injury (including maternity allowance); *or*
- you are irreconcilably estranged from your parents; *or*
- you have been in custody or care; *or*
- your parents cannot be found; *or*
- it is not reasonably practicable for your parents to send parental contributions to the UK, or they would be placed in jeopardy if they did so; *or*
- you are an orphan; *or*
- you are a member of a religious order living in a house of that order. **Note:** this provision will no longer apply to students from 1 September 2009.

If you are considered an independent student, only your gross taxable income for the academic year, less various disregards (including earnings from part-time work), is taken into account.

If your spouse or civil/cohabiting partner is considered part of the assessable household, her/his income is assessed in a similar way to that of parents (see p27).[34]

Any income from your spouse or civil/cohabiting partner is added to your income to form the household income to be taken into account.

As with dependent students, the household income figure is then used to determine how much the household is expected to contribute to your costs and, therefore, how much support you will receive from the Government.

'Current system' students: pre-2008 cohorts

If you start your course in the 2006/07 or 2007/08 academic years, and are not subject to any of the gap year provisions (see p19), the assessed income will first reduce any maintenance grant or special support grant you are due to receive.

In 2008/09, if your household income is £18,360 or less, you will receive the maximum maintenance or special support grant. If your income is between £18,361 and £39,305 you will receive a reduced amount of the applicable grant (the minimum amount is £50). For every £6 of household income between £18,360 and £27,810, £1 is deducted from the grant. For every £9.50 of household income above £27,810, £1 is deducted from the grant until the maximum household income of £39,305 is reached. No grant is payable if household income is £39,305 or more.[35]

Income above £39,780 reduces other support at a rate of £1 for every £9.50 of income above £39,780.[36] Any supplementary grants for dependants will be reduced first, then the 25 per cent of the student loan that is means tested and finally any grant for travel costs.[37]

This assessment also applies if you start a course in the 2008/09 academic year or later but have previously studied at HE level.

'Current system' students: 2008 cohort

If you start your course in the 2008/09 academic year or later and have not previously studied at HE level, the assessed income will first reduce any maintenance grant or special support grant you are due to receive.

If your household income is £25,000 or less, you will receive the maximum maintenance or special support grant. If your income is between £25,001 and £60,005 you will receive a reduced amount of the applicable grant (the minimum amount is £50). For every £6 of household income between £25,001 and £34,450, £1 is deducted from the grant. For every £21.12 of household income above £34,450, £1 is deducted from the grant until the maximum household income of £60,005 is reached. No grant is payable if household income is £60,005 or more.[38]

Income above £61,060 will reduce the income-assessed 25 per cent of the applicable basic rate of student loan at a rate of £1 for every £9.50 of additional income.

Other income-assessed support is reduced in a different way. Support is reduced at a rate of £1 for every £9.50 of income above £39,780.[39] Any supplementary grants for dependants will be reduced first, then any long courses loan payable, and finally any grant for travel costs.[40]

'Old system' students

If you are funded under the system available to students who started courses between 1998 and 2005, the following income assessments are applied.

Higher education grant

The income assessment for the HE grant is separate from that for other support.[41] If your household income is £16,750 or less, you will receive the maximum grant. If your income is between £16,751 and £22,734 you will receive a reduced amount of the grant (the minimum amount is £50). For every £6.30 of household income above £16,751, £1 will be deducted from the grant until the maximum household income of £22,735 is reached. No grant is payable if household income is £22,735 or more.

Dependent students

If you are a dependent student (see p27), or your spouse, civil partner or cohabiting partner's income is taken into account, your household income is calculated as for 'current system' students.

If your household income is less than £23,660, no contribution applies. Once household income reaches £23,660, a £45 contribution towards your support becomes payable. After this, £1 is deducted from your support for every £9.50 of household income above this amount.[42]

The contribution is applied first to the grant for tuition fees, then to any grants for dependants, then to the income-assessed portion of the student loan and finally to any grant for tuition fees, until all income-assessed support is eliminated.[43]

Independent students

If you are a single independent student (see p28 for the definition of independent), the income thresholds are different. As with 'current system' students, only your own estimated gross taxable income (less various disregards) for the current academic year is taken into account. If your income is less than £11,020 no contribution is payable, but your student support is reduced by £1 for every £9.50 of income above this level in the same order as for dependent students.[44]

Institutional bursaries

A 'current system' student who is receiving the full maintenance or special support grant of £2,835 and whose university or college charges fees of more than £2,835 should be eligible for a minimum non-repayable bursary, equal to any fee amount charged above £2,835. Therefore, the maximum mandatory bursary for 2008/09 is £310. However, many institutions offer more than this minimum mandatory bursary. You should contact your university or college for more information.

2. Part-time undergraduates

Support for part-time students is different from that for full-time students. The support offered is the same for both new and existing part-time undergraduate students. The personal and course eligibility requirements apply as for full-time students (see pp19 and 21).[45] To be eligible for this package, a student must be studying a course that is at least 50 per cent of a full-time course – ie, it takes no longer than twice the time of the equivalent full-time course to complete.[46]

Grant for fees

If you are a part-time undergraduate student (including students from the European Union (EU) – see p20) you may be eligible for an income-assessed grant.[47] The maximum amount of grant for which you are eligible depends on the intensity of study for each academic year of the course.

Maximum grant for part-time fees 2008/09

Course intensity	Maximum grant available 2008/09[48]	Maximum grant available 2009/10[49]
Less than 60%	£785	£805
60–74%	£945	£970
75% or more	£1,180	£1,210

Grant for course costs

A grant for course costs of up to £255 (£260 in 2009/10) is available to students from low-income backgrounds to help with the costs of books, equipment and travel.[50] The amount of grant available is not affected by the intensity of study. This is not available to EU students.

Fee waiver

This provision is only available to students who were in receipt of a part-time fee waiver in the 2003/04 and 2004/05 academic years. If you are such a student, are studying at least 50 per cent of an equivalent full-time course and are on a low income, you may be able to apply for a fee waiver from your institution if your fees are more than the maximum fee support provided by your local authority. Continuing EU students are also eligible to apply for this help.

From the start of the 2006/07 academic year, part-time students have been able to apply for help from the new Additional Fee Support Scheme, a part of the Access to Learning Fund (see p33).

Assessment of income

In 2008/09, if your income is below £16,090, you are eligible for the maximum grant for fees and course costs. If your income is between £16,090 and £24,280, you will receive some help with fees and course costs. If your income is between £24,280 and £26,825 you will receive some help with course costs, but not with fees. The exact amount you receive depends on your income. If your income is £26,825, you will receive a course grant of £50. Only your and your partner's (if you have one) income is taken into account as household income. Your parents' income is ignored regardless of your age.[51]

If you are married or in a civil partnership, or aged 25 or over and living with a partner (including a same-sex partner) or have dependent children, the following amounts will be deducted from your income:[52]
- £2,000 for your partner;
- £2,000 for your eldest child;
- £1,000 for every other child.

Disabled students' allowance

If you are studying at an intensity of at least 50 per cent of an equivalent full-time course and have a disability, you can apply for a disabled students' allowance. The amount a local authority can award for non-medical help and other general expenditure is, however, reduced according to the workload of a part-time course.

Maximum amounts approved by the local authority 2008/09[53]

Non-medical personal helper(s)	£15,000 per academic year
Major items of specialist equipment	£5,030 for duration of the course
Other expenditure	Up to £1,260 per academic year
Extra travel expenditure resulting from disability	Full reimbursement

Maximum amounts approved by the local authority or SFE 2009/10[54]

Non-medical personal helper(s)	£15,390 per academic year
Major items of specialist equipment	£5,161 for duration of the course
Other expenditure	Up to £1,293 per academic year
Extra travel expenditure resulting from disability	Full reimbursement

Part-time taster modules

If you are studying between 10 and 49 per cent of an equivalent full-time course and have no previous experience of higher education, you may be eligible for help with tuition fees for a module or academic year (whichever is the shorter). The maximum amount payable is at the discretion of your university or college. You should contact the Access to Learning administrator at your college or university. EU students are also eligible to apply for this help.

3. Hardship funds

Higher education institutions are allocated money to provide hardship funds for 'home' (see p21) undergraduate and postgraduate students in financial difficulty. Repayable loans and non-repayable grants can both be issued by the funds.

Access to Learning Fund

Non-repayable grants are available on a needs-assessed basis if you are experiencing financial difficulty serious enough to mean you may have to leave your course. The funds can help with living and study costs such as childcare, rent, books and utility bills, or with large one-off and exceptional costs such as major housing repairs, and emergency situations such as fire or bereavement.

Priority is given to students with children, mature students, students from low-income families, disabled students, final year students and those who have left care. However, all students who meet the personal and course requirements for undergraduate student support are eligible, including healthcare students and those in receipt of dance and drama awards. You must, however, have applied for your full entitlement of a student maintenance loan and received the first instalment where you are eligible for one.

The funds cannot be used to meet the costs of tuition fees charged to full-time undergraduate students or to make up for non-receipt of a parental contribution to a grant or loan.

A grant would not normally exceed £3,500, although institutions have some discretion in exceptional circumstances. Individual institutions have different application processes and different pressures on the funds and no sum is guaranteed. However, there is an appeals process should you need to challenge the fund administrator's decision.

Additional Fee Support Scheme

This scheme is available to help 'home' and European Union students meet the costs of their part-time fees while studying. Local Fund administrators have discretion on how much assistance to pay and to whom. Students should contact the Fund administrator at their institution for further information.

Notes

1. **Full-time undergraduates**

1 E(MA) Regs
2 Reg 2 E(SS) Regs
3 s25 HEA 2004
4 Sch 1 Part 2 E(SS) Regs
5 For a definition of 'relevant family member' see Sch 1, para 1 E(SS) Regs
6 Sch 1, para 8 E(SS) Regs
7 Sch 1, para 10 E(SS) Regs
8 Reg 5 and Sch 2 E(SS) Regs
9 Reg 28 E(SS) Regs
10 Reg 32 E(SS) Regs
11 Reg 17 E(SS) Regs
12 Reg 21 E(SS) Regs
13 Reg 61 E(SS) Regs
14 Regs 65-70 E(SS) Regs
15 Reg 67-72 E(SS)No.2 Regs
16 Regs 71 and 77 E(SS) Regs
17 Regs 73 and 79 E(SS)No.2 Regs
18 If you have taken out more than five student loans, you will repay your loan in 84 monthly instalments.
19 Reg 55 E(SS) Regs
20 Reg 58 E(SS) Regs
21 Reg 42 E(SS) Regs
22 Reg 44 E(SS) Regs
23 Reg 43 E(SS) Regs
24 s79(f) CA 1989
25 Reg 39 E(SS) Regs
26 Reg 40 E(SS) Regs
27 Reg 41 E(SS)No.2 Regs
28 Sch 4 E(SS) Regs
29 Sch 4 para 3 E(SS) Regs
30 Sch 4 para 4 E(SS) Regs
31 Sch 4 para 1 E(SS)No.2 Regs
32 Sch 4 para 5(4)–(5) E(SS) Regs; Sch 4 para 5(3)–(4) E(SS)No.2 Regs

33 Sch 4 para 2 E(SS) Regs
34 Sch 4 para 6 E(SS) Regs
35 Reg 57 E(SS) Regs
36 Sch 4 para 9 E(SS) Regs
37 Regs 97 and 100 E(SS) Regs
38 Reg 56 E(SS) Regs
39 Sch 4 para 9 E(SS) Regs
40 Regs 96 and 99 E(SS) Regs
41 Reg 62 E(SS) Regs
42 Sch 4 para 8(1) E(SS) Regs
43 Reg 98 E(SS) Regs
44 Sch 4 para 8(2) E(SS) Regs

2. **Part-time undergraduates**

45 Reg 132 E(SS) Regs
46 Reg 134(1)(c) E(SS) Regs
47 Reg 136 E(SS) Regs
48 Reg 137 E(SS) Regs
49 Reg 137 E(SS)No.2 Regs
50 Reg 136(1)(b) E(SS) Regs
51 Reg 137 E(SS) Regs
52 Reg 138 E(SS) Regs
53 Reg 140 E(SS) Regs
54 Reg 140 E(SS)No.2 Regs

Chapter 3

Undergraduate student support: Wales

This chapter covers:
1. Full-time undergraduates (below)
2. Part-time undergraduates (p39)
3. Hardship funds (p41)

Basic facts
- Undergraduate students are able to apply for a mixture of grants and loans for fees and living costs, depending on their personal circumstances.
- Support differs for full- and part-time students.
- The support available in England and Northern Ireland is different to that available in Wales.
- Separate provisions apply to healthcare, social work and initial teacher training students.
- A Financial Contingency Fund is available for those in financial difficulty.

The type of financial support you can receive when you are learning depends on several factors, including when you begin your course, the length of the course, the discipline you are studying, whether the course is full time or part time, where you normally live when you apply for support, where you will be studying, your age and if you have previously received funding for a course.

If you are a student on an NHS-funded healthcare course, a course of initial teacher training or a course leading to a qualification in social work, your support will vary (see Chapter 6).

1. Full-time undergraduates

Full-time undergraduates in Wales on eligible courses (see p36) and who are personally eligible (see p36) can apply for financial assistance from the Welsh Assembly. Separate provision is available for part-time undergraduates (see p39).

Who is eligible for support

In order to receive financial support you must be 'personally eligible' (see below) and studying an eligible course (see below).

Personal eligibility

To be personally eligible for support from the Welsh Assembly you must meet the residency rules.[1] These are the same as for England, except that, where appropriate, you must be normally resident in Wales on the first day of the first academic year.

Course eligibility

Broadly, the course must be full time (as defined by the education provider) and be:[2]

- a first degree;
- a higher education (HE) diploma;
- a BTEC higher national certificate (HNC) or higher national diploma (HND);
- a course of initial teacher training;
- a course for the further training of teachers, or youth or community workers;
- a course to prepare for certain professional examinations of a standard higher than A level, or BTEC or HNC/HND where a first degree is not required for entry;
- a course not higher than a first degree, but higher than those described in the above bullet point.

Students who entered higher education on or after 1 September 1998 and before 1 September 2006

If you began your course on or after 1 September 1998 and before 1 September 2006, or you were treated as a continuing student when you started in the 2006/07 academic year, you will receive financial help under the old rules for student support. This is, in the main, identical to the support available for 'old system' students in England (see p18).[3]

However, if you are eligible for funding under this system as a Welsh-domiciled student there are some differences. In addition to the support available for all English and Welsh students, you may be able to receive an Assembly learning grant for 'old system' students.

Assembly learning grant for 'old system' students

Students who started their education in either the 2002/03 or the 2003/04 academic years, and who are on a low income, may be eligible for a means-tested Welsh Assembly learning grant of up to £1,500.[4] A grant of at least £450 is available if you are on a full-time course and your family income is below £17,250. If your household income is below £11,491, £750 is available. The full £1,500 will be offered if your household income is less than £5,745. The grants are administered through Welsh local authorities but you can attend any institution in the UK.

If you are an 'old system' student, and you started your higher education in September 2004 or later, you should apply for the £1,000 HE grant in the first instance (see p22).[5] However, if your household income is less than £5,745, you will receive a £500 'top-up' Assembly learning grant to bring your total grant funding to £1,500.

Assessment of income

The means test for 'old system' Welsh students is broadly the same as that for English students.[6]

Students who entered higher education on or after 1 September 2006

Tuition fees

Eligible, 'new system' Welsh-domiciled students and non-UK European Union students studying in Wales will pay flexible fees of up to £3,145 in the 2008/09 academic year. They will also receive a tuition fee grant of up to £1,890, so that the most that eligible students will pay is £1,255 for the year.[7] You may be eligible for a tuition fee loan to cover the remainder.[8] If you are eligible for fee support but not for a fee grant you can receive a fee loan up to the level of the fee charged.[9]

If you choose to study in England or Northern Ireland, you will pay up to £3,145. Fees for Welsh-domiciled students in Scotland are fixed at £1,775 a year for all courses except medicine, which is fixed at £2,825 a year. In all cases, eligible Welsh-domiciled students can take out tuition fee loans to cover this cost.

The maximum loan available will match the fee you are charged. The fee loan is not means tested on your income or the income of anyone in your household. However, the loan will be added to your total student loan debt (including any loans taken out for living costs) and you must start your repayments once you have graduated, or otherwise left the course, and are earning at least £15,000 a year (if you are working in the UK).

If you wish to pay all, or part, of the fee in cash in advance, you can do so. Your institution will expect some indication of how you intend to pay your fees when you register.

Help with tuition fees for part-time courses is also available (see p39).

Assembly learning grant for 'current system' students[10]

The Assembly learning grant for 'current system' students is a non-repayable, means-tested allowance of up to £2,835. The maximum amount is payable to students with a household income of less than £18,370 a year, and a partial amount is paid on a sliding scale to students with a household income of up to £39,300.

Part of the grant substitutes the student loan for living costs. If you receive an Assembly learning grant, the amount of loan for living costs you can receive is reduced, pound for pound, up to a maximum of £1,255. If you receive more than £1,255 Assembly learning grant, the student loan is not reduced further (see below for more details of loans for living costs).

Example

Gordon receives an Assembly learning grant of £1,540. The maximum amount of loan for living costs he can receive will be reduced by £1,255.

If you are entitled to apply for means-tested benefits, you should apply for the special support grant instead of the Assembly learning grant (see below). If you are not entitled to apply, but your partner is, the Assembly learning grant will be included as income in any benefits claim. See Chapter 20 for more details.

Special support grant

In order to provide extra support for students regarded as particularly vulnerable, a separate grant is available if you are a full-time student eligible to claim means-tested social security benefits.[11]

Most full-time students cannot receive such benefits. Some students, however, can claim – eg, if you are a lone parent, or you and your partner are both full-time students and have one or more children, or you receive disability living allowance, or you are deaf. See the relevant benefits chapter for details of which students can claim means-tested benefits.

If you can claim means-tested benefits, you should claim the special support grant rather than the Assembly learning grant. Like the Assembly learning grant for 'new system' students, the special support grant is a non-repayable, means-tested allowance of up to £2,835. The maximum amount is payable to students with a household income of less than £18,370 a year. A partial amount is paid on a sliding scale to students with a household income of up to £39,300.

Unlike the Assembly learning grant, however, the special support grant does not substitute any part of the student loan and it is not taken into account when calculating your entitlement to means-tested benefits.

Student loans for living costs

Student loans for living costs are available to eligible Welsh-domiciled students on the same terms and rates as for students in England (see p23).

Supplementary grants

A number of other grants and allowances are available to particular groups of students with extra needs.

Students with dependants

Students with dependent children may be able to receive a parents' learning allowance[12] and/or a childcare grant[13] on the same basis as students in England (see p25).

If you have an adult dependant(s) 'wholly or mainly financially dependent' on you, you may be eligible for an adult dependants' grant.[14] Again, this is awarded on the same basis as in England (see p25).

Students with children should also apply for child tax credit (see Chapter 18).

Disabled students' allowance

If you are disabled and have extra costs associated with your course because of your disability, you may be entitled to extra help to pay for them. This is also awarded on the same basis as in England (see p26).[15]

Grants for travel costs

Medical and dental students on placement and students who must travel abroad may be entitled to help with the cost of travel. This is awarded on same basis as in England.[16]

Assessment of income

The means test for 'new system' Welsh students is the same as that for English students who started in the 2006/07 or 2007/08 academic years (see p27).[17]

---

2. **Part-time undergraduates**

New and existing part-time undergraduate students can qualify for grants for fees and living costs. The personal and course eligibility requirements are the same as for full-time students (see pp19 and 21). To be eligible for this package a student must be studying a course that is at least 50 per cent of a full-time course.

Grant for fees

If you are a part-time undergraduate student (including students from the European Union (EU) – see p20), you may be eligible for a means-tested grant for fees.[18] The maximum amount of grant to which you are eligible depends on the intensity of study for each academic year of the course (see table on p40).

Grant for course costs

A grant for course costs of up to £1,050 is available to students from low-income backgrounds to help with the costs of books, equipment and travel.[19] The amount of grant available is affected by the intensity of study (see table on p40). This is not available to EU students. It does not affect your entitlement to means-tested benefits.

Part-time fee and course grants

Course intensity	Maximum fee grant	Maximum course grant	Total maximum support
50–59% of the equivalent full-time course	£620	£1,050	£1,670
60–74% of the equivalent full-time course	£745	£1,050	£1,795
75% or more of the equivalent full-time course	£930	£1,050	£1,980

Assessment of income[20]

If you are single and you have no dependants, the following assessment applies to you. If your income is £16,109 or less, you are eligible for the maximum grant for fees and course costs. If your income is between £16,110 and £24,295, you will receive some help with fees and course costs. If your income is between £24,295 and £26,915, you will receive some help with course costs, but not with fees. The exact amount you receive depends on your income. Only your and your partner's (if you have one) income is taken into account as household income. Your parents' income is ignored.

If you are married or in a civil partnership, or aged 25 or over and living with a partner (including a same-sex partner) or have dependent children, the following amounts are added to the above income limits:

- £2,000 for your partner;
- £2,000 for your eldest child;
- £1,000 for every other child.

The Student Finance Wales booklet *A Guide to Financial Support for Part-time Students in Higher Education 2008/09* provides further details, including examples.

Disabled students' allowance

If you are studying at an intensity of at least 50 per cent of an equivalent full-time course and have a disability, you may also apply for a disabled students' allowance.[21] The amount a local authority can award for non-medical help and other general expenditure is, however, reduced according to the workload of a part-time course.

See p26 for further information.

Fee waiver

This is available to part-time students undertaking 10 credits or more who are in receipt of a means-tested benefit, whose sole income is benefits or who are registered jobseekers. Students who already have a first degree are not eligible to apply. This scheme is administered by the universities and colleges.

3. Hardship funds

Higher education institutions are allocated money to provide hardship funds for 'home' (see p21) undergraduate and postgraduate students in financial difficulty. Repayable loans and non-repayable grants can both be issued by the funds.

Financial Contingency Fund

Non-repayable grants are available on a needs-assessed basis if you are experiencing financial difficulty serious enough to mean you may have to leave your course. The Financial Contingency Fund can help with living and study costs such as childcare, rent, books and utility bills, or with large one-off and exceptional costs such as major housing repairs and emergency situations such as fire or bereavement.

Priority is usually given to students with children, mature students, students from low-income families, disabled students, final year students and those who have left care. However, all students who meet the personal and course requirements for undergraduate student support are eligible to apply, including healthcare students and those in receipt of dance and drama awards. You must, however, have applied for your full entitlement of a student loan if you are eligible for one.

The funds cannot be used to meet the costs of tuition fees charged to full-time undergraduate students or to make up for non-receipt of a parental contribution to a grant or loan.

A grant would not normally exceed £3,500, although institutions have some discretion in exceptional circumstances. Individual institutions have different application processes and different pressures on the funds and no sum is guaranteed. However, there is an appeals process should you need to challenge the Fund administrator's decision.

Notes

1. **Full-time undergraduates**
   1   Sch 1 ALGL(HE)(W) Regs
   2   Reg 5 and Sch 2 ALGL(HE)(W) Regs
   3   ALGL(HE)(W) Regs
   4   E(ALGS)(W) Regs
   5   Reg 35 ALGL(HE)(W) Regs
   6   Sch 5 ALGL(HE)(W) Regs
   7   Reg 18 ALGL(HE)(W) Regs
   8   Reg 22 ALGL(HE)(W) Regs
   9   Reg 21 ALGL(HE)(W) Regs
   10 Reg 36 ALGL(HE)(W) Regs
   11 Reg 37 ALGL(HE)(W) Regs
   12 Reg 28 ALGL(HE)(W) Regs
   13 Reg 27 ALGL(HE)(W) Regs
   14 Reg 26 ALGL(HE)(W) Regs
   15 Reg 24 ALGL(HE)(W) Regs
   16 Reg 31 ALGL(HE)(W) Regs
   17 Sch 5 ALGL(HE)(W) Regs

2. **Part-time undergraduates**
   18 Reg 82(4) ALGL(HE)(W) Regs
   19 Reg 82(1) ALGL(HE)(W) Regs
   20 Reg 82(5) ALGL(HE)(W) Regs
   21 Reg 83 ALGL(HE)(W) Regs

Chapter 4

Undergraduate student support: Northern Ireland

This chapter covers:
1. Full-time undergraduates (below)
2. Part-time undergraduates (p49)
3. Hardship funds (p49)

Basic facts
- Undergraduate students are able to apply for a mixture of grants and loans for fees and living costs, depending on their personal circumstances.
- There are differences in support for full- and part-time students.
- The support available in Northern Ireland is different to that in England and Wales.
- Separate provisions apply to healthcare, social work and initial teacher training students.
- Hardship funds are available for those in financial difficulty.

The type of financial support you can receive when you are learning depends on several factors, including: when you begin your course, the length of the course, the discipline you are studying, whether the course is full time or part time, and your age.

If you are a student on an NHS-funded healthcare course, a course of initial teacher training or a course leading to a qualification in social work, your support will vary (see Chapter 6).

1. Full-time undergraduates

Student awards for Northern Irish-domiciled students studying in Northern Ireland, mainland Britain or the Republic of Ireland are administered by the Department for Employment and Learning Northern Ireland. Applications for support are processed by five education and library boards (ELBs). You should apply to the ELB which covers the area in which you normally live, rather than where you intend to study.

The rules on personal eligibility and course eligibility for Northern Irish students are the same as for students in England (see pp19 and 21), except that students must be resident in Northern Ireland before the start of the academic year.

Student support

Students who entered higher education on or after 1 September 1998 and before 1 September 2006

If you began your course on or after 1 September 1998 and do not fit into any of the circumstances outlined above, you will receive financial help under the old rules for student support, which are, in the main, identical to the support available for 'old system' students in England (see p18).[1]

This system also applies to new students who are attending institutions in the Republic of Ireland.

There are, however, some differences, which are outlined below.

Tuition fees

The maximum fee you will have to pay in the 2008/09 academic year is £1,255.[2] The Government may pay some, or all, of the fee depending on your family's income. If you are assessed to make a contribution, you may be eligible for a student loan for fees up to the amount of the fee charged.[3] See p45 for more details.

If you are a Northern Irish student attending a course at a publicly funded college in the Republic of Ireland, you will have your tuition fees paid by the Irish Government. In addition, the college may charge a registration fee of €825 (2007/08 rates) to cover examination and student services fees, which can be claimed back from your ELB.[4] Therefore, it is important that you apply to your ELB to ensure this charge will be paid, even if you do not intend to apply for financial help towards living costs.

Higher education bursary

If you have a low income you may be eligible for a non-repayable, means-tested bursary of up to £2,000 to help with your living costs.[5]

The full amount is available if you have a household income of less than £11,275, whereas a partial amount is available on a sliding scale if your family's income is between £11,275 and £22,551. If you have a family income of more than £22,551, you are not eligible to receive the bursary.

Any bursary you receive will affect the amount of student loan you can have (see p45).

Your bursary is paid in three instalments over the course of the academic year.

Student loan

You can apply for a partially means-tested student loan to help cover living costs and other expenses. These are income-contingent loans (see p23).

Maximum amount of income-contingent loan 2008/09[6]

	Full year	Final year
London	£6,475	£5,895
Elsewhere	£4,625	£4,280
Parental home	£3,580	£3,235

You may be entitled to additional amounts of loan for any extra weeks of attendance over the standard 30 weeks and three days.

A quarter of the loan is means tested on your household income. In addition, if you are entitled to the full rate of bursary (see above), the amount you can be loaned is reduced by £1,500. If you are entitled to a partial bursary, the amount of loan you can take out is reduced by the amount of the bursary you receive.[7]

The loan is repayable at the end of your studies. The amount of money you pay back each month for an income-contingent loan depends on your earnings. Once you earn above £15,000 a year, repayments begin at the rate of 9 per cent of all income above this threshold. For example, if you earn £16,000 a year, you will pay back 9 per cent of £1,000 (ie, £90 a year or £7.50 a month).

Care leavers' grant[8]

You may be eligible for this grant if you left care before 1 September 2005 and entered higher education before your 21st birthday. The care leavers' grant is available because you may not have the same access to financial help or to a parental home as other students during the long vacation. If you are eligible for the grant at the start of your course you remain eligible for help throughout the remainder of your course, even if you are older than 21 by the end.

In order to be eligible, the ELB must be satisfied that no parental contribution is required for the means-tested elements of student support – eg, help with tuition fees. You should qualify for a care leavers' grant if, since the age of 16, you have been provided with accommodation for any continuous period of three months prior to beginning your course, or if you have been in custody or care as a result of a court order.

Provided you meet these criteria and you have not been under the guardianship of your parents since that time, you are eligible for up to £100 a week in the long vacation (usually the summer) of every continuous year of your studies. This does not include the vacations immediately before you start, or after you complete, your course.

The amount you receive is at the ELB's discretion and, although not subject to a means test, will be paid according to need. For example, your ELB may consider the other support you receive, such as help from the social services department or hardship funds from your place of study.

Other support

The childcare grant, parents' learning allowance, adult dependants' grant, and disabled students' allowance are all available to Northern Irish undergraduates on the same basis as students in England.[9] See pp25–26 for further details of these forms of support.

Students who entered higher education on or after 1 September 2006

If you began your course on or after 1 September 2006 and are not otherwise treated as if you had started before this date (eg, you had secured a deferred entry place from the 2005/06 academic year), you will receive financial help under the current rules for student support.[10] The exception to this rule is if you are studying in the Republic of Ireland, in which case you will be funded as an 'old system' student.

Tuition fees

Eligible, 'current system' Northern Irish-domiciled students studying in Northern Ireland, Wales or England will pay variable fees of up to £3,145 in the 2008/09 academic year. You are eligible for a tuition fee loan to cover these.[11]

Fees for Northern Irish-domiciled students in Scotland are fixed at £1,775 per year for all courses except medicine, in which case the fee is fixed at £2,825 per year. In all cases, eligible Northern Irish-domiciled students can take out tuition fee loans to cover this cost.

The maximum fee loan available will match the fee you are charged. The fee loan is not means tested on your income or the income of anyone in your household. However, the loan will be added to your total student loan debt (including any loans taken out for living costs) and you will start repayments once you have graduated or otherwise left the course and are earning at least £15,000 a year.

If you wish to pay all, or part, of the fee in cash, you can do so. Your institution will expect some indication of how you intend to pay your fees when you register.

Help with tuition fees for part-time courses is also available (see p31).

If you wish to study in the Republic of Ireland, see the information for 'old system' students on p44.

Maintenance grant

The maintenance grant for 'current system' students is a non-repayable, means-tested allowance of up to £3,335. The maximum amount is payable to students with a household income of £18,360 or less a year, and a partial amount is paid on a sliding scale up to a household income of £39,305.[12]

If you are entitled to apply for means-tested benefits, you should apply for the special support grant instead of the maintenance grant (see p48). If you are not entitled to apply, but your partner is, the maintenance grant will be included in benefits claims for your household.

Part of the maintenance grant substitutes the student loan for living costs. This means that if you receive any maintenance grant, the amount of loan for living costs you can receive is reduced, up to a maximum of £1,760. The formula for this can be complex, and you should seek advice from your ELB, students' union or university advice service.

If you are in receipt of a full maintenance grant of £3,335, the maximum amount of student loan for living costs is reduced by £1,760.

If you are in receipt of a maintenance grant of between £1,260 and £3,335, the loan will be reduced by £1,260 plus the difference between the calculation of the maintenance grant under the Northern Irish and English regulations. The difference arises because in Northern Ireland students can receive a higher amount of bursary and the means test is applied in different ways.

To calculate this figure, you must first calculate what you would receive under both systems.

In Northern Ireland, this calculation is: £2,075 *minus* (household income *minus* £18,360 *divided by* £4.55). The £2,075 is the maximum rate of Northern Irish grant less £1,260.

In England, the calculation is: £1,575 *minus* (household income *minus* £18,360 *divided by* £6). The £1,575 is the maximum rate of English grant less £1,260.

Subtracting the second figure from the first will give you the amount you should add to £1,260 and subtract from the total available amount of loan for living costs.[13]

If the maintenance grant you receive is less than £1,260, the loan is reduced by the amount of the grant payable. You will receive a grant of £1,260 or less if your assessable household income is greater than £27,810.

Examples

Gail is a single, independent student studying in Belfast. She starts her course in October 20087. She has an assessable household income of £2,000. She receives the maximum grant of £3,335 and can take out a student loan of up to £2,865 (the maximum rate of £4,625 less £1,760).

Anne is 18 and lives with her parents in Armagh. She starts her course in Belfast in October 2008. Her assessable family income is £21,500. The maintenance grant received is calculated as follows.
£2,075 – (£21,500 – £18,360 ÷ £4.55). This works out as £2,075 – £690.11, so Anne receives £1,384.89.
Under the English regulations, Anne's grant would have been calculated as follows.
£1,575 – (£21,500 – £18,360 ÷ £6). This works out as £1,575 – £523.33 = £1,051.67.

Therefore, the maximum rate of loan for living costs Anne can receive is reduced by £1,260 plus the difference between the English and Northern Irish regulations.
£1384.89 – £1,051.67 = £333.22. Therefore, the maximum rate of loan is reduced by £1,593.22. As a student living in the parental home, this means Anne can take out a loan of up to £1,986.78. This will be rounded down to the nearest £5.

John is 19 and starts his course in Derry in October 2008. He receives a maintenance grant of £800. The maximum amount of loan he can receive is reduced by £800.

For more details of student loans for living costs, see below.

Special support grant

In order to provide extra support to students regarded as particularly vulnerable, a separate grant is available if you are a full-time student eligible to claim means-tested social security benefits.[14]

Most full-time students cannot receive such benefits but if, for example, you are a lone parent, or you and your partner are both full-time students and have one or more children, or you receive disability living allowance, or you are deaf, you may be able to claim one or more means-tested benefits. See Chapters 12, 14 and 15 for full details of which students can claim means-tested benefits.

If you can claim means-tested benefits, you should claim the special support grant instead of the maintenance grant. Like the maintenance grant, this is a non-repayable, means-tested allowance of up to £3,335. The maximum amount will be payable to students with a household income of less than £18,360 a year. A partial amount will be paid on a sliding scale up to a household income of £39,305.

Unlike the maintenance grant, the special support grant does not substitute any part of the student loan and it is not taken into account when calculating your entitlement to means-tested benefits.

Student loan

Student loans for living costs are available to eligible 'current system' students on the same terms and rates as for 'old system' students, except that up to £1,760 of the loan may be substituted for the maintenance grant that is paid to the student. See p45 for rates of loan and p47 for details of the loan substitution. If you receive a special support grant, no part of your loan is substituted.

Other support

The childcare grant, parents' learning allowance, adult dependants' grant, and disabled students' allowance are all available to Northern Irish undergraduates on the same basis as students in England. See pp25–26 for further details of these forms of support.

You may also be entitled to a bursary from your institution.
Northern Irish undergraduates can also apply for a care leavers' grant (see p45).

2. Part-time undergraduates

Part-time students in Northern Ireland receive funding on the same basis as part-time students in England.[15]

3. Hardship funds

Higher education institutions are allocated money to provide hardship funds for 'home' (see p21) undergraduate and postgraduate students in financial difficulty. Repayable loans and non-repayable grants can be issued by the funds.

Support funds

Non-repayable grants are available on a needs-assessed basis if you are experiencing financial difficulty serious enough to mean you may have to leave your course. The funds can help with living and study costs such as childcare, rent, books and utility bills, or with large one-off and exceptional costs such as major housing repairs and emergency situations such as fire or bereavement. These are known as support funds in Northern Ireland, although similar funds are available elsewhere.

Priority is usually given to students with children, mature students, students from low-income families, disabled students, final year students and those who have left care. However, all students who meet the personal and course requirements for undergraduate student support are eligible, including healthcare students. You must, however, have applied for your full entitlement of a student loan if you are eligible for one.

The funds cannot be used to meet the costs of tuition fees charged to full-time undergraduate students or to make up for non-receipt of a parental contribution to a grant or loan.

A grant would not normally exceed £3,500, although institutions have some discretion in exceptional circumstances. Individual institutions have different application processes and different pressures on the funds and no sum is guaranteed. However, there is an appeals process should you need to challenge the fund administrator's decision.

Notes

1. Full-time students

1 E(SS)(NI) Regs
2 Reg 30 E(SS)(NI) Regs
3 Regs 33–34 E(SS)(NI) Regs
4 Reg 30(7) E(SS)(NI) Regs
5 Reg 62 E(SS)(NI) Regs
6 Reg 65 E(SS)(NI) Regs
7 Reg 68 (3)-(4) E(SS)(NI) Regs
8 Reg 44 E(SS)(NI) Regs
9 Regs 41–57 E(SS)(NI) Regs
10 Reg 2 E(SS)(NI) Regs
11 Regs 18–23 E(SS)(NI) Regs
12 Reg 59 E(SS)(NI) Regs
13 Reg 66 E(SS)(NI) Regs
14 Reg 60-61 E(SS)(NI) Regs

2. Part-time students

15 Regs 125-141E(SS)(NI) Regs

Chapter 5

Postgraduate student support

This chapter covers:
1. Studentship rates (below)
2. Disabled students' allowance (p53)
3. Postgraduate student support in Northern Ireland (p53)

If you are a UK student undertaking a postgraduate course, you have a legal right to receive financial support in one situation only: if you are studying on a postgraduate course of initial teacher training (eg, a Postgraduate Certificate in Education) – see p66. English and Welsh students may also be able to receive a bursary for postgraduate study in social work (see p72), but this financial help is not available to Northern Irish students undertaking study in the UK.

State support for other postgraduate courses is very limited. Individual scholarships or 'studentships' are available from seven research councils but the demand far outstrips supply and funding is not guaranteed. Inter-disciplinary studentships are also offered by some funders, such as the Economic and Social Research Council and the Natural Environment Research Council. See Appendix 2 for the addresses of the award-making bodies.

Funding for postgraduate students in Northern Ireland is different to that in England and Wales – see p53 for further details.

1. Studentship rates

Research councils fund research and Masters studentships, covering fees and maintenance. The following are the basic rates for maintenance in 2008/09. They do not include any grant for tuition fees, which is usually paid in addition. The rate for this in 2008/09 is £3,300. Other schemes may be available, and eligibility and residence conditions will apply – contact the relevant research council for information (see Appendix 2).

Body	Research studentships	Masters studentships	
AHRC	£14,940	£11,040	London
PPMS	£12,940	£9,040	Outside London
		£10,420	London
		£8,420	Outside London
ESRC	£14,940	–	London
	£12,940	–	Outside London
NERC	£14,940	£10,280	London
	£12,940	£8,240	Outside London
MRC[1]	£14,940	£14,940	London
	£12,940	£12,940	Outside London
EPSRC[2]	£12,940	–	
Engineering	£14,400	–	Engineering doctorates only
STFC	£14,940	–	London
	£12,940	–	Outside London
BBSRC[3]	£14,940	£14,940	London
	£12,940	£12,940	Outside London
	£19,970	£19,970	Students with veterinary degrees only

AHRC = Arts and Humanities Research Council

BBSRC = Biotechnology and Biological Sciences Research Council

EPSRC = Engineering and Physical Sciences Research Council

ESRC = Economic and Social Research Council

MRC = Medical Research Council

NERC = Natural Environment Research Council

PPMS = Professional Preparation Masters Scheme

STFC = Science and Technology Facilities Council (formerly the Partial Physics and Astronomy Research Council)

Additional allowances may be available if you have dependants or are a mature student, and some research councils will fund part-time study. The relevant research council can offer guidance on the full range of support available.

Note: the application deadline for almost all awards made through the research councils is usually several months in advance of the start of the course, and you should make your application as early as possible.

2. **Disabled students' allowance**

Both full- and part-time postgraduate students studying 'recognised' taught and research courses are eligible for a disabled students' allowance. A recognised course is one which normally requires a first degree qualification to enter, is at least one academic year long, is provided by a publicly funded institution and is not a course of initial teacher training. Your course should be eligible for an award from a research council or be equivalent to a course which is eligible for awards. Part-time courses should be for longer than a year, but no more than twice as long as an equivalent full-time course. Existing and new students are eligible and there is no age limit, but residency conditions will apply.

One allowance of up to £10,000 a year in 2008/09[4] (rising to £10,260 in 2009/10[5]) is available for specialist equipment, non-medical personal helpers and/or additional travel costs, subject to a needs assessment. Contact your local authority or Student Finance England (see Appendix 2) for more details.

3. **Postgraduate student support in Northern Ireland**

There are no concessionary fees for postgraduate courses in Northern Ireland. You should contact the university or college where you want to study to check on any sources of funding for your course. **Note:** postgraduate funding is no longer available for UK students wishing to study in the Republic of Ireland.

Funding is generally in the form of studentship awards. To be considered for funding you must comply with the three-year residency requirement for undergraduates (see p17).

If you are a suitably qualified graduate you may compete for an award, but there are always more applicants than awards. Further information can be obtained in the booklet *Awards for Postgraduate Study*, available from the Department for Employment and Learning Northern Ireland (DELNI). Closing dates for the different awards vary between 1 May and 30 June and are strictly observed. Check the closing date with the postgraduate office at the university you will be attending.

Studentship awards

These grants are awarded for postgraduate research degrees (eg, MPhil, PhD) and for approved courses of advanced study (eg, Masters degrees). You can obtain approved course lists from the universities. Most students benefiting from these awards have degree classifications of 2:1 or above, although you may be accepted for a taught Masters degree in science and technology if you have a lower second class honours degree.

Studentship awards are for fixed amounts and are not means tested. Approved fees and maintenance costs are included. The basic rate of the maintenance grant payable in 2008/09 is £12,900. Additional allowances may also be paid for dependants and students with special needs.

If you are a science and technology student working on a research project, you may also apply through DELNI for a Co-operative Award in Science and Technology that involves sponsorship from industry. Details are available from DELNI. The basic maintenance grant of £12,900 is supplemented by a payment from the collaborating body of at least 40 per cent.

Studying in Northern Ireland

If you are seeking research funding and want to study in Northern Ireland, you must apply directly to the university for a place on a course and an award. Being offered a place does not automatically mean that you will obtain funding. Closing dates for applications are at the discretion of the institution (and are generally around April/May), but late applications may be accepted subject to availability of places. Grants are awarded by DELNI for all fields except agriculture and medicine.

Studying elsewhere in the UK

If you plan to study elsewhere in the UK, you may be able to receive funding through various research councils – you need to approach the university where you want to study. The university will then advise you which research council to apply to and when application forms are available. Closing dates vary between councils.

Bursary awards for particular courses

Postgraduate Certificate in Education

See the information on initial teacher training in Northern Ireland on p70.

European Social Fund

Institutions hold updated lists of postgraduate courses (one-year vocational courses) that offer places attracting European Social Fund funding. To meet the criteria, students must be unemployed graduates under 25 years of age. Your circumstances and the class of your degree are taken into account when awards are being made. Apply directly to the institution for this funding.

Notes

1. Studentship rates

1 The MRC and EPSRC have changed their method of funding. Individual institutions are now allocated block grants from which they then set the number of studentships and the level of stipend. A minimum level of stipend is set as indicated in the table, with institutions deciding whether to grant more than this depending on local circumstances.

2 See note I. Note that the EPSRC sets no minimum payment for Masters studentships.

3 The BBSRC has a similar scheme to the MRC and EPSRC for its doctoral (research) studentships only. The minimum level of bursary is set as indicated.

2. Disabled students' allowance

4 Reg 156 E(SS) Regs

5 Reg 156 E(SS)No.2 Regs

6

Chapter 6

Vocational courses and other sources of student support

This chapter covers:

1. Healthcare students in England and Wales

If you are studying an allied health profession, or a profession complementary to dentistry, nursing or midwifery, you may be eligible for an NHS bursary and any applicable supplementary allowances. You may also be eligible if you are studying medicine or dentistry, but only for the latter years of pre-registration training.

There are two types of bursary. The type you are able to receive depends on the level of course you are studying. Diploma-level students are eligible for a non-means-tested bursary, while degree-level students are eligible for a means-tested award. Each type of bursary also has additional allowances for specific groups. To be eligible for either, you must also fulfil the personal residency requirement for higher education students in England (see p19). **Note:** the provisions for Turkish workers and their families do not apply.

Both types of bursary are funded in England by the NHS Student Grants Unit, based in Fleetwood. In Wales nursing and midwifery students are eligible for the non-means-tested bursary and this is processed by the university. The means-tested bursary and the childcare allowance for all students is processed by the NHS (Wales) Student Awards Unit, based in Cardiff. In addition to receiving either of the two bursaries, all NHS students who meet the criteria are now eligible for financial support from the Access to Learning Fund (see p33) for study in England

and the Financial Contingency Fund for study in Wales. In both cases, the NHS pays your tuition fees for you.

Eligible courses
- Allied health professions: chiropody, dietetics, occupational therapy, orthoptics, physiotherapy, prosthetics and orthotics, radiography, speech and language therapy.
- Professions complementary to dentistry: dental auxiliary, dental hygiene, dental therapy.
- Audiology.[1]
- Degree-level nursing and midwifery.
- Diploma-level nursing, midwifery or operating department practice (including conversion courses for second-level nurses who have not practised for a year or more).
- Medicine and dentistry (the latter stages of pre-registration training only).

Changes in 2007/08

The bursary scheme was updated for the 2007/08 academic year in the light of recent age discrimination legislation. There were new provisions for NHS-funded healthcare students who require maternity leave (see p63). The changes only affect you if you started your course in the 2007/08 academic year or later. Students who started before this date are covered by the previous system. This chapter therefore refers to 'old' and 'new' system students.

There were new provisions for NHS-funded healthcare students who require maternity/paternity leave and adoption leave (see p63). These new provisions affect all students enrolled onto a pre-registration course and who are in receipt of the maintenance element of the NHS bursary regardless of when they started their course.

Diploma-level students

Diploma-level students receive the non-means-tested bursary. The level of bursary you receive does not depend on your income. In England the bursary is available to students on a nursing, midwifery or operating department practice higher education diploma course. In Wales, the bursary is available to nursing and midwifery students. In Wales, operating department practice students have their tuition fees paid by the NHS and receive a training salary instead of the non-means-tested bursary.

If you are eligible for this bursary, the NHS also pays your fees. The bursary is paid in 12 equal monthly instalments across the academic year. There are three rates of bursary; the rate you receive depends on where you live.

Maximum amounts of non-means-tested bursaries 2008/09

	'Old system' students	'New system' students
London	£7,374	£7,629
Elsewhere	£6,275	£6,531
Parental home	£6,275	£6,531

There are additional allowances available if you are a diploma student.

Extra weeks' allowance

The bursary assumes that you are required to attend the course for 45 weeks a year. However, if, as part of your course, you must move to London to attend a practice placement, the bursary will be increased by £17 a week for the length of the placement.

Older students' allowance

If you are an 'old system' student, and were 26 or over before the beginning of your first academic year,[2] you will receive an additional £733. If you turn 26 during your course, you do not become eligible in later years. This cannot be claimed in addition to the single parent addition (see p59). This is not available for 'new system' students.

Dependants' allowances

If you have adults or children wholly or mainly financially dependent on you, you may be eligible for extra dependants' allowances. However, the income of your dependant(s) is taken into account and so eligibility for this allowance is means tested.

Dependants' allowances 2008/09

'New system' students:

Spouse or civil partner (or other adult dependant, or first child if there is no spouse or any adult dependants)	£2,181
Each additional dependant	£525

'Old system' students:

Spouse or civil partner (or other adult dependant, or first child if there is no spouse or any adult dependants)	£2,181
Child aged under 11[3]	£461
Child aged 11–15	£916
Child aged 16–17	£1,213
Child aged 18+	£1,738

Single parent addition

If you are an 'old system' student and a lone parent, you are entitled to an additional £1,076. This is not paid in addition to the older students' allowance. 'New system' students should apply for the parents' learning allowance.

Parents' learning allowance

If you are a 'new system' student and have a dependent child(ren), you can claim an additional £1,076. This is available to all 'new system' student parents, including those with partners, but is means tested.

Childcare allowance

If you have responsibility for a child under the age of 15 (or 17 if s/he has special educational needs) and you use registered or approved childcare, you can apply for a childcare allowance. You cannot receive the childcare allowance if you also receive the childcare element of working tax credit (see Chapter 19).

The grant can cover up to 85 per cent of your actual costs of childcare, with a maximum payment of £123.25 a week for one child or £182.75 a week for two or more children.

The childcare grant is means tested; the amount you receive depends on your income and that of any dependants.

Initial expenses allowance

If you are a first-year student, you are given an additional one-off payment of £55 at the beginning of your course.

Practice placement costs

The cost of travel between your home and a practice placement site that is not part of the college, plus additional residential costs where appropriate, may be reimbursed to you. Only the amount that exceeds the cost of travel between your term-time residence and place of study is reimbursed. Your college will have details of how these expenses should be claimed.

Disabled students' allowance

If you have a disability, you can claim a disabled students' allowance from the NHS on the same basis as students in other forms of higher education (see p26).

Degree-level students

A means-tested bursary is available if you are studying for a degree-level qualification in any of the healthcare disciplines outlined on p57. If you meet the personal eligibility criteria your fees will be paid. The amount of money you receive for living costs depends on your (and your partner's) income. If you are a dependent student (see p27) your parents' income is taken into account. The living costs include a basic amount for, for instance, rent and food. A means-tested bursary-holder may also be eligible for a reduced-amount undergraduate student loan. This loan is not subject to a means test and an application should be made through your local authority or Student Finance England.

Employed students do not usually qualify for bursaries, but may qualify for student support payable by the Department for Innovation, Universities and Skills.

Maximum amounts of means-tested bursaries 2008/09

	'Old system' students	'New system' students
London	£3,050	£3,306
Elsewhere	£2,483	£2,739
Parental home	£2,031	£2,287

Reduced rate student loans 2008/09[4]

	All students – full year	All students – final year
London	£3,185	£2,435
Elsewhere	£2,265	£1,765
Parental home	£1,700	£1,290

As with diploma students, there is a range of additional allowances available. However, the rates for degree-level students are generally different.

Extra weeks' allowance

The bursary is paid for a notional academic year of 30 weeks and three days. However, should your course require additional attendance over and above this, further allowances are paid. The rate for each additional week is as follows, and is the same for both 'old system' and 'new system' students.

Extra weeks' allowance 2008/09

London	£103
Elsewhere	£80
Parental home	£53

If your required attendance in an academic year is 45 weeks or more, an allowance for all 52 weeks is paid.

Older students' allowance

If you are an 'old system' student, and were aged 26 or over before the beginning of your first academic year,[5] you will receive an additional allowance. If you turn 26 during your course, you do not become eligible in later years. This cannot be claimed in addition to the single parent addition. It is also payable to diploma students attending accelerated programmes for graduates, regardless of age.

Older students' allowance 2008/09

Age before first academic year

26	£437
27	£757
28	£1,123
29+	£1,485

Dependants' allowances

If you have adults or children wholly or mainly financially dependent on you, you may be eligible for extra dependants' allowances. However, the income of your dependants is taken into account and so eligibility for this allowance is means tested.

Dependants' allowances 2008/09

'New system' students:

Spouse or civil partner (or other adult dependant, or first child if there is no spouse or any adult dependants)	£2,573
Each additional dependant	£525

'Old system' students:

Spouse (or other adult dependant, or first child if there is no spouse or any adult dependants)	£2,573
Child aged under 11[6]	£538
Child aged 11–15	£1,076
Child aged 16–17	£1,431
Child aged 18+	£2,059

Single parent addition

If you are an 'old system' student and a lone parent you are entitled to an additional £1,270. This is not paid in addition to the older students' allowance. 'New system' students should apply for the parents' learning allowance.

Parents' learning allowance

If you are a 'new system' student and have a dependent child(ren), you can claim an additional £1,270. This is available to all student parents, including those with partners, but is means tested.

Two homes grant

This allowance of £896 is payable if you have dependants and must maintain a home other than the one where you live when attending the course. This grant is being phased out and students who start their course after 1 September 2008 will not be able to apply for it.

Childcare allowance

This is paid on the same basis as the childcare allowance for non-means-tested NHS bursary students. See p26 for details.

Practice placement costs

The cost of travel between your home and a practice placement site that is not part of the college, and additional residential costs where appropriate, may be reimbursed to you. Only the amount that exceeds the cost of travel between your term-time residence and place of study is reimbursed. Your college will have details of how these expenses should be claimed.

Disabled students' allowance

If you have a disability you can claim a disabled students' allowance from the NHS on the same basis as students in other forms of higher education (see p26).

NHS hardship grant

In addition to institutional hardship funds such as the Access to Learning Fund (see p33), the NHS operates a limited hardship fund for medicine and dentistry students eligible for the means-tested bursary. You should contact the Student Grants Unit to apply for the NHS hardship fund.

European Union nationals

If you are a national of a European Union (EU) member state, you may be eligible for NHS bursary support as follows.

Non-UK EU nationals and their children who satisfy the three-year residence criteria in the 'UK and Islands' will be treated as if they were UK students and are eligible for support for both maintenance and fees. They are not required to have settled status. If their residence in the UK was mainly for the purpose of full-time higher education, they may still be eligible for a NHS bursary (maintenance grant and tuition fees) if they can show that they were ordinarily resident in a European Economic Area country or Switzerland immediately prior to their period of ordinary residence in the UK.

EU students who are not ordinarily resident in the UK under the terms described, may be awarded an 'EU fees only' award, under which they have the cost of their tuition fees met, but are not eligible for a student loan, hardship funds or the maintenance element of the NHS bursary.

Part-time students

Part-time students on NHS-funded degree courses are eligible for 75 per cent of the means-tested NHS bursary. The part-time diploma students' bursary is the appropriate portion of full-time study.

The full rate is paid if you have additional costs resulting from a disability and for reimbursing the costs of attending a clinical placement.

Students who are pregnant or who have recently given birth

If you are an NHS-funded student, have enrolled on your course, and require maternity leave, you can be paid your bursary for a period of up to 45 weeks (known as a 'maternity allowance'). Seconded students and EU nationals on fees-only awards cannot receive this help as they are not eligible for the bursary or any of the supplementary grants.

For more information see www.nhsstudentgrants.co.uk.

---

2. Healthcare students in Northern Ireland

If you are planning to study an allied health professions degree course in Northern Ireland, you can apply for funding from the Department of Health, Social Services and Public Safety (DHSSPS). Under these arrangements you will not have to pay tuition fees and will be eligible to apply for an income-assessed bursary to cover living costs and a reduced rate, non-income-assessed student loan. As in England and Wales, medical and dental students in their final years of study are also funded through this system. Students from European Union states who are studying in Northern Ireland are also exempt from paying tuition fees, but they are not eligible for a bursary or loan to cover living costs.

The amount of bursary you receive depends on your household income. Additional allowances may be available if you have dependants or a disability. Your local education and library board (ELB) will be able to advise. The rates for 2008/09 are as follows.

Bursary rates 2008/09

Full-year rates	Bursary	Loan
Living away from parental home	£2,300	£2,265
Living at parental home	£1,875	£1,700

Final-year rates		
Living away from parental home	£2,300	£1,765
Living at parental home	£1,875	£1,290

The ELBs deal with the bursary arrangements on behalf of the DHSSPS. If you are a Northern Irish student you should, therefore, apply to your ELB. If you live in England, Scotland or Wales, you should apply to the North Eastern ELB.

Nursing and midwifery students

Full-time pre-registration nursing and direct entry midwifery students taking up a commissioned DHSSPS place on a course leading to entry on the Nursing and Midwifery Council register are entitled to receive a bursary while undertaking the course. Students receiving a bursary do not pay tuition fees, but they are not eligible for support from their ELB, and nor do they have access to their institution's support fund.

The bursary system changed for new students after 1 September 2007, but 'old system' students who started their course before that date remained funded under the original rules.

Both schemes comprise a non-means-tested basic rate, additional means-tested allowances, travel expenses for costs incurred while on clinical placements and one-off payments of £110 for uniform and £80 for books. Disabled students' allowances are also payable where appropriate, at the same rate as for other higher education students (see p26). The rates are determined annually.

Note: a general review of the bursary scheme is being conducted and changes may be made for this or future academic years. Contact the DHSSPS for further information (see Appendix 2).

Bursary rates 2008/09: 'old system' students

Basic award (not means tested)	
Aged under 26 years at the start of the course	£5,910
(this rate applies for the duration of the course)	
Aged 26 years and over at the start of the course	£6,655
Additional dependants' additions (means tested)	
Partner or other adult dependant (or first child if no other dependant)	£2,220
Child aged under 11	£465
Child aged 11–15	£925
Child aged 16–17	£1,230
Child aged 18+	£1,765
Single parents' allowance (not means tested)	£1,100

Bursary rates 2008/09: 'new system' students

Basic award (not means tested)	£5,910
Additional dependants' additions (means tested)	
Partner or other adult dependant (or first child if no other dependant)	£2,220
Each subsequent child	£525
Parents' learning allowance *(not means tested)*	£1,100
Contribution to childcare	Up to £1,215

3. Initial teacher training in England

There are three main routes for initial teacher training (ITT) in England that lead to qualified teacher status:

- Bachelor of Education (BEd) – an undergraduate degree, usually for four years' full-time study or equivalent, with qualified teacher status gained after a year's successful teaching;
- Postgraduate Certificate in Education (PGCE) – a postgraduate degree, usually for one year or part-time equivalent, with qualified teacher status gained after a year's successful teaching;
- School-Centred Initial Teacher Training (SCITT). This can be undertaken through two routes:
  - the graduate teacher programme – up to one year of postgraduate training while working as a teacher to gain qualified teacher status; *or*
  - the registered teacher programme – up to two years of undergraduate degree study while training and working as a teacher to gain qualified teacher status.

Each route has a different funding mechanism.

Bachelor of Education

The principal financial assistance available if you are studying a BEd qualification is the basic undergraduate student support package as outlined in Chapter 2. This includes all supplementary grants and access to the hardship funds.

There are no further incentives for BEd study in 2008/09. The Secondary Shortage Subject Scheme (SSSS) incentive in England has been discontinued for new students since the 2007/08 academic year. However, if you are a student who started before that date and previously received support through the SSSS, you may still be able to receive help – speak to your institution about the transitional arrangements.

Postgraduate Certificate in Education

If you are on a full- or part-time PGCE and meet the personal and residential eligibility criteria for undergraduate student support (see p19) you are entitled to the same support package as new undergraduate students. You are also eligible for assistance from the Access to Learning Fund. As with undergraduate students, there are also several incentive packages for which you may be eligible.

Tuition fees

In England, PGCE students are, like new undergraduates, liable for variable fees of up to £3,145, but eligible UK students can take out a loan to cover the cost of these.[7] In addition, for eligible English-domiciled students, the first £1,260 of the maintenance or special support grant is not means tested.

Teacher training bursary

A salary of £4,000 a year is available if you are undertaking a primary postgraduate ITT course and are not already employed as a teacher. This rises to £6,000 for secondary ITT courses, and to £9,000 if you are training to teach a secondary shortage subject: maths, science, information and communications technology, design and technology, modern languages, religious education or music. If you are on a one-year course, you are paid in monthly instalments between October and June. If your course is part time, you are paid in instalments in accordance with the length of your training. Payments are made by the training provider.

If you are on a modular course, you are eligible provided you are not already employed as a teacher in a school or within further or higher education. In this instance, one payment of half the total amount (ie £,2000, £3,000 or £4,500 if you are training to teach a shortage subject) is made after you have registered for the first assessment module, and the second is paid after you achieve qualified teacher status.

If you are a full-time trainee, the salary is not taxable and you do not have to pay national insurance contributions. If you are a part-time trainee, the salary may be taxable, depending on your total income for the year. It will be included in any calculation for means-tested benefits.

Students from the European Union are eligible for this incentive.

'Golden hello'

This is an incentive to encourage you to train in certain shortage subject areas (maths, science, information and communications technology, design and technology, engineering, manufacturing, modern languages, religious education or music). The money is paid if you have successfully achieved qualified teacher status and are entering your second year of teaching in one of the shortage areas, provided the second year is within 12 months of the induction year. The post must be in a publicly funded school in England, a non-maintained special school, or an academy. The position must also be permanent or on a fixed-term contract of more than a term's duration. The amount you receive depends on the subject. For maths and science, the payment is £5,000. The amount for other subjects is £2,500. The incentive is paid in a lump sum with your salary and is taxable. You should inform the school that you are eligible to receive the incentive.

Graduate teacher programme

If you are a graduate aged 24 or over, the graduate teacher programme allows you to train as a teacher in maintained schools while still earning a living.

Salary

When you start on the programme you receive a salary from the school in which you are based. The level of salary to be paid by the school is agreed by the governing body and may be at a rate based on the scales for either qualified or unqualified teachers, but must be no lower than the minimum salary grade for unqualified teachers of around £15,000. If you are on this scheme you are not eligible for the training salary or the 'golden hello' outlined on p66.

Training grant

In addition, the school receives £4,920 a year for the cost of your training. This can be used to cover the cost of an initial training needs assessment, tuition fees, supply cover, mentoring training, learning resources and materials. This funding cannot be used as a wage supplement.

Registered teacher programme

This scheme is similar to the graduate teacher programme, but if you have yet to complete the necessary degree-level qualification you can continue to study for this in addition to your teacher training within a maintained school.

Salary

The school agrees your salary level, but it must be no lower than the minimum salary grade for unqualified teachers of around £15,000.

Training grant

As with the graduate teacher programme, the school receives a £9,100 training grant. This can be used for the purposes specified above, including meeting the costs of your degree course fees.

Repayment of teachers' loans

This was a pilot scheme for newly qualified teachers who took teaching posts in the academic years 2002/03, 2003/04 or 2004/05. If you are eligible and you work in a shortage subject (see p66), you will have your student loan repaid. The scheme only applies if you spend at least half of your teaching time teaching the shortage subjects.

To be eligible you must:

- be employed in England or Wales in a teaching post at a maintained school, a non-maintained special school, a city technology college, a city college for the technology of arts or a city academy;
- have begun employment between 1 July 2002 and 30 June 2005;
- be employed to teach one or more of the shortage subjects for at least half of your teaching time within a normal school week.

More information is available at www.teachernet.gov.uk/teachersloans. The scheme has not been extended and is, therefore, unavailable to those teachers who started employment after 30 June 2005, unless they could not start work before that date because they were pregnant or had recently given birth.

4. Initial teacher training in Wales

In Wales, there are two main routes for initial teacher training (ITT) that leads to qualified teacher status.

- Bachelor of Education (BEd) – an undergraduate degree, usually for four years' full-time study or equivalent, with qualified teacher status gained after a year's successful teaching.
- Postgraduate Certificate in Education (PGCE) – a postgraduate degree, usually for one year or part-time equivalent, with qualified teacher status gained after a year's successful teaching.

Bachelor of Education

The principal financial assistance available if you are studying a BEd qualification is the basic undergraduate student support package for Welsh students as outlined in Chapter 3. This includes all supplementary grants and access to the hardship funds. In addition to this support, students in Wales may be eligible for certain incentive packages, which are outlined below.

Secondary undergraduate placement grants

Grants of £1,000 are available if you are on an undergraduate teacher training course in Wales and are studying one of the secondary shortage subject areas (maths, science, modern foreign languages, design and technology, information technology, Welsh, music and religious education).

If you are studying in a non-shortage area, £600 is payable. The only course currently offering this is English including drama. The grant is paid to you through the teacher training provider in two instalments in each year of the course.

Welsh medium incentive supplement

In order to help those students who need additional assistance to raise their competence and confidence, a £1,500 grant is available to undergraduate or postgraduate students undertaking secondary ITT in Wales using the Welsh language.[8] This increases to £1,800 for maths and science courses. Once qualified, you are expected to take up a secondary school teaching post using the Welsh language. Your institution assesses your eligibility and advises you on the application process.

Postgraduate Certificate of Education

If you are on a full- or part-time PGCE and meet the personal and residential eligibility criteria for undergraduate student support (see p19), you are entitled to the same support package as new undergraduate students. Note that £1,255 of the full maintenance grant of £2,825 is not means tested, but the remaining £1,570 does depend on family income. You are also eligible for assistance from the Financial Contingency Fund. As with undergraduate students, there are also several incentive packages for which you may be eligible.

Tuition fees

Eligible, 'new system' Welsh-domiciled PGCE students studying in Wales will pay flexible fees of up to £3,145 in the 2008/09 academic year, but the university will also receive a tuition fee grant of up to £1,890. The most you will therefore pay is £1,255 for the year.[9] You are eligible for a tuition fee loan to cover the remainder.[10] If you are eligible for fee support but not for a fee grant, you can receive a fee loan up to the level of the fee charged.[11]

Teacher training grant

If you undertake a PGCE course in Wales you are eligible for a teacher training grant during the period of study and may be eligible for an additional teaching grant on taking up employment as a qualified teacher.

The rate of grant depends on the subject you are training to teach. If you are eligible and training to be a secondary maths or science teacher, you will receive a £7,200 training grant and a £5,000 teaching grant.

If you are eligible and training to teach one of the other priority secondary subjects (modern languages, design and technology, ICT, and Welsh as a second language), you will receive a £7,200 training grant and a £2,500 teaching grant.

All other secondary PGCE courses (including English, drama, art, geography, history, and PE) offer a £4,200 training grant for eligible students. All primary PGCE courses receive a £2,200 training grant.

If you are a full-time trainee, the salary is not taxable and you do not have to pay national insurance contributions. If you are a part-time trainee, the salary may be taxable, depending on your total income for the year. It will be included in any calculation for means-tested benefits.

Students from the European Union (EU) are eligible for this incentive.

PGCE(FE)

This is a long-running pilot scheme for full-time PGCE students training to teach in further education studying at a Welsh institution and has been extended for 2008/09. Full-time students receive a bursary of £6,000, with an extra £1,000 available for those training to teach science, maths and sports science subjects. It is not means tested and open to EU students. As with other PGCE courses, if you meet the personal and residential criteria for undergraduate student support, you can apply for the same support package as undergraduate students.

Welsh medium incentive supplement

This is available on the same terms as for undergraduate students (see p69).

Repayment of Teachers' Loans scheme

The Repayment of Teachers' Loans scheme has closed to new applicants. However, existing teachers on this scheme still benefit.

5. Initial teacher training in Northern Ireland

Students accepted on a course of initial teacher training in Northern Ireland in the 2008/09 academic year, including Postgraduate Certificate in Education (PGCE) courses, receive the same funding as 'new system' undergraduate students (see Chapter 4). This means that PGCE students are liable for tuition fees, but can take out a loan to cover these.

You can make an application for funding through an education and library board. The additional financial incentives available for undergraduate and PGCE study in England and Wales are not available in Northern Ireland, but Northern Irish students studying in England or Wales can claim these.

6. Social work students

England

Students studying an undergraduate diploma or degree in social work in England may be eligible for a non-means-tested bursary from the Department of Health. The NHS Business Services Agency (BSA) administers these bursaries on its behalf.

If you are a full-time undergraduate studying at an institution in England you may be eligible to receive this assistance in addition to the Department for Innovation, Universities and Skills student support package (see p17).

Undergraduate support

Support for undergraduates studying social work is made up of several elements.

Tuition fees

If you are an 'old system' student (ie, you are not required to pay variable tuition fees – see p22) and are liable to make a contribution towards your tuition fees after your local authority has made a financial assessment for your student support, this is paid on your behalf by the NHS BSA directly to your university or college.

If you are a 'new system' student (and, therefore, required to pay variable tuition fees – see p22) the NHS BSA does not pay your tuition fees on your behalf. Instead, you receive a higher rate of bursary (see below), which contains a tuition fee contribution that you can use to pay part of the fee. You do not, however, have to do this.

Basic grant

This gives you additional money for living costs. The amount you receive depends on where you study and whether or not you are a 'new system' student (see p22). A fixed contribution of £575 is paid as part of the basic grant to cover the costs of travel to placements.

If you are an 'old system' student, you can get £3,075 if you are studying at an institution outside London, or £3,475 if you are studying at a university or college in London or at the University of London. Essentially, the amount of loan you receive from your local authority or Student Finance England (SFE) determines the rate of basic grant you receive.

If you are a 'new system' student, the basic grant rates rise to £4,575 outside London and £4,975 within London.

Both types of bursary are paid for 52 weeks and will be taken into account in benefits calculations. The element paid for travelling expenses should be disregarded.[12] However, this is not usually specifically identified so benefits offices may take the full bursary into account. Speak to an adviser for assistance.

Part-time students

If you are a part-time undergraduate student you will have your tuition fees paid by the NHS BSA. You can receive the 'incentive to train' bursary at half the rate for full-time study. Students who started in 2006/07 or later academic years receive half the 'new system' students' rate. All students are also eligible for help with placement costs. You are not eligible for other forms of support.

Postgraduate support

In addition to the undergraduate bursary, the NHS BSA also administers support for students studying a postgraduate level course, such as the Masters in Social Work, or for students studying an undergraduate degree or diploma who already have a first degree. The bursary can help with extra study and living costs, and there is additional help if you have children or a disability.

Tuition fees

Your tuition fees of up to £3,300 are paid in full by the NHS BSA, direct to the institution. These are not means tested.

'Incentive to train' bursary

Although unable to apply for local authority support, eligible postgraduate students can receive the undergraduate 'incentive to train bursary' at the 'old system' students' rate including the placement travel expenses allowance.

Additional graduate bursary

This is a means-tested grant paid in addition to the 'incentive to train' bursary. Up to £3,928 is available to students studying in London or at the University of London, with up to £2,544 available to those studying elsewhere.

The grant is means tested on your unearned income and any taxable income of a partner, if you have one.

Students with dependants

You can receive the adult dependants' grant, the parents' learning allowance and the childcare grant on the same basis as higher education (HE) undergraduates receiving local authority or SFE support.

Disabled students' allowance

Postgraduate social work students can apply for a disabled students' allowance at the same rates as for HE undergraduates.

Part-time students

Part-time postgraduate students have their tuition fees paid by the NHS BSA. They can receive the 'incentive to train' bursary at half the rate for full-time study, plus help with placement costs. They are not eligible for other forms of support.

How to apply

In the first instance, if you are an undergraduate, you should apply to your local authority for student support. When it has assessed your application and you have received notification of this (sometimes known as an award notification), you should contact the NHS BSA for an application form for the bursary. Postgraduates should apply direct to the NHS BSA.

Application forms are also available from the NHS BSA website at www.ppa.org.uk/swb.

Wales

Students in Wales studying for qualifications in social work may qualify for financial help from the Care Council for Wales (CCW).

Undergraduate support

If you are studying for an undergraduate degree or diploma in social work you should first apply for student support through your local authority, as do other undergraduate students (see Chapter 3). CCW advises that once the assessment has been done, you do not actually take out the full tuition fee loan as it provides a tuition fee element of £1,255. If you study in Wales you may be eligible for the tuition fee grant to complete the payment of fees up to £3,145. If you study outside Wales you would then need to borrow £1,890 to cover fees of £3,145.

The CCW can offer funding in addition to any support received from your local authority. If you are liable to make a contribution towards your tuition fees after your local authority has made its financial assessment, this is paid on your behalf by the CCW directly to your university or college.

You will also receive a non-means-tested bursary to help cover your living costs of £2,500 in 2008/09. If you are studying part time, the bursary is calculated on a *pro rata* basis.

In addition, a practice learning grant of £500 is available to help meet the costs of travel to placements. If your travel costs to placements are more than £500, you can apply to the CCW for reimbursement of these extra costs. However, you should keep all receipts as you may be asked to submit these as proof of expenditure.

To apply, you should contact the CCW for an application form or visit www.ccwales.org.uk.

Postgraduate support

If you are on a postgraduate diploma or Masters course in Wales you should apply, in the first instance, for the basic undergraduate bursary from the CCW, including the practice learning grant.

While you cannot receive undergraduate support through your local authority, the CCW may be able to offer an additional graduate bursary, of up to £2,510 in 2008/09. The exact amount will depend on your personal circumstances. You can apply for the adult dependants' grant, the parents' learning allowance and the childcare grant from CCW at the same time as the additional graduate bursary.

If you have a disability you may be eligible for extra help through the postgraduate disabled students' allowance (see p53).

The CCW will also pay your tuition fees of up to £3,300.

Northern Ireland

If you are studying for a degree in social work in Northern Ireland, you can apply for an incentive grant from the Social Services Inspectorate (see Appendix 2). Non-means-tested grants of £4,000 plus a further £500 towards placement expenses are available for each year of the course.

You will have to pay tuition fees, but the funds are in addition to any money made available by your education and library board as part of the main undergraduate support system, including loans for fees.

7. Dance and drama awards

The Department for Innovation, Universities and Skills (DIUS) has set up a scholarship programme to ensure that talented dance and drama students can attend courses at the leading dance and drama institutions in England, in cases where fees and living costs would otherwise be prohibitively expensive.[13] Dance and drama awards fund studies in HND and HNC courses in dance, drama and production. Funding is available through selected, approved specialist schools for between one and three years of study. You must be aged 16 and over for dance courses, or 18 and over for drama-related courses. There are 525 awards granted each year, and they are generally issued to those who show exceptional talent in an audition.

The residency rules for other higher education support apply and students from England, Wales and Scotland can apply for full support, whilst students from Northern Ireland can apply for help with fees only. A separate scheme operates in Northern Ireland for help with other costs (see below).

If you are a recipient of an award most of your fees will be paid, but you will have to make a contribution. In 2008/09 this is £1,255. If you have a low family income you can apply for extra assistance with your fees from Learner Support Services, a company which administers the scheme on behalf of the DIUS. The award may also provide support for your living costs depending on your circumstances. Other allowances may be available if you have extra costs associated with a disability or childcare expenses. More information on the awards is available through the participating dance and drama schools or from www.direct.gov.uk/danceanddrama (where a list of the participating schools can also be found).

Northern Ireland

The dance and drama (Northern Ireland) awards form part of the Northern Ireland further education awards scheme (see Chapter 4). They provide assistance for courses at one of the 21 accredited providers in mainland Britain (as there is no provision in Northern Ireland). If a student receives a main dance and drama award which pays for the majority of the fees charged, s/he can also apply to the Western Education and Library Board for a dance and drama (Northern Ireland) award for help with the remainder of the fee and maintenance.

The maximum available is £5,333 for those living in lodgings in London. For more information, see www.welbni.org.

8. **Alternative sources of finance**

Career development loans[14]

The Department for Innovation, Universities and Skills (DIUS) in participation with three major banks (Barclays, The Co-operative and the Royal Bank of Scotland) operates a deferred repayment loan system. You can borrow between £300 and £8,000 towards fees and other expenses if you are on a vocational full-time, part-time or distance learning course lasting up to two years (and including up to one year's practical work experience where it is part of your course). Degree and postgraduate courses are included.

The interest charged will vary depending on the bank, when you apply and the length of repayment, but is typically between 12 and 14 per cent a year. Throughout your period of study and up to one month after completing or leaving the course, the DIUS pays the interest on the loan for you. Repayments are fixed and can be spread between one and five years. If you are registered unemployed at the end of the first month of completing your course, you may apply to the bank for deferment of repayment for up to five months initially, and for two further extensions of six months each. More information on career development loans can be found at www.direct.gov.uk/cdl.

Career development loans are not available in Northern Ireland and students normally resident in Northern Ireland but undertaking study elsewhere in the UK may also find they are ineligible, although if you have been resident in Great Britain for a minimum of three months and your reason for residence is not solely for the purposes of education, you should be able to apply.

Professional studies loans

Three of the major high street banks (HSBC, NatWest and Lloyds TSB) offer professional studies loans. Some schemes are specifically aimed at study in certain fields (eg, medicine, dentistry, law, veterinary science and architecture). However, some banks now offer loans for general vocational study. Loans of up to £25,000 are available. Interest rates and repayment terms are variable, and you can often defer repayment until after the completion of your course, although the debt will continue to accrue interest. You may be required to be an existing customer of the bank concerned. Contact a local branch or visit the website of any of the banks on p75 for more information.

The professional studies loans scheme is not available in Northern Ireland.

Business school loan scheme

The Association of MBAs runs this scheme in conjunction with NatWest. It is available to those studying for a Masters in Business Administration or equivalent, full time, part time or by distance learning. Repayment is deferred until the completion of your course, but the debt continues to accrue interest. For further information, contact NatWest on freephone 0800 200 400, or visit the Association's website at www.mbaworld.com. Some individual business schools also have a loan scheme with HSBC. Contact the school where you want to study to see if it participates.

The business school loan scheme is not available in Northern Ireland.

Charities

It is unlikely that a course lasting more than one year could be financed entirely by trust fund help. Educational charities and trusts are, however, in a position to provide supplementary help to students who may be without funding for part of their course or who, for various reasons, need help over and above that provided by public funds.

Educational charities and trusts often have specific, even unusual, terms of reference. They may be restricted to helping, for example, students only:
- on certain courses of study; *or*
- above or below a certain age (often 21 or 25); *or*
- from particular parts of Britain or countries of the world; *or*
- in defined occupations, professions or industries, or who have a parent working in one of these.

A student does not usually receive more than about £300 from any one charity, although higher amounts are not unknown. Charities more often make single, rather than recurrent, payments. Payments tend to be:
- for particular items – eg, tools or equipment; *or*
- for a specific purpose – eg, childcare; *or*
- those which the charity or trust believes might make the difference between completion and non-completion of the course.

Charities are more sympathetic to students whose need for assistance results from sickness or unforeseen circumstances than to students who have mismanaged their money or who have started a course knowing they had insufficient funds.

Many charities only give assistance to first-time students. Assistance is more difficult to find if you are a postgraduate or taking a second undergraduate course.

Applications often take some time to process so it is wise to apply for support well in advance of the course start date.

Further information

There are a number of publications that contain details of charities and trusts, including:

- *The Educational Grants Directory* (Directory of Social Change);
- *A Guide to Grants for Individuals in Need* (Directory of Social Change);
- *Directory of Grant Making Trusts* (Directory of Social Change);
- *Charities Digest* (Waterlow's Legal Publishing);
- *The Grants Register* (Palgrave Macmillan) – this is particularly relevant to postgraduate student awards for both the UK and overseas;
- *Study Abroad* (UNESCO);
- *International Awards 2001+* (Association of Commonwealth Universities);
- *British and International Music Yearbook* and the *British Music Education Yearbook* (both published by Rhinegold).

Many of these publications can be found in local public libraries, or university or college libraries. Advice centres may also carry some, particularly the *Education Grants Directory*.

There are also some useful websites listing charities and educational grants, including:

- Hotcourses database at www.scholarship-search.co.uk;
- Funderfinder at www.funderfinder.org.uk.

Students in need should also consult their local authority, students' union, careers service, Citizens Advice Bureau, town hall and local clergy as they may know of other trusts. In addition to awarding scholarships and prizes in specific subjects, colleges may have funds available for students in financial difficulties and unable to apply to the Access to Learning Fund or Learner Support Fund, so it may be useful to consult your institution's student service. Students in Northern Ireland should contact the Adult Learner Finance Project for Northern Ireland through the duty information officer at the Educational Guidance Service for Adults (EGSA).

Educational Grants Advisory Service

For more advice on alternative sources of funding, contact the EGSA. If you provide information on your personal background, course and requirements, you will be matched with any appropriate trusts or charities.

However, EGAS generally cannot help overseas students or students wishing to study outside the UK. You can phone the advice line on 020 7254 6251, open from 10am–12pm and 2pm–4pm Mondays, Wednesdays and Fridays only. You can also apply for help online. See Appendix 2 for the full contact details.

Adult Learner Finance Project

For further information on alternative sources of funding in Northern Ireland, you can also contact the Adult Learner Finance Project for Northern Ireland through EGSA. Telephone 028 9024 4274 or email info@egsa.org.uk. See Appendix 2 for the full contact details.

Notes

1. Healthcare students in England and Wales

1 Audiology courses must be recognised by either the British Association of Audiological Technicians, the British Association of Audiological Scientists or the British Society of Hearing Therapists.
2 This is not necessarily the first day of your course.
3 The age of the child used for determining the level of allowance is that on the day before the start of the academic year, unless s/he is born during that year.
4 Reg 70 SS Regs
5 This is not necessarily the first day of your course.
6 The age of the child used for determining the level of allowance is that on the day before the start of the academic year, unless s/he is born during that year.

3. Initial teacher training in England
7 Reg 21 SS Regs

4. Initial teacher training in Wales
8 E(WMTTIS) Regs
9 Reg 18 ALGL(HE)(W) Regs
10 Reg 22 ALGL(HE)(W) Regs
11 Reg 21 ALGL(HE)(W) Regs

6. Social work students
12 **IS** Reg 62(2)(h) IS Regs
   HB Reg 59(2)(g) HB Regs
   CTB Reg 46(2)(g) CTB Regs

7. Dance and drama awards
13 E(G)(DD)(E) Regs

8. Alternative sources of finance
14 s2 ETA 1973

Part 2

Benefits and tax credits

Chapter 7

Carer's allowance

This chapter covers:
1. What is carer's allowance (below)
2. Who is eligible (below)
3. Amount of benefit (p84)
4. Claiming carer's allowance (p84)
5. Challenging a decision (p84)
6. Other benefits and tax credits (p85)

Basic facts

– Carer's allowance (CA) is paid to people who care for someone with a disability.
– Students are eligible to claim if they are not in full-time education.
– The amount of CA you get is not affected by any savings you may have, but you cannot get CA if you work and earn more than £95 a week.
– You do not need to have paid any national insurance contributions to qualify for CA, but you can receive national insurance credits while receiving it.
– Getting CA qualifies you for a carer premium with income support, income-based jobseeker's allowance, housing benefit and council tax benefit, or a carer addition with pension credit.
– Claims are administered by the Department for Work and Pensions Carers Allowance Unit. You can make your claim at local Jobcentre Plus offices.

1. What is carer's allowance

Further Information

This chapter gives an outline of the carer's allowance rules and focuses on issues relevant to students. For more detailed information on the rules, see CPAG's *Welfare Benefits and Tax Credits Handbook*.

Carer's allowance is paid to people who spend at least 35 hours a week looking after a disabled person (adult or child). The disabled person must be getting attendance allowance, constant attendance allowance or the middle or highest rate of disability living allowance care component. The amount you get is not means tested, but counts as taxable income when assessing your student loan, grant or other student support income.

2. Who is eligible

You qualify for carer's allowance (CA) if:[1]
- you are 16 or over;
- you spend at least 35 hours a week caring for someone;
- the person for whom you care gets the middle or highest rate disability living allowance care component, attendance allowance or constant attendance allowance;
- you are not earning over £95 a week after deductions;
- you satisfy residence and presence conditions, and are not a 'person subject to immigration control' for benefit purposes.

You are not eligible if you are in full-time education – ie, you are studying more than 21 hours a week (see below).

There is no upper age limit for CA.

Breaks from caring

If you have been providing care for at least 35 hours a week in 22 of the last 26 weeks (14 of the last 26 weeks if either you or the disabled person were in hospital) you can still get CA. Effectively, you can have a four-week break from caring every six months (a 12-week break if either you or the disabled person were in hospital for at least eight weeks).[2]

What is 'full-time education'

You are regarded as being in **'full-time education'** if you attend a course of education at a university, college or other educational establishment for 21 hours or more a week.[3] These 21 hours include not just classes, lectures and seminars, but also individual study for course work. Meal breaks and unsupervised study are ignored. However, you are regarded as being engaged in **'supervised study'** if you are doing course work, whether at home or at college, alone or in the presence of a supervisor.[4] **'Unsupervised study'** is work beyond the requirements of the course.

Students and carer's allowance

When you start college or university you should inform the Department for Work and Pensions (DWP) (in Northern Ireland, the Department for Social

Development). The DWP normally requires details of your course, including its length and written confirmation of exactly how many hours of study a week students are expected to do. It is advisable to send a copy of your timetable to the DWP with a letter from the head of the appropriate department at the institution, who will be asked to estimate the weekly hours of study required. It is unusual for an institution to have a fixed amount of regular hours expected on its courses; normally a timetable is issued to a student, with a requirement to study independently throughout the terms and vacations. It is, therefore, always worth checking with your department exactly how many hours are expected in addition to the college timetable.

If your college or university says that it expects students to spend 21 hours or more a week in supervised study and classes, the DWP will normally conclude that it is full-time education. Although decision makers can consider the specific facts of your case, including your own evidence of your hours of study, in practice it is difficult to persuade the DWP that, in practice, you study fewer hours than the standard required for your course. The fact that you might work more quickly than average or are unable to spend so many hours on course work because of your caring responsibilities would not, therefore, be sufficient for you to count as a part-time student.

If you are not required to attend all of the modules on your full-time course because of prior accreditation, or if you have already completed some of the course requirements in advance (eg, you were previously attending the course part time, or completed extra modules in the summer vacation, or are repeating a year because you failed a module), this should be taken into account by the DWP and the appropriate time deducted from the compulsory hours.

If your course is part time but you spend more time than the standard amount expected on it, this should not exclude you from CA as long as the college or university regards your course as part time. If you have to care for someone, you may need to change your registration to that of a part-time student.

Taking a break from full-time study

'Attending' a course means being enrolled on and pursuing a course.[5] You are treated as still being in full-time education during short and long vacations and until the course ends, you abandon it or are dismissed from it. You are also still regarded as being full time during temporary interruptions.[6]

If you have to take time out to care for someone, you might not be able to get CA unless you have finally abandoned your course or have changed your mode of registration on the course from full time to part time (see p283). However, you can claim jobseeker's allowance for up to a maximum of 12 months once your caring responsibilities have ended and you are waiting to return to your course (providing you meet the other rules of entitlement – see Chapter 15).

3. **Amount of benefit**

You get £50.55 a week (2008/09 rate). You can claim an extra £30.20 for an adult dependant who does not earn too much. An **'adult dependant'** is a spouse or civil partner who lives with you, or someone who lives with you and looks after your child (eg, an unmarried partner).

If your partner is the carer, s/he can claim an addition in her/his carer's allowance for you as her/his dependant. Your student support income is not counted as 'earnings' and so does not disqualify her/him from the increase.

4. **Claiming carer's allowance**

You can make a claim for carers allowance (CA) online at www.dwp.gov.uk/carersallowance. Alternatively, you can claim on Form DS700, available from local Jobcentre Plus offices, the Carer's Allowance Unit on 01253 856 123 or from the Benefit Enquiry Line on freephone 0800 882 200. In Northern Ireland, the form is available from the Disability and Carers Service, Castle Court, Royal Avenue, Belfast BT1 1HR, telephone 028 9090 6186. Alternatively you can use the freephone number 0800 220 674.

Your claim can be backdated for up to three months if you qualified during that earlier period. Your claim may be backdated further if you claim within three months of the person for whom you care being awarded a qualifying benefit (eg, attendance allowance or disability living allowance). In this case, your CA can be backdated to the first day from when the qualifying benefit is payable.

Getting paid

CA is usually paid directly into a bank (or similar) account. Which account it goes into is up to you. If you do not want your benefit to be paid into an account that is overdrawn, give the DWP details of an alternative account if you have access to, or can open, one.

If you are overpaid CA, you might have to repay it.

5. **Challenging a decision**

If you think a decision about your carer's allowance is wrong (eg, because the decision maker got the facts or law wrong, or your circumstances have changed since the decision was made), there are a number of ways you can try to get the decision changed.

- You can seek a revision or a supersession of the decision. In some cases you have to show specific grounds. In others, you must apply within a strict time limit.
- You can appeal to an independent tribunal. There are strict time limits for appealing – usually one month from the date you are sent or given the decision. You can make a late appeal in limited circumstances.

If you are considering challenging a decision, you should seek advice as soon as possible.

6. **Other benefits and tax credits**

The disabled person's benefit

Your entitlement to carer's allowance (CA) depends on the person for whom you care continuing to get her/his disability benefit. If her/his benefit stops, your benefit will also stop. To avoid being overpaid, make sure you tell the Carer's Allowance Unit (or the Social Security Agency in Northern Ireland) if the disabled person's benefit stops.

It is not always financially prudent to claim CA. Although it may be more money for you, it may result in the person for whom you care losing some income support (IS), income-based jobseeker's allowance (JSA), income-related employment and support allowance (ESA), pension credit (PC), housing benefit (HB) or council tax benefit (CTB). If s/he lives alone, s/he may also be getting a severe disability premium included in these benefits (additional amount with PC). This will be lost as soon as CA is paid to you for looking after her/him. The severe disability premium/additional amount is roughly the same amount as CA, so it is always worth checking who would be better off claiming the extra help, the carer or the disabled person.

Also, if you become a full-time student and no longer qualify for CA, check whether the disabled person can qualify for the severe disability premium.

Overlapping benefits

Although you cannot receive CA at the same time as another income-replacement benefit, such as incapacity benefit, contribution-based JSA, contribution-based ESA, retirement pension, bereavement benefits, maternity allowance or severe disablement allowance, if you are eligible for more than one benefit you get the one which is worth the most.

Getting a carer's premium

If you are eligible for IS, income-based JSA, ESA, PC, HB or CTB as a part-time or full-time student, getting CA entitles you to a carer's premium (carer's addition with PC). If you are awarded CA, you should inform the local benefit office that pays your IS, JSA ESA, or PC, or the local authority if you get HB or CTB so that your benefit can be recalculated to include the carer's premium (carer's addition with PC). There is a good chance that your benefit will increase as a result of this addition.

Notes

2. Who is eligible
1 s70 SSCBA 1992
2 Reg 4(2) SS(ICA) Regs
3 Reg 5(2) SS(ICA) Regs
4 Reg 5(2) SS(ICA) Regs; *Flemming v Secretary of State for Work and Pensions* [2002] EWCA Civ 641, 10 May 2002; *Bronwyn Wright-Turner v Department for Social Development* [2002] NICA 2
5 *Flemming v Secretary of State for Work and Pensions* [2002] EWCA Civ 641, 10 May 2002
6 Reg 5(3) SS(ICA) Regs

Chapter 8

Child benefit

This chapter covers:
1. What is child benefit (below)
2. Who is eligible (p88)
3. Amount of benefit (p91)
4. Claiming child benefit (p91)
5. Challenging a decision (p92)
6. Other benefits and tax credits (p92)

Basic facts
– Child benefit is paid to people who are responsible for a child or a 'qualifying young person'.
– Both full-time and part-time students can claim child benefit.
– If you are under 20, someone else may be able to claim child benefit for you if you are studying.
– Child benefit is not means tested.
– Claims are administered by HM Revenue and Customs.

1. What is child benefit

Further information
This chapter gives an outline of the child benefit rules and focuses on issues relevant to students. For more detailed information on the rules, see CPAG's *Welfare Benefits and Tax Credits Handbook*.

Child benefit is paid to people who are responsible for a child or 'qualifying young person'. You do not have to have paid national insurance contributions to qualify for child benefit. It is not means tested, so the amount you get is not affected by your student loan, grant or other income.

2. **Who is eligible**

You qualify for child benefit if:[1]
- you are responsible for a child or 'qualifying young person' – ie:
  - s/he lives with you; *or*
  - you contribute to the cost of supporting her/him at a rate of at least the amount of child benefit for her/him.

  You do not have to be the child's parent; *and*
- you have priority over other potential claimants. Only one person can get child benefit for a particular child. There is an order of priority for who receives it where two or more people would otherwise be entitled; *and*
- you and the child or 'qualifying young person' satisfy presence and residence conditions; *and*
- you are not subject to immigration control for benefit purposes.

Being a student, whether full or part time, does not affect your entitlement to child benefit.

If you are a 'qualifying young person' someone else may be able to claim child benefit if s/he is responsible for you. You cannot, however, claim child benefit for yourself.

If a qualifying young person receives incapacity benefit, income support, income-based jobseeker's allowance, income-based employment and support allowance, working tax credit or child tax credit in her/his own right, any child benefit paid for the young person stops.

If a young person lives with a partner, or is married or in a civil partnership, you can get child benefit for her/him if s/he lives with you or you still contribute to her/his support, but only if her/his partner is in 'relevant education' (see p89) or approved training. The young person's partner cannot be the claimant.

Special rules apply in some circumstances – eg, if your child is being looked after by a local authority or if s/he is in detention.

Who counts as a child

Anyone aged under 16 counts as a 'child' for child benefit purposes, whether or not s/he goes to school. As long as you meet the other qualifying conditions, child benefit can be paid for her/him.[2] Child benefit can also be paid for a child after s/he reaches 16 until at least 31 August after her/his 16th birthday and then for as long as s/he continues to count as a 'qualifying young person'.

Who counts as a qualifying young person

A 'qualifying young person' is someone who:[3]
- is aged 16 and has left 'relevant education' (see p89) or training. This only applies up to 31 August after her/his 16th birthday (but see p89); *or*

- is aged 16 or 17, has left education or training and satisfies the extension period rule (see p90); *or*
- is aged 16 or over but under 20 and either:
  - is on a course of full-time non-advanced education which was not provided as a result of her/his employment; *or*
  - is on approved training which was not provided under a contract of employment (in England, Entry to Employment or Programme-Led Apprenticeships; in Wales, Skillbuild, Skillbuild+ or Foundation Modern Apprenticeships; or in Northern Ireland Access or Training for Success: Professional and Technical Training).[4]

The young person must have begun the course of full-time non-advanced education or approved training before reaching 19, or have been accepted or enrolled to undertake the education or training before that age; *or*

- is aged 16 or over but under 20 and:
  - has finished a course of full-time non-advanced education, but has been accepted or is enrolled on another such course; *or*
  - has finished a course of full-time non-advanced education or approved training, but has been accepted or is enrolled to take further approved training.

This does not apply if the courses or training are provided as a result of her/his employment; *or*

- is aged 16 or over but under 20 and has left 'relevant education' (see below) or approved training but has not passed her/his 'terminal date' (see p90).

If your child counts as a qualifying young person on more than one of the above grounds, s/he counts as a qualifying young person until the last date that applies.[5]

If you stop being entitled to child benefit for your child because s/he no longer counts as a qualifying young person, but s/he later satisfies one of the above conditions again and so counts as a qualifying young person once more, child benefit can again become payable for her/him. **Note:** in some cases, you can continue to claim during such an interruption – eg, if your qualifying young person is ill.

In the rest of this chapter the term 'child' is used to mean both children under 16 and qualifying young people aged 16 or over.

Relevant education

'**Relevant education**' is defined as education which is full time and non-advanced. For the purpose of deciding if your child is in relevant education, HM Revenue and Customs considers that the definition of 'full time' given on p160 applies, but this is not actually stated in the legislation. It may, therefore, be possible to argue, for example, that unsupervised, as well as supervised, study should be counted when assessing if such a course is full time.

The extension period rule

If your child is 16 or 17, s/he continues to count as a qualifying young person, and so child benefit can continue to be paid for her/him, during an 'extension period' if:[6]

- s/he has left education or training; *and*
- s/he is registered as available for work, education or training with the Careers or Connexions service, Ministry of Defence or, in Northern Ireland, the Department for Employment and Learning or an education and library board. In some circumstances, s/he can also be registered with a corresponding body in another European Economic Area state; *and*
- s/he is not in remunerative work (ie, work of 24 hours a week or more for payment, or in expectation of payment); *and*
- you were entitled to child benefit for her/him immediately before the extension period started; *and*
- you apply in writing within three months of the date your child's education or training finished.

In this context, 'education' and 'training' are not defined and so may mean any kind of education or training.

The extension period starts from the Monday after your child's course of education or training ends and lasts for 20 weeks from that date. If your child reaches 18 during the extension period, unless s/he counts as a qualifying young person on another ground (see p88), your child benefit for her/him ends from the first child benefit payday on or after s/he reaches 18.[7]

The terminal date rule

If your child leaves 'relevant education' (see p89) or approved training before reaching 20, s/he continues to count as a qualifying young person until either:[8]

- the first Sunday on or after her/his 'terminal date' (see below); *or*
- if s/he reaches 20 before that date, the Sunday on or after her/his 20th birthday (unless her/his 20th birthday is on a Monday, in which case s/he counts as a qualifying young person until the Sunday before her/his birthday).

This means that, unless s/he continues to count as a qualifying young person on another ground or is returning to sit an exam (see p91), the general rule is that you stop receiving child benefit for her/him on that date.

Your child's **'terminal date'** is the first of the following dates which falls after the date her/his 'relevant education' or approved training finished:

- the last day in February; *or*
- the last day in May; *or*
- the last day in August; *or*

- the last day in November.

A child who returns to sit an external examination in connection with her/his course of relevant education is treated as still being in relevant education until the date of the last exam.[9]

19-year-olds

If your child is on a course of full-time non-advanced education or approved training, s/he can only count as a qualifying young person once s/he is 19 if s/he began (or was accepted or enrolled on) that course of education or training before that age.[10] If s/he did, so long as you meet the other qualifying conditions, you continue to be entitled to child benefit for her/him until the first terminal date falling after the end of the course or training, or her/his 20th birthday if this comes first.

Even if HM Revenue and Customs does not accept that your child counts as a qualifying young person while on a new course, it may be possible to argue that s/he should count as a qualifying young person for a period after s/he leaves the new course under the terminal date rule if s/he then leaves that course or training before reaching 20.[11] If your claim is refused, seek advice.

3. **Amount of benefit**

Weekly rate from April 2008

Eldest eligible child	£18.80
Other children (each)	£12.55

If you are living with a partner and your family includes stepchildren or the children of your partner, and you each receive child benefit for your respective children, only one of you can receive the higher rate for the eldest child – the one with the eldest child.

4. **Claiming child benefit**

Child benefit is administered by HM Revenue and Customs (the Revenue). You claim child benefit on Form CH2, which can be obtained from the Child Benefit Office on 0845 302 1444 (0845 603 2000 in Northern Ireland), any Revenue enquiry centre, the Revenue's website (www.hmrc.gov.uk) or from Jobcentre Plus offices.

You should submit your claim to the Child Benefit Office, PO Box 1, Newcastle upon Tyne NE88 1AA, or take the form to a Revenue enquiry centre or Jobcentre Plus office. In some cases, you might be able to claim child benefit online.

You should make a claim within three months of becoming eligible. This is because your claim can usually only be backdated for up to three months. You do not have to show any reason why your claim was late.

Getting paid

Child benefit is usually paid directly into your bank (or similar) account. Which account it goes into is up to you. If you do not want your benefit to go into an account that is overdrawn, give the Revenue details of an alternative account if you have access to, or can open, one.

If you are overpaid child benefit, you might have to repay it.

5. **Challenging a decision**

If you think a decision about your child benefit is wrong (eg, because the decision maker got the facts or law wrong, or your circumstances have changed since the decision was made), there are a number of ways you can try to get the decision changed.

- You can seek a revision or a supersession of the decision. In some cases you have to show specific grounds. In others, you must apply within a strict time limit.
- You can appeal to an independent tribunal. There are strict time limits for appealing – usually one month from the date you are sent or given the decision. You can make a late appeal in limited circumstances.

If you are considering challenging a decision, you should seek advice as soon as possible.

You cannot appeal against some decisions, such as a decision on which of two people whose claims have equal priority should get child benefit. However, you can ask for a revision or a supersession of such a decision.

6. **Other benefits and tax credits**

If you qualify for child benefit, you may also qualify for tax credits and means-tested benefits. Child benefit is:

- paid in addition to non-means-tested benefits;
- ignored as income for tax credits purposes.

Child benefit is ignored as income for pension credit purposes. It is also ignored as income for income support (IS) and income-based jobseeker's allowance (JSA) if you are getting child tax credit (CTC). However, if you have been getting IS or income-based JSA since before 6 April 2004 which includes amounts for your child(ren), child benefit is taken into account as income until you are awarded CTC, unless you have a child under one, in which case £10.50 of your child benefit is ignored.

Child benefit is taken into account when working out housing benefit (HB) and council tax benefit (CTB).

If you receive child benefit you count as responsible for a child for IS, income-based JSA, and, usually, for HB and CTB. This can help you qualify for these benefits while you are a full-time student in some circumstances (see Chapters 12, 14, 15 and 23).

Notes

2. Who is eligible

1 ss141–147 SSCBA 1992
2 s142(1) SSCBA 1992; reg 4 CB Regs
3 s142(2) SSCBA 1992; regs 2–8 CB Regs
4 Reg 1(3) CB Regs
5 Reg 2(2) CB Regs
6 Reg 5 CB Regs
7 Reg 14 The Child Benefit and Guardian's Allowance (Administration) Regulations 2003 No.492; reg 5(3) CB Regs
8 Reg 7 CB Regs
9 Reg 7(2) case 2.1 CB Regs
10 Reg 3(4) CB Regs
11 This is because in the rules on terminal dates there is no requirement that a course of education or training must be started before a person is 19.

Chapter 9

Disability living allowance

This chapter covers:
1. What is disability living allowance (below)
2. Who is eligible (p95)
3. Amount of benefit (p99)
4. Claiming disability living allowance (p99)
5. Challenging a decision (p100)
6. Other benefits and tax credits (p101)

Basic facts
– Disability living allowance (DLA) is paid in order to assist disabled people with personal care and mobility needs.
– The amount you get is not affected by your income or capital, and all student support is ignored when working out entitlement.
– It has a care component and a mobility component.
– Adults, young people and children can all qualify for DLA.
– A person can receive either one or both components providing s/he meets the eligibility criteria.
– It is available to both full-time and part-time students who meet the basic eligibility criteria.
– Receipt of DLA enables a full-time student to be eligible for income support, housing benefit and council tax benefit or for increased amounts of these benefits.
– Claims for DLA are administered by the Department for Work and Pensions Disability Living Allowance Unit in Blackpool.

1. What is disability living allowance

Further information
This chapter gives an outline of the disability living allowance rules and focuses on issues relevant to students. For more detailed information on the rules, see CPAG's *Welfare Benefits and Tax Credits Handbook*.

Disability living allowance (DLA) is a benefit available to disabled people aged under 65 when they first claim, who require help with personal care or have mobility difficulties. You do not have to have paid national insurance contributions to qualify for DLA. It is not means tested, so the amount you get is not affected by your student grant or loan, or any other income you receive. It is available to both full- and part-time students who meet the basic eligibility criteria.

DLA has two components.

- **Care component.** This is for help with personal care needs and is payable at three different rates.
- **Mobility component.** This is payable at two different rates depending upon the severity of your walking problems.

DLA is payable to the person with the disability rather than her/his carer. The carer may be eligible to receive carer's allowance, providing that the disabled person receives the middle or highest rate care component of DLA (see Chapter 7).

2. Who is eligible

To qualify for disability living allowance (DLA) you must:

- be under the age of 65 when you make the claim (attendance allowance is available to people above this age for care needs only). There is no lower age limit for the care component. The lower age limit for lower rate mobility component is five, and for the higher rate mobility component three;
- meet the disability test for the care and/or mobility component;
- unless you are terminally ill (see below), have satisfied the disability test for a continuous period of three months immediately before the start of the award and be likely to satisfy it for the next six months; *and*
- satisfy residence and presence tests and not be a 'person subject to immigration control' for benefit purposes. You can get further advice from UKCISA (see Appendix 2).

You are regarded as **'terminally ill'** if you have a progressive disease and can reasonably be expected to die within six months as a result of that disease. If this is the case, you can claim under what are known as the 'special rules' or someone can claim under these rules on your behalf.

Care component

The level of help you need determines the rate of care component you receive.

Lowest rate

You can qualify for this if you require care in connection with your bodily functions for a 'significant' period of the day (whether during a single period or a number of periods) or you meet the 'cooking test.'

You should count as requiring care for a significant portion of the day if it would take an hour in total to provide the help you need. This can be continuous or made up of short periods of time – eg, if you need help for 20 minutes three times a day.[1]

For the cooking test you have to be 16 or over and show that you are so severely physically or mentally disabled that you cannot prepare a cooked meal for yourself, assuming you had the ingredients. Your ability to chop food, use taps, carry pans or use a cooker are all relevant.

Middle rate

You can qualify for this if you require:
- frequent daytime attention in connection with your bodily functions (for more than one hour);[2] or
- continual daytime supervision in order to avoid substantial danger to yourself or others;[3] or
- prolonged (20 minutes or more) or repeated night-time attention; or
- supervision at night in order to prevent danger to yourself or others that requires another person to be awake for a prolonged period or at frequent intervals to watch over you.

Highest rate[4]

You can qualify for this if you need care or supervision during the day and the night, and you meet both a daytime *and* a night-time middle rate criteria, or if you are terminally ill (see p95) and claiming under the special rules (see p99).

Attention and bodily functions

'**Attention**' is active help from another person to assist you with personal tasks concerning your bodily functions that you are unable to do for yourself. '**Bodily functions**' include breathing, sitting, seeing, hearing, eating, drinking, washing, going to the toilet, getting out of bed or a chair, taking medication and communicating. Any help in connection with impaired bodily function can count if it involves personal contact (physical or verbal in your presence) and it is reasonably required.

For example, a blind student might need the help of a notetaker or reader, or a guide around campus or around town. A deaf student might need an interpreter. A student with arthritis might need help getting in and out of chairs. However, you must need the help of another person to qualify for DLA; if you need to use artificial aids only you will not qualify.

You cannot get help for domestic chores, unless someone is helping you do them for yourself.

If you have dyslexia, you could argue that you qualify for DLA but only if you need someone to be with you to help you read and write – ie, someone sitting beside you reading to you, or helping you develop writing skills.[5]

Continual supervision

'**Continual supervision**' is regular or frequent supervision, but does not necessarily have to be non-stop. The supervision does not have to stop the danger to the disabled person, but should reduce the risk of harm. You must show that there is a real risk of danger without the help of the other person. The person providing the supervision need not always be active or awake, but needs to be ready to act should help be required.

Having a social life

The kind of help you need must be reasonably required. This means you need it to enable you as far as possible to live a normal life. You can include help needed to take part in social activities, sport, recreation, cultural or political activities, so long as the help is required in connection with a bodily function.

Mobility component

To qualify for DLA mobility component you must be able to benefit from 'enhanced facilities for locomotion' – ie, that you are interested in going out, can get out from time to time and would benefit from outdoor journeys. There are two rates of mobility component and the level you receive depends on the severity of your disability.

Lower rate[6]

You can qualify for this if you can walk but are so severely mentally or physically disabled that, disregarding your ability to use familiar routes, you cannot take advantage of your ability to walk outdoors without the guidance or supervision of another person most of the time.

You can still qualify if you are able to manage on familiar routes. If you cannot manage without guidance or supervision on unfamiliar routes or if you cannot manage anywhere, you should qualify. For example, a blind student may qualify even though s/he has learned the route to and from home and college if s/he still needs guidance in other places.

Higher rate

You can qualify for this if:
- you are unable to walk; *or*
- you are virtually unable to walk outdoors;[7] *or*
- you are totally blind and have an 80 per cent hearing loss;[8] *or*

- you have no legs or feet (from birth or because of amputation); or
- the exertion required to walk would constitute a danger to your life or be likely to lead to a serious deterioration in your health; or
- you have a severe mental impairment and highly disruptive and dangerous behavioural problems, and you are in receipt of the highest rate of DLA care component.[9]

Unable/virtually unable to walk

Being **'unable to walk'** means that you cannot literally put one foot in front of another.

Most disputes about mobility component involve the interpretation of **'virtually unable to walk'**. You have to show that your ability to walk out of doors is so limited, taking into account the distance, speed, length of time and manner in which you walk without feeling severe discomfort, that you are virtually unable to walk. Any walking done when you are suffering pain or severe discomfort must be discounted.

Exertion required to walk.

You can qualify for the higher rate mobility component if the **'exertion required to walk'** could lead to a danger to your life or a serious deterioration in your health. You need to show that you would never recover, or that recovery would take a significant period of time or require some medical intervention. For example, if you have a serious lung, heart or chest condition you may qualify.

Under-16-year-olds

For a child to be eligible for the care component of DLA:[10]

- her/his needs must be substantially greater than those a child in normal physical and mental health requires at the same age; or
- s/he must have substantial care, supervision, or watching over needs which other children of her/his age in normal physical or mental health do not have.

Note: those under 16 cannot qualify for DLA on the basis of the 'cooking test'.

For a child to be eligible for the mobility component at the lower rate s/he must need substantially more guidance or supervision than a child of the same age in normal physical and mental health.[11]

Students and disability living allowance

Full-time and part-time disabled students are eligible to claim DLA. It does not affect your eligibility for, or the amount of, student support income. In addition, entitlement to DLA can help you qualify for means-tested benefits.

If you become a student, this may result in the Department for Work and Pensions (DWP) reconsidering whether you are still entitled to DLA, although this is not standard practice. However, the DWP might assume that if you are now capable of a full-time course, your health has improved and you no longer have the same care or mobility needs. If this happens and your DLA is affected, see p100 for information about challenging the decision.

3. Amount of benefit

Weekly rate from April 2008	£
Care component (lowest rate)	17.75
Care component (middle rate)	44.85
Care component (highest rate)	67.00
Mobility component (lower rate)	17.75
Mobility component (higher rate)	46.75

4. Claiming disability living allowance

You can make a claim for disability living allowance (DLA) online at www.dwp.gov.uk/eservice/.

Alternatively, you can request an application pack from the Benefit Enquiry Line on 0800 882 200 (textphone 0800 243 355) or your local Jobcentre Plus office. Providing you make the claim within six weeks of requesting the form, if eligible, you will receive DLA for all of this period.

The claim pack is extensive and repetitive in places, but it is important to give as much information as you can about your disability. Give examples of all the things you cannot do or have difficulties with. You will be asked about your leisure activities and hobbies, and the help you need. Make sure to put down all the help you need, whether you undertake hobbies or not and any help you need with studying. It does not matter whether or not you are already receiving the help; it is what you need that counts.

Claiming under the special rules

You are allowed to claim under the special rules if you are regarded as 'terminally ill' – ie, if you have a progressive disease and could reasonably be expected to die within six months as a result.

In these circumstances there is no requirement to satisfy the disability test for the three-month qualifying period and the highest rate care component of DLA is paid straight away. The Department for Work and Pensions (DWP) aims to deal with these claims within eight working days.

Note: you do not qualify for the mobility component automatically. However, you should claim this based on your mobility needs.

Awards are made for a fixed period of three years but, if there is already a mobility component award in place, the period of the special rules award may be adjusted to end at the same time.

Getting paid

DLA is usually paid directly into your bank (or similar) account. Which account it goes into is up to you. If you do not want your benefit to go into an account that is overdrawn, give the DWP details of an alternative account if you have access to, or can open, one.

If you have been overpaid DLA, you might have to repay it.

5. **Challenging a decision**

If you think a decision about your disability living allowance (DLA) is wrong – eg, because the decision maker got the facts or the law wrong, or your circumstances have changed since the decision was made, there are a number of ways you can try to get the decision changed.

- You can seek a revision or a supersession of the decision. In some cases you have to show specific grounds. In others, you must apply within a strict time limit.
- You can appeal to an independent tribunal. There are strict time limits for appealing – usually one month from the date you are sent or given the decision. You can make a late appeal in limited circumstances.

If you are considering challenging a decision, you should seek specialist advice as soon as possible.

Note: when you ask for an award of DLA to be revised or you appeal (in respect of one or both components), the Department for Work and Pensions (DWP) or tribunal can look at your entitlement to both components of DLA, whether or not you want it to. You run the risk of having your award reduced or of one or both components being removed altogether. You should, therefore, seek advice or consider fully all the circumstances before applying for a revision or appealing. If you have only been awarded DLA for a set period, it may instead be worth waiting to apply for a higher rate when you make your next (renewal) claim.

If the DWP assumes that because you are a student, you no longer have the same care or mobility needs and your DLA is affected, you can challenge the decision. See above for what you should consider before you do so. If you do challenge the decision, bear the following in mind.

- Let the DWP (or appeal tribunal) know if you took up the course for therapeutic reasons and are only able to do it with the support of disability services or the disabled students' allowance.
- It is sometimes worth providing a copy of the disabled students' allowance report as evidence of the difficulties you have with studying and the support you need if your DLA entitlement is in dispute.

6. **Other benefits and tax credits**

Disability living allowance (DLA) is usually paid in full in addition to any other social security benefits or tax credits. Constant attendance allowance overlaps with the care component and war pension mobility supplement overlaps with the mobility component. You are paid the higher of these.

If you are in receipt of DLA you are eligible for housing benefit (HB) and council tax benefit (CTB) even if you are a full-time student. You are also eligible for income support (IS) if you made a claim before 27 October 2008. After this date, you are eligible to claim income-related employment and support allowance (ESA) if you are not already in receipt of IS.

In addition, receiving DLA entitles you to a disability premium and, if you receive the middle or highest rate care component and satisfy other conditions, a severe disability premium, and an enhanced disability premium if you receive the highest rate care component. If you are getting ESA, you will receive the work-related activity component. The amount of the premium or component depends on the rate and the components of DLA you receive.

If your child receives DLA (at any rate), you qualify for a disabled child premium and an enhanced disability premium with HB/CTB if s/he receives the highest rate care component. If you have two children receiving DLA, you should receive one of these premiums for each child, depending on how many they qualify for. You can also get the disability/severe disability element of child tax credit.

If you are receiving working tax credit, DLA enables you to qualify for the disability and severe disability elements.

If you are still receiving allowances for your children with your IS or income-based jobseeker's allowance, you can also get a disabled child premium if your child gets any rate of DLA, and possibly an enhanced disability premium if your child receives the highest rate care component.

When you make a claim for a means-tested benefit or tax credits it is, therefore, important to inform the local Department for Work and Pensions office, local authority or HM Revenue and Customs that you, your partner or child are receiving DLA.

Notes

2. Who is eligible

1 CDLA/58/1993
2 s72(1)(b)(i) SSCBA 1992 and CA/281/1989
3 s72(1)(b)(ii) SSCBA 1992 and R(A) 2/75
4 s72(4)(a) SSCBA 1992
5 CDLA/1983/2006; CDLA/3204/2006
6 s73(1)(d) SSCBA 1992
7 s73(1)(a) SSCBA 1992; reg 12 DLA Regs
8 s73(2) SSCBA 1992
9 s73(3) SSCBA 1992; reg 12(5) and (6) DLA Regs
10 s72(6)(b) SSCBA 1992; CA/92/1992
11 s73(4) SSCBA 1992

Chapter 10

Employment and support allowance

This chapter covers:

Basic facts

– Employment and support allowance (ESA) replaced incapacity benefit and income support for people making a new claim on grounds of disability from 27 October 2008.
– It is for people who have limited capability for work, according to a work capability assessment.
– There is an income-related and a contributory ESA, including a contributory 'ESA in youth'.
– Part-time students who have limited capability for work and full-time students who get disability living allowance are eligible for income-related ESA.
– Part-time and full-time students can claim contributory ESA if they have paid sufficient national insurance contributions.
– Full-time students aged 19 or over and part-time students can claim ESA in youth after 28 weeks of limited capability for work, which began when they were under 20 (or sometimes 25) without having any national insurance contributions.
– In some circumstances, full-time students under 19 can get ESA in youth.

1. **What is employment and support allowance**

Further information

This chapter gives an outline of the employment and support allowance rules and focuses on issues relevant to students. For more detailed information on the rules, see CPAG's *Welfare Benefits and Tax Credits Handbook*.

Employment and support allowance (ESA) is a new benefit for people who have limited capability for work because of illness or disability. It was introduced on 27 October 2008. People who were already claiming incapacity benefit or income support on incapacity or disability grounds when ESA was introduced continue to receive these benefits, although the Government plans eventually to transfer all of these claimants to ESA.

There are two types of ESA – contributory ESA and income-related ESA. Contributory ESA is for people who have paid national insurance contributions, or whose period of limited capability for work starts when they are young. Income-related ESA is means tested and is for people who have limited capability for work and are on a low income. It is possible to receive one or both types of ESA.

2. **Who is eligible**

To qualify for employment and support allowance (ESA) you must meet all the basic conditions.[1]

- You have limited capability for work (see p108).
- You are aged 16 or over and under age 60 if you are a woman, or age 65 if you are a man.
- You are in the UK (although some absences are allowed – see CPAG's *Welfare Benefits and Tax Credits Handbook*).
- You satisfy the rules for contributory ESA (see below) or income-related ESA (see p106).
- You are not working, although some 'permitted work' is allowed (see CPAG's *Welfare Benefits and Tax Credits Handbook*).

Contributory employment and support allowance

Contributory ESA is not means tested. To qualify, you must meet the basic conditions above and either:[2]

- have paid sufficient national insurance (NI) contributions (see CPAG's *Welfare Benefits and Tax Credits Handbook* for details); *or*
- you can get ESA in youth. This depends on:

 – your age when you began your period of limited capability for work;
 – your age when you make your first claim; *and*
 – whether or not you are a full-time student (see below).

You must also satisfy residence and presence tests and not be a 'person subject to immigration control' (see CPAG's *Welfare Benefits and Tax Credits Handbook* for details).

ESA is payable after 196 days (28 weeks) of limited capability for work.

Under age 19

Students in full-time education under age 19 are not eligible for contributory ESA except a very small minority who can qualify through their NI contributions and those whose course is not counted because it is designed for people with disabilities (see below).

You can get ESA in youth as soon as you reach your 19th birthday if you are still in full-time education. You must have had limited capability for work for 28 weeks before benefit can be paid, but these weeks can fall before your 19th birthday.

Students under age 19 in part-time education are eligible for ESA in youth. You can claim from age 16. You can serve the 28-week qualifying period before you reach age 16, so your benefit can start from your 16th birthday.

Full-time education

You are treated as being in **'full-time education'** if you attend a course of education for 21 hours or more a week. Count classes, lectures, seminars and periods of supervised study. Do not count lunch breaks, private unsupervised study or work at home.[3] You continue to be treated as being in full-time education during any temporary interruption of your studies.

Disabled students should ignore any hours of tuition that would not be received by someone of the same age who is not disabled. Any such special teaching does not count towards the 21 hours.[4]

Aged 19

At age 19 students can get ESA in youth regardless of whether they are studying full or part time. If you have already had limited capability for work for 28 weeks when you reach your 19th birthday, you can claim and be paid ESA straight away.

Aged 20 or over

If you already get ESA in youth you can continue to get it after age 20. If you have not already claimed, you must start your claim no later than the end of a continuous period of 196 days (28 weeks) of limited capability for work that began before your 20th birthday. You have a further three months to send in your claim form. After that, you can only make a new claim for contributory ESA if:

- you have paid sufficient NI contributions; *or*
- you are 25 or under and a former student. There is an age exception that allows certain people to claim up to age 25 when they have left their course (see below).

Age exception

Normally, to claim contributory ESA after age 20 you must have sufficient NI contributions, but there is an age exception for students. You can claim if you are under 25 and give up or finish a course that you started before your 20th birthday and you have had limited capability for work for 28 weeks. The following rules specify when your course must have started and finished, and by when you need to claim. You claim once you have left your course.[5]

- You were registered on a course of full-time education, or certain kinds of training, three months or more before your 20th birthday. Any course counts, from secondary school education to university undergraduate or postgraduate degrees. If you are studying part time because your disability prevents you from doing a full-time course, you are regarded as full time for this rule. The law does not say what 'full time' means or give a set number of hours. The Department for Work and Pensions (DWP) may ask you for evidence from the educational institution.
- You attended the course in the first academic term after registration.
- You were still attending the course within the last two complete tax years before the benefit year in which you claim ESA. A tax year runs from 6 April and a benefit year runs from the first Sunday in January. For example, if you claim ESA in 2008, you must have attended the course at some point on or after 6 April 2005. You are regarded as still attending the course while taking time off temporarily because of illness or a domestic emergency.
- You start your claim no later than the end of a continuous period of 196 days (28 weeks) of incapacity that started before your 25th birthday. You have another three months to send in your claim form.

Income-related employment and support allowance

Income-related ESA is means tested. You are eligible if you are a part-time student and have limited capability for work. If you are a full-time student, you are only eligible if you get disability living allowance (DLA).

To qualify for income-related ESA while studying you must satisfy the basic conditions on p104 and all the following conditions.[6]

- You are either a full-time student (see p107) who is entitled to DLA (either component, at any rate – see Chapter 9) or a part-time student;[7] *and*
- Your income is less than the set amount the law says you need to live on (known as your 'applicable amount') – see p109; *and*
- You have no more than £16,000 capital; *and*
- Your partner (if you have one) is not working 24 hours or more a week; *and*

- You are 'habitually resident' in the UK, Ireland, Channel Islands or Isle of Man, have a 'right to reside' in the UK, and are not a 'person subject to immigration control'. These terms are explained in CPAG's *Welfare Benefits and Tax Credits Handbook*. Further advice is available from UKCISA (see Appendix 2).

Full-time student

You are a full-time student if you are:[8]
- under 20 and a 'qualifying young person' (see below); *or*
- 19 or over and a full-time student (unless you are aged 19 and count as being a qualifying young person) (see below); *or*
- under 19 in full-time advanced education (see p108).

Under 20 and a qualifying young person

You are a qualifying young person if you are 19 or under and attending a full-time course of non-advanced education which you were accepted on, enrolled on or started when you were under 19. If you are accepted on, enrol on or start the course on or after your 19th birthday, you are not a qualifying young person (see below). 'Non-advanced education' is anything below degree, HNC or HND level, and includes school-level courses. Your course is classed as 'full time' for income-related ESA if it is for more than 12 hours a week during term time. These 12 hours include classes and supervised study, but not meal breaks or unsupervised study either at home or at college. You may count as a qualifying young person in a gap between courses or for a period after you have finished a course – see p88.

19 or over and a full-time student

You count as a full-time student if you are undertaking a full-time course of study at an educational establishment.[9]

If you attend a **further education** college and your course is government funded you will usually count as a part-time student as long as your course comprises 16 guided learning hours or less a week. 'Guided learning hours' include all supervised study – eg, classes, lectures, tutorials and structured assessment periods. They do not include unstructured or unsupervised study time – eg, studying at home or in a library. A document called a 'learning agreement' is used to provide proof of course hours. It is important to use the official learning agreement. The hours on this document are calculated as an average figure and may differ from the hours on your timetable. Ask about your learning agreement at your college or check with your course tutor. The local authority uses your learning agreement to decide whether or not you are studying full time.

In Northern Ireland, the definition of a full-time course depends on the institution's definition of 'full time'. A letter from the institution stating that your course is part time should be sufficient when applying for ESA.

Students in **higher education** are counted as full-time students if the college or university says the course is full time. Ask at your college, or check with the course tutor or the registry department for evidence of whether you are registered on a full- or part-time course.

If your course is only for a few hours each week, you should argue that it is not full time, but a course could be full time even if you only attend a few lectures a week.

Under 19 in full-time advanced education

If you are under 19 and in full-time advanced education rather than in non-advanced education, the rules on when you count as full time are the same as for those aged 19 or over (see p107).

3. **Limited capability for work**

One of the basic rules of entitlement to employment and support allowance (ESA) is that you must be assessed as having 'limited capability for work'. This means that because of your mental or physical condition it is unreasonable to require you to work. This is normally assessed at a medical known as the 'work capability assessment'. The work capability assessment also assesses whether you have 'limited capability for work-related activity'. If you do, your ESA includes an extra amount called a 'support component', which is paid to the most disabled people. If you do not, your ESA includes a 'work-related activity' component and you are expected to attend work-focused interviews, and failure to engage may result in a reduction of benefit.

Full-time students who get disability living allowance (DLA) and who are claiming income-related ESA are treated as having limited capability for work and do not have to satisfy this part of the test.[10] However, this does not apply to all full-time students. If you are a qualifying young person under 20 and claiming income-related ESA (see p106), you have to satisfy this test. Similarly, if you are claiming contributory ESA (including ESA in youth), but not income-related ESA, you still have to pass the limited capability for work test, even if you get DLA. All students, unless they get the support component, have to attend work-focused interviews. These include agreeing an action plan of activities to help you find work. At present, however, your benefit will not be reduced if you do not undertake any of these.

4. **Amount of benefit**

Employment and support allowance (ESA) is payable after three 'waiting days' (apart from ESA in youth, which has a 196-day qualifying period). You are paid a limited amount of ESA during an initial 'assessment phase' (in most cases, this is expected to last 13 weeks) and are paid more in the 'main phase' that follows.

The exact amount of ESA you are paid depends on:

- whether you are claiming contributory ESA or income-related ESA;
- whether you are in the assessment or the main phase;
- which of the two possible additional components you get after the assessment phase. These are a support component of £29 a week and a work-related activity component of £24 a week.

In the assessment phase, for **contributory ESA** you get a basic allowance. For **income-related ESA**, the amount you get depends on your needs (your applicable amount) and how much income you have.

In the main phase, an additional component (either the work-related activity component or the support component) is added. In income-related ESA, it is added to your applicable amount and, as in the assessment phase, your income is subtracted from your applicable amount. In contributory ESA, it is added to the basic allowance.

Contributory employment and support allowance

Weekly rate from October 2008[11]	£
Assessment phase, basic allowance (under 25)	47.95
Assessment phase, basic allowance (25 or over)	60.50
Main phase, basic allowance (16 or over)	60.50
Main phase, support component	29.00
Main phase, work-related activity component	24.00

Income-related employment and support allowance

The amount of income-related ESA you get depends on your circumstances and, if you have one, the circumstances of your partner.[12] The amount also depends on your income and capital. You should go through the following steps to work out the amount of ESA to which you are entitled.

Step 1: capital

If your capital is over £16,000 you cannot get income-related ESA. Some kinds of capital are ignored. For details, see CPAG's *Welfare Benefits and Tax Credits Handbook*.

Step 2: work out your applicable amount

This is an amount for basic weekly needs. It is made up of:[13]

- personal allowances (see p110);
- premiums (see p111);
- work-related activity or support component (see p112);
- housing costs (see p112).

Step 3: work out your weekly income

Chapter 20 explains how your loan, grant or other income is taken into account and how to work out your weekly income.

Step 4: deduct weekly income from applicable amount

If your income is less than your applicable amount, ESA equals the difference between the two.

If your income is the same as or more than your applicable amount, you cannot get ESA. You can claim again if your income goes down – eg, during the long vacation.

Income-related ESA tops up contributory ESA if you are entitled to both and the income-related amount is higher.

Applicable amount

Work out your applicable amount by adding together your personal allowances, premiums, the component that applies to you in the main phase, and eligible housing costs. Note that benefit rates are uprated in April each year, but it is usually possible to find out what the new rates will be from the beginning of December. Check the Department for Work and Pensions website at www.dwp.gov.uk for a press release on social security uprating, or see CPAG's *Welfare Rights Bulletin*.

Personal allowance

Your personal allowance is made up of one personal allowance at either the single, lone parent or couple rate depending on your situation. The amount depends on your age and whether you are in the assessment phase or the main phase.

Circumstances	Assessment phase £ per week	Main phase £ per week
Single		
Under 25	47.95	60.50
25 or over	60.50	60.50
Lone parent		
Under 18	47.95	60.50
18 or over	60.50	60.50
Couple		
Both under 18 (higher rate)	72.35	94.95
Both under 18 (if not eligible for higher rate)	47.95	60.50
One under 18, one 18 or over (higher rate)	94.95	94.95
One under 18, one 18–24 (if not eligible for higher rate)	47.95	60.50

One under 18, one 25 or over (if not eligible for higher rate)	60.50	60.50
Both 18 or over	94.95	94.95

If you are both under 18, you get the higher rate if:
- one of you is responsible for a child; *or*
- you and your partner would both be eligible to claim income-related ESA if you were single; *or*
- your partner would qualify for income support (IS) if s/he were single; *or*
- your partner would qualify for income-based jobseeker's allowance (JSA) or severe hardship payments of JSA.

If one of you is under 18 and the other is 18 or over, you get the higher rate if the younger person would:
- qualify for IS or income-related ESA if s/he were single; *or*
- qualify for income-based or severe hardship payments of JSA.

Premiums

Qualifying for premiums depends on your circumstances. You can qualify for a:
- pensioner premium (see pxvi for amounts);
- carer's premium of £27.75;
- enhanced disability premium for an adult of £12.60 (£18.15 for a couple);
- severe disability premium of £50.35.

If you or your partner are aged 60 or over you qualify for a **pensioner premium**. If you are single you get £63.55 and if you are in a couple you get £94.40. In the main phase, these amounts are reduced by the amount of the work-related activity component or support component that you qualify for.

You qualify for a **carer's premium** if you are entitled to carer's allowance (CA). If you are entitled to CA but not paid it because it overlaps with another benefit, you still qualify. You get two premiums if both you and your partner qualify.

You qualify for a **disability premium** if you or your partner get the highest rate disability living allowance (DLA)care component or you get the support component of ESA.

Severe disability premium is for severely disabled people who live alone, or can be treated as living alone. You qualify for this premium if you get the middle or highest rate DLA care component and no one gets carer's allowance for looking after you. You will not get it if you live with another person aged 18 or over – eg, a friend or parent, unless they are separately liable for rent, or you only share a bathroom or hallway, or in some other circumstances. See CPAG's *Welfare Benefits and Tax Credits Handbook* for details.

If you have a partner, you will not qualify unless s/he also qualifies in her/his own right or is registered blind. If you both qualify, you get two premiums.

Components

In the main phase, you receive one of either the work-related activity or support components. The work-related activity component is £24. The support component is £29. It is possible to lose the whole of the work-related activity component if you do not take part in the required assessments/interviews.

Housing costs

If you own your own home, ESA can help with the cost of mortgage interest payments. Normally, help only starts once you have been getting ESA for 39 weeks, although there are some exceptions to this. For help with your rent, you need to claim housing benefit (HB – see Chapter 12). For an outline of the rules, see p170 and for full details, see CPAG's *Welfare Benefits and Tax Credits Handbook*.

Example

Doreen is 19 and has cerebral palsy. She gets the lowest rate DLA care component and lives with her parents. In January 2009 she starts a full-time NVQ Level 3 course. She claims ESA. She is eligible for contributory ESA in youth and income-related ESA.

Assessment phase:
Contributory ESA
Doreen gets £47.95 basic allowance.

Income-related ESA
Step 1 Doreen has no savings or capital.
Step 2 Her applicable amount is:
Basic allowance for herself = £47.95.
Step 3 Her weekly income is:
Contributory ESA = £47.95 (DLA is disregarded).
Step 4 The amount of contributory ESA is the same as the amount of income-related ESA to which she is entitled, so she gets contributory ESA of £47.95.

Main phase:
Contributory ESA
Doreen is assessed as having limited capability for work and as being in the work-related activity group. In the main phase of ESA, she gets £60.50 basic allowance and £24 work-related activity component (£84.50 in total).

Income-related ESA
Step 2 Her applicable amount is:
Basic allowance for herself (£60.50) and work-related activity component (£24) = £84.50
Step 3 Her weekly income is:
Contributory ESA = £84.50 (DLA is disregarded).
Step 4 The amount of contributory ESA is the same as the amount of income-related ESA to which she is entitled, so she gets contributory ESA of £84.50.

5. Claiming employment and support allowance

You start your claim by phoning a Jobcentre Plus contact centre (although paper claim forms should also be available if it is not suitable for you to use the telephone). Phone the national number on 0800 055 6688 (textphone 0800 023 4888) and your call will be routed to your local centre.

In Northern Ireland you should contact your local social security office.

You are usually interviewed after you claim. You need to send in medical certificates from your GP until you are assessed under the work capability assessment. If you need to serve a 28-week qualifying period before you can get employment and support allowance (ESA), ask your doctor for a backdated medical certificate and send this with your claim.

Either member of a couple can make a claim for income-related ESA for both, but whoever claims must be eligible in her/his own right. You claim contributory ESA for yourself only.

Claims for ESA can be backdated for up to three months.

6. Challenging a decision

If you think a decision about your employment and support allowance (ESA) is wrong (eg, because the decision maker got the facts or law wrong, or your circumstances have changed since the decision was made), there are a number of ways you can try to get the decision changed.

- You can seek a revision or a supersession of the decision. In some cases you have to show specific grounds. In others, you must apply within a strict time limit.
- You can appeal to an independent tribunal. There are strict time limits for appealing – usually one month from the date you are sent or given the decision. You can make a late appeal in limited circumstances.

As EMA is a new benefit, and students are subject to specific rules, you should look closely at any decision to make sure it is correct. If you are considering challenging a decision, you should seek advice as soon as possible.

7. Other benefits and tax credits

You cannot get employment and support allowance (ESA) if you are getting statutory sick pay (SSP) from an employer.[14] SSP runs out after 28 weeks, after which you can claim ESA.

You cannot get ESA if you are getting income support (IS) or jobseeker's allowance (JSA). You can claim contributory ESA if your partner is getting IS or JSA.[15] You are excluded if you get joint-claim JSA. You cannot get income-related ESA if your partner gets IS, income-based JSA or pension credit.

Income-related ESA passports you to full housing benefit and council tax benefit, Healthy Start food vouchers and vitamins if you are pregnant, free school meals and regulated social fund payments. ESA also passports you to other health benefits (see Chapter 11) and discretionary social fund payments (see Chapter 17).

Notes

2. **Who is eligible**
  1 s1 WRA 2007
  2 Sch 1 paras 1-4 WRA 2007
  3 DMG para 57132 vol 10
  4 Reg 12 ESA Regs
  5 Reg 9 ESA Regs
  6 Sch 1 para 6 WRA 2007
  7 Reg 18 ESA Regs
  8 Regs 14-16 ESA Regs
  9 Reg 131 ESA Regs

3. **Limited capability for work**
  10 Reg 33(2) ESA Regs

4. **Amount of benefit**
  11 s2 WRA 2007; reg 67(2) and (3) ESA Regs
  12 s4 WRA 2007Reg 67 and Sch 4 ESA Regs

7. **Other benefit and tax credits**
  13 s20 WRA 2007
  14 s1(3)(f) WRA 2007

Chapter 11

Health benefits

This chapter covers:
1. What are health benefits (below)
2. Who is eligible (p116)
3. Claiming health benefits and refunds (p122)
4. Challenging a decision (p123)
5. Overseas students (p123)

Basic facts

– People under 19 and in full-time education can get free prescriptions, sight tests, vouchers for glasses and dental treatment.
– Prescriptions are free in Wales. In addition, you can get a free dental examination if you are under 25, or are 60 or over.
– Other students can get help if they are on a low income or in certain other circumstances.

---

1. **What are health benefits**

Further information

This chapter gives an outline of the health benefit rules and focuses on issues relevant to students. For more detailed information on the rules, see CPAG's *Welfare Benefits and Tax Credits Handbook*.

Although most health treatment is free under the NHS for UK residents, there are fixed charges for some NHS services and treatments. These include:
- prescriptions;
- sight tests;
- glasses or contact lenses;
- dental treatment;
- wigs or fabric supports; *and*
- fares to hospital.

You are exempt from the charges in specified circumstances, or if your income is sufficiently low. As a student, you are not automatically exempt from paying these charges unless you fall into one of the categories listed below. Otherwise, you can apply for a 'remission certificate' under the low income scheme (see p120). If you get one, part or all of the charges are waived, depending on your income. For information about claims, see p122.

Note: you may also qualify for vouchers for Healthy Start food and for free vitamins. See p119 for further information.

2. **Who is eligible**

You are automatically exempt from NHS charges if:[1]

- you or a member of your family receive income support (IS), income-based jobseeker's allowance (JSA), income-related employment and support allowance (ESA) or the guarantee credit of pension credit (PC); *or*
- you or a member of your family receive:
  - child tax credit (CTC); *or*
  - CTC and working tax credit (WTC); *or*
  - WTC including a disability or severe disability element,
  and your gross annual income is £15,050 or less a year; *or*
- you are a war disablement pensioner and you need the item or service because of your war disability.

Note:
- There are other categories of people who are exempt – eg, if you are a permanent resident in a care home, a hospital inpatient, an asylum seeker, 16 or 17 and being financially maintained by a local authority, or if you are in prison or a young offenders institution.
- You may also be exempt from some charges because of your age or a specific health condition – see the individual types of charge below.
- If you are not exempt on any of the grounds listed above or below, you may be entitled to a full or partial remission of charges on grounds of low income (see p120), but you have to apply for a 'remission certificate'.

If you are exempt because you receive tax credits

If you are exempt from NHS charges because you receive tax credits, you should be sent an NHS tax credits exemption certificate automatically. This could be up to six weeks after you are awarded tax credits. If you have an award of tax credits, but have not yet been sent your certificate, you can sign the relevant treatment forms to say you do not have to pay. You can use your award letter as evidence of this. If this is not accepted and you are charged, be sure to keep your receipts so you can claim a refund (see p123). If there is a delay in getting your exemption certificate you should seek advice.

If you are getting CTC but are exempt from charges because you are getting IS, income-based JSA or the guarantee credit of PC, you do not get an NHS tax credits exemption certificate. However, if you stop getting IS, income-based JSA or the guarantee credit of PC because, for example, of your student income, you need a certificate. You should let HM Revenue and Customs know about your change in circumstances as soon as possible. It notifies the NHS Business Services Authority in Newcastle upon Tyne, who issues you with a certificate.

Free prescriptions

The cost of a prescription in England and Northern Ireland is £7.10.[2] Prescriptions are free in Wales if they provided in Wales or if you have an entitlement card (ie, because you live in Wales, but your doctor is in England). In Northern Ireland, plans have been announced to scrap prescription charges in 2010. From January 2009, the cost will be reduced to £3.

Otherwise, you qualify for free prescriptions if:[3]
- you are in one of the exempt groups listed on p116; or
- you are aged under 16, or under 19 and in full-time education (see below); or
- you are aged 60 or over; or
- you are pregnant or have given birth within the last 12 months (see p122); or
- you have one or more of the following specific medical conditions:
  - a continuing physical disability which prevents you from leaving home except with the help of another person;
  - epilepsy requiring continuous anti-convulsive therapy;
  - a permanent fistula, including caecostomy, ileostomy, laryngostomy or colostomy, needing continuous surgical dressing or an appliance;
  - one of the following conditions: diabetes mellitus (except where treatment is by diet alone), myxoedema, hypoparathyroidism, diabetes insipidus and other forms of hypopituitarism, forms of hypoadrenalism (including Addison's disease) for which specific substitution therapy is essential, myasthenia gravis; or
- your income is low enough (see p120).

'Full-time education' means full-time instruction at a recognised educational establishment – eg, a school, college or university. If you are studying elsewhere, or you have finished your A levels and are waiting to start college or university, check to see if you are exempt because you are on a low income.

Pre-payment certificates

If you are likely to need a lot of prescriptions, but are not exempt from payment, you can reduce the cost by buying a pre-payment certificate. A holder of a pre-payment certificate does not have to pay any further charges for prescriptions for the duration of the certificate, regardless of how many are required.[4]

A three-month certificate saves money on more than four prescriptions, while a 12-month certificate saves money on more than 14 prescriptions. Applications can be made in England by post on Form FP95, available from chemists, some doctors' surgeries and relevant health bodies. This should be sent to the address on the form. Applications can also be made by telephone on 0845 850 0030 or online at www.ppa.nhs.uk and at registered pharmacies. In Northern Ireland, you can purchase a certificate from most pharmacies.

Free sight tests

You qualify for a free NHS sight test if:[5]
- you are in one of the exempt groups listed on p116; *or*
- you are under 16, or under 19 and in full-time education (see p122); *or*
- you are aged 60 or over; *or*
- you are registered blind or partially sighted; *or*
- you have been prescribed complex or powerful lenses; *or*
- you have diabetes or glaucoma or are at risk of getting glaucoma; *or*
- you are 40 or over and are the parent, sibling or child of someone who has glaucoma; *or*
- you are a patient of the Hospital Eye Service; *or*
- your income is low enough.

Note: you may also qualify for a voucher towards the cost of buying or repairing glasses or contact lenses.[6]

Free dental treatment and dentures

If you live in Wales and are under 25 or are 60 or over, you qualify for free dental examinations.[7] Otherwise, you qualify for free dental treatment (including check-ups) and appliances (including dentures) if:[8]
- you are in one of the exempt groups listed on p116; *or*
- you are aged under 18, or are under 19 and in full-time education (see p122); *or*
- you are pregnant or have given birth within the last 12 months (see p122); *or*
- you are a patient of the Community Dental Service; *or*
- your income is low enough.

Note: you may also qualify for reduced-cost treatment and appliances on the grounds of low income.

Free wigs and fabric supports

You qualify for free wigs or fabric supports if:[9]
- you are in one of the exempt groups listed on p116; *or*

- you are under 16, or under 19 and in full-time education (see p122); *or*
- you are a hospital inpatient when the wig or fabric support is provided; *or*
- these are provided in Wales or you have an entitlement card; *or*
- your income is low enough.

Fares to hospital

You qualify for help with the costs of travel to hospital or any other establishment for NHS treatment or services if:[10]
- you are in one of the exempt groups listed on p116; *or*
- you live in the Isles of Scilly; *or*
- your income is low enough.

Note:
- You may also qualify for partial help with fares on the grounds of low income.
- In some cases, you can get help with the costs of travel to obtain NHS treatment abroad.

Healthy Start food and vitamins

You qualify for Healthy Start **food vouchers** if:[11]
- you are more than 10 weeks pregnant and:
  - you are under 18; *or*
  - you are 18 or over and you (or a member of the family) are entitled to IS, income-based JSA, income-related ESA, or CTC, provided in the latter case that gross income for CTC purposes does not exceed £15,575 and there is no entitlement to WTC; *or*
- you are a mother aged 18 or over and have 'parental responsibility' for a child under one (or it is less than a year since her/his expected date of birth) and you (or a member of the family) are entitled to IS, income-based JSA or CTC, provided in the latter case that gross income for CTC purposes does not exceed £15,575 and there is no entitlement to WTC.
  If you qualify for vouchers for more than one child under this rule – eg, if you have twins, you get vouchers for each;
- you have a child under four and you (or a member of the family) are entitled to IS, income-based JSA or CTC, provided in the latter case that gross income for CTC purposes does not exceed £15,575 and there is no entitlement to WTC.

In practice, this means that each week you get one voucher for each of your children aged between one and four, two vouchers for each of your children under one (or within one year of their expected date of birth), plus one voucher if you are pregnant. Vouchers are worth £3 each and can be exchanged at registered food outlets for liquid cow's milk and cow's milk-based infant formula, fresh fruit and vegetables (including loose, pre-packed, whole, sliced, chopped or mixed fruit or vegetables, but not fruit or vegetables to which salt, sugar, herbs or other flavouring has been added).

You qualify for free **vitamins** if you qualify for Healthy Start food vouchers.[12]

The low income scheme

The NHS Business Services Authority has a means test to determine whether you qualify for either a full or partial remission certificate. The means test is roughly based on the applicable amounts for IS (see Chapter 14), but there are some differences.

Applications for help under the low income scheme should be made to the NHS Business Services Authority on Form HC1 (HC1W in Wales), available from Jobcentre Plus offices, NHS hospitals, some doctors' surgeries, some chemists, many students' union advice centres or at www.ppa.nhs.uk.

Calculating entitlement

To qualify for help, you must have less than £16,000 capital (£17,250 in Wales), or less than £21,500 (£22,000 in Wales) if you live permanently in a care home.[13]

If your income (see below) does not exceed your requirements (see p121) by more than 50 per cent of the current cost of a prescription (at the time of writing this was £3.55), you receive a full remission certificate (an HC2 – or HC2W in Wales).[14] If your income exceeds your requirements by more than this amount, you receive a partial remission certificate (an HC3 – or HC3W in Wales), depending on the level of excess as follows:[15]

- a remission of dental charges and charges for wigs and fabric supports which are higher than three times your excess income;
- a voucher for glasses or lenses, reduced by an amount equal to twice your excess income;
- a reduction in the cost of a sight test to the amount of your excess income, if lower, plus the amount by which the cost exceeds the NHS sight test fee;
- a reduction by the amount of your excess income in the amount you can get for hospital fares.

If you qualify for a remission certificate, it is normally valid for 12 months. If you are a full-time student, your certificate is normally valid until the end of your course or the start of the next academic year. You should make a repeat claim shortly before the expiry date. Remember that if you qualify for IS or income-based JSA over the summer vacation, you are automatically exempt from NHS charges during that period.

Calculating income

Income is calculated in the same way as for IS, with some modifications.[16] The income that is taken into account is your own and that of your partner, where appropriate. Your parents' income is not taken into account. However, any money given to you by your parents may be taken into account when assessing eligibility. Information about how your income is calculated and how student income is treated is in Chapter 22.

Calculating requirements

Your requirements are based on those used for calculating the applicable amount for IS (see Chapter 14).[17]

This is an amount for basic weekly needs. Chapter 14 gives details of how to qualify for each premium. Your requirements are made up of:

- **personal allowances**
  - single person aged under 25   £47.95
  - single person aged 25 or over   £60.50
  - single person aged 60 or over   £124.05
  - lone parent aged under 60   £60.50
  - lone parent aged 60 or over   £124.05
  - couple aged under 60   £94.95
  - couple aged 60 or over   £189.35
- **premiums**
  - carer (as for IS);
  - disability (as for IS, except that you can include a disability premium after 28 weeks of incapacity for work, rather than 52 weeks);
  - enhanced disability for an adult (as for IS);
  - severe disability (as for IS).
- **weekly rent** less any housing benefit (HB) and non-dependant deductions;
- **weekly council tax**, if you are liable, less any council tax benefit;
- **mortgage interest**, endowment payments and capital repayments on your home, as well as on loans to adapt a home for a disabled person, deducting any non-dependant deductions;
- **amounts for children**. If you have children you are likely to be exempt from charges through getting a qualifying benefit like IS, JSA or CTC. If you get CTC but are not exempt from charges, your children are not included in the low income assessment.

If your income is less than or no more than £3.55 (half the cost of a prescription in England) higher than your needs, you are entitled to health benefits. If your income is more than £3.55 higher than your needs, you will not get free prescriptions, but you might get partial help with other charges.

Example

Oliver is 21, and a third-year full-time undergraduate in Wales. His income is, assessed to be £89.32 a week.

His requirements are calculated as his personal allowance (£47.95) plus his weekly rent (£85). This gives a total of £132.95. This is more than his income, so he receives full help with health costs. As a Welsh-domiciled student, however, Oliver qualifies for free prescriptions and, as he is under 25, free dental examinations.

Deborah is 24, and a second-year full-time undergraduate in London. Her income is assessed to be £187.20 a week.

Her requirements are calculated as her personal allowance (£47.95) plus her weekly rent (£150). This gives a total of £197.95. This is £10.75 more than her income, so she receives full help with health costs.

3. Claiming health benefits and refunds

How and where you claim help with NHS charges depends on your circumstances. Some of these are shown below.

Under 19 and in full-time education

To claim the exemption from NHS **prescription charges**, you must sign the declaration form on the back of the prescription. To claim a free **sight test**, you must sign the optician's form before your test.

To claim free **dental treatment**, you must tell the dental receptionist before your treatment that you think you are exempt from charges. You should complete a form at this point. Remember in Wales, if you are under 25 you qualify for free dental examinations.

Pregnant women and recent births

To claim free **dental treatment** and **prescriptions**, you must apply for a maternity exemption certificate on a form available from your midwife, health visitor or doctor.

You must claim **Healthy Start food and vitamins** in writing. You should complete the form in the Healthy Start application leaflet (HS01). This is available from maternity clinics and some doctor's surgeries or from 0870 555 455. Information about Healthy Start and a downloadable claim form are also available at www.healthystart.nhs.uk. Your claim form must be countersigned by a health professional (eg, a midwife or health visitor) who certifies that you have been given appropriate advice about healthy eating and breastfeeding.

Prescribed condition

To claim free **prescriptions** because you have a prescribed condition, you must apply for an exemption certificate on a form available from your doctor, hospital or pharmacist.

The low income scheme

Applications for help under the low income scheme should be made to the NHS Business Services Authority on Form HC1, available from Jobcentre Plus offices, NHS hospitals, some doctors' surgeries, some chemists, many students' union advice centres or at www.ppa.nhs.uk.

Refunds

If you pay for an item or service that you could have got free of charge or at a reduced cost, you can apply for a refund. You must apply within three months of payment, although the time limit can be extended if you can show good cause for applying late (eg, you were ill).[18]

For a refund of prescription charges use Form FP57, which you must get when you pay for the prescription at the pharmacy or dispensing chemist. A bilingual version (WP57) is available in Wales.

For other items and services use Form HC5, available from post offices, Jobcentre Plus offices, NHS hospitals and some doctors' surgeries.

If you wish to have your costs refunded on the basis of low income, but do not already have an HC2 or an HC3 remission certificate (see p122), you should send a completed HC1 form with the HC5 form.

4. Challenging a decision

If you think a decision about your health benefits is wrong:
- you can ask for a formal review. You should write to the Review Section, NHS Business Services Authority, PO Box 993, Newcastle upon Tyne NE99 2TZ. You can also request a review online at www.ppa.nhs.uk;
- because decisions about health benefits are based on your circumstances at the time you apply for a certificate, you should consider making a fresh claim, or reporting the change in your circumstances, if you think you would now be entitled to more help with NHS charges.

If there are delays in obtaining a certificate, you can complain to the customer services manager. If necessary, you could pay for the treatment or items you need then try to obtain a refund (see above).

5. Overseas students

Many overseas students can get free NHS treatment and help with NHS charges. Detailed information is available at www.ukcisa.org.uk.

Asylum seekers

If you are an asylum seeker or a dependant of an asylum seeker and receiving support from either the Border and Immigration Agency or a local authority, you are eligible for full exemption from NHS charges. If you are getting asylum support, you should be sent an HC2 certificate with your first support payment. If you are not supported by the Border and Immigration Agency or a local authority, you should apply using an HC1 form.

European Economic Area students and Swiss nationals

If you are a student from any part of the European Economic Area (EEA) or Switzerland you can get NHS treatment during a temporary stay in the UK on the same basis as UK residents, provided that you have a European health insurance card. You can also get help with NHS charges on the same basis as UK residents.

Other overseas students

If you are a non-EEA overseas student on a course lasting six months or longer, you qualify for NHS treatment and help with NHS charges on the same basis as UK residents. In addition, any immediate family members with you in the UK also qualify.

Health benefits are not classed as public funds and, therefore, do not affect your immigration status.

If you are an overseas student on a course lasting less than six months, you cannot usually get free NHS treatment or help with NHS charges. However, you can get emergency treatment, treatment of certain communicable diseases and compulsory psychiatric treatment free through the NHS, but other treatments and services incur a charge. You are, therefore, strongly advised to take out adequate medical insurance for the duration of your stay in the UK.

Notes

2. **Who is eligible**
   1 Regs 3-5 NHS(TERC) Regs; regs 3-5
      NHS(TERC)(W) Regs
   2 Regs 3-6 NHS(CDA) Regs
   3 Regs 4 and 5 NHS(TERC) Regs;
      NHS(CDA) Regs; NHS(FP&CDA)(W)
      Regs
   4 Reg 9 NHS(CDA) Regs
   5 Reg 13 NHS(GOS) Regs; reg 3
      NHS(OCP) Regs
   6 Regs 9 and 15 NHS(OCP) Regs
   7 Reg 3 NHS(DC)(W) Regs
   8 Regs 4 and 5 NHS(TERC) Regs; regs 4
      and 5 NHS(TERC)(W) Regs; Sch 2
      NHS(DC) Regs; reg 9 and Sch 5
      NHS(DC)(W) Regs
   9 Regs 4 AND 5 NHS(TERC) Regs;
      NHS(CDA) Regs; NHS(FP&CDA)(W)
      Regs
   10 Regs 3, 5 and 9 NHS(TERC) Regs; regs 3
      and 5 NHS(TERC)(W) Regs
   11 Reg 3 HSS&WF(A) Regs
   12 Reg 3 HSS&WF(A) Regs
   13 Sch 1 NHS(TERC) Regs; Sch 1
      NHS(TREC)(W) Regs
   14 Reg 5 NHS(TERC) Regs; reg 5
      NHS(TERC)(W) Regs
   15 Reg 6 NHS(TERC) Regs; reg 6
      NHS(TERC)(W) Regs
   16 Reg 16 and Sch 1 NHS(TERC) Regs; reg
      15 and Sch 1 NHS(TERC)(W) Regs
   17 Reg 17 and Sch 1 NHS(TERC) Regs; reg
      16 and Sch 1 NHS(TERC)(W) Regs

3. **Claiming health benefits and refunds**
   18 Reg 11 NHS(TERC) Regs; reg 10
      NHS(TERC)(W) Regs; reg 10 NHS(CDA)
      Regs; Sch 1 para 1 NHS(FP&CDA)(W)
      Regs; regs 6 and 20 NHS(OCP) Regs; reg
      7 NHS(DC) Regs; reg 10 NHS(DC)(W)
      Regs

Chapter 12

Housing benefit

This chapter covers:

Basic facts

– Housing benefit (HB) helps with the rent. In Northern Ireland, it also helps with rates.
– Full-time students under aged 19 are eligible if they are not on a higher education course.
– Full-time students aged 19 are usually eligible if they are finishing a non-advanced course that they started before they reached 19.
– Other full-time students can claim – eg, if they get income support or income-based jobseeker's allowance, are a lone parent, have certain disabilities, or are 60 or over.
– Student couples with a child can claim throughout the year.
– Students' partners are eligible to claim.
– There can be limits to the rent covered by HB.
– HB is a means-tested benefit. The amount you get is affected by your grant, loan or other income and your level of savings.
– Claims are administered by local authorities.

1. What is housing benefit

Further information

This chapter gives an outline of the housing benefit rules and focuses on issues relevant to students. For more detailed information on the rules, see CPAG's *Welfare Benefits and Tax Credits Handbook*.

Housing benefit (HB) helps with the rent. In Northern Ireland, it helps with both rent and rates. You can get help with rent in private, housing association or local authority accommodation, but not if you live with your parents. There are limits to the level of rent that HB will cover.

Most full-time students cannot claim HB, but part-time students can claim.

HB is means tested, so your loan and other income affect the amount you get.

2. Who is eligible

To qualify for housing benefit (HB), you must satisfy the basic rules (see below), your payments must be eligible for HB (see p129) and you must be a student who is eligible to claim (see p130).

Basic rules

As well as being a student who is eligible to claim HB (see p130), you must also meet all the following conditions to qualify.
- You or your partner are liable to pay rent (see below).
- You or your partner pay rent for the home in which you normally live (see p128).
- The payments you make (eg, your rent) are eligible for HB (see p129).
- You satisfy presence and residence conditions and are not a 'person subject to immigration control' for benefit purposes. You can get further advice from UKCISA (see Appendix 2).
- Your capital is no more than £16,000. There is no capital limit if you are aged 60 or over and getting the pension credit guarantee credit.
- Your income is sufficiently low (see Chapter 20).

Liable for rent

You must be liable for rent. If you are jointly liable for the rent with others (eg, you have each signed the tenancy agreement), the amount of HB you get is based on your share of the rent (although, less commonly, it may not be an equal share if that seems reasonable to the local authority).

If you are a couple it does not matter whose name is on the rent agreement, either of you can claim. So if you are a student who is eligible for HB, you can claim for both of you. If you are not eligible for HB, your non-student partner can claim for both of you.

There are some circumstances in which a local authority has the discretion to treat you as liable for the rent even if you are not legally liable – eg, if you have taken over paying the rent from someone else, or to treat you as not liable for the rent when you are legally liable – eg, if your agreement to pay rent is not on a commercial basis.

Your normal home

Usually you can only get HB for one home, and that is the place where you normally live. There are rules that can help you if you are temporarily away from home, are liable for rent on more than one home, have just moved home and in some other situations. The rules that specifically help students are outlined below.

You are away from your term-time home

You cannot get HB for any weeks in the summer vacation when you are away from your term-time home unless you would live there anyway even if you were not studying. To continue to get HB for weeks of absence, you must argue that your main purpose in living there is not simply to make it easier to attend the course – eg, you were settled there before the course, or you are independent of or estranged from your parents.[1] However, if your grant or loan covers the summer vacation, your HB does not stop for weeks of absence.[2] HB also does not stop if you have to go into hospital.

If you leave your home during the academic year (or any time if you live there not just to facilitate attendance on the course), you can continue to get HB as long as you intend to return, you do not sub-let, and you are not likely to be away for more than 52 weeks.[3] You cannot use this provision if you can get HB under the 'two-homes rule' described on p129. The two-homes rule is more generous in any case because it is not time-limited.

Examples
John flat-shares in Sheffield while attending university. He gets HB as a disabled student. During the summer vacation he goes home to his parents in Leicester for seven weeks. His HB stops for those seven weeks. He should give the local authority the dates he intends to be away.

Donna has always lived in Cardiff and is attending her local college. She is a lone parent and gets HB. She regularly visits family in Aberystwyth during vacations. Her HB continues during her absence.

You have two homes

Liable for rent on one home

If you are a single or lone-parent student who can claim HB and you live in one home so that you can attend your course and another home at other times but you are only liable to pay for one of these, you are treated as occupying the home for which you pay. You can get HB for that place even while you are not there. **Note:** you cannot get HB under this rule if you pay rent for both homes, or if you pay rent for one and a mortgage on the other.[4]

Example

Emily's usual home is in Bristol, where she lives with her 18-year-old daughter, who is at college. She has to pay rent for her Bristol home. Emily is studying at Leeds University and lives rent-free with a cousin while in Leeds. Emily is eligible to claim HB for her Bristol home throughout the year. Whether any HB is payable, and at what times, depends on the amount of her student support.

Liable for rent on two homes

If you have to pay rent for two homes, there are some circumstances in which you can get HB paid for both.

- If you have moved into a new home before the tenancy has expired on the old one and you cannot reasonably avoid having to pay rent on your old home, you can get HB paid for both for up to four weeks.[5]
- If you qualify for HB on two homes because a move was delayed while you were adapting your new home for the needs of a disabled member of your family, you can get HB paid for both for up to four weeks.[6]
- If you have had to leave your home because of a fear of violence and are intending to return to your former home, you can get HB for up to 52 weeks.[7]
- If you are in a couple and one of you is a student eligible for HB, and you have to live in two separate homes, you can get HB on both homes indefinitely if the local authority decides it is reasonable.[8]

Eligible payments

You can get HB to help pay the rent – eg, to a private landlord, local authority, housing association or co-operative. You can also get HB for some other types of payment – eg, site rent for a caravan or mobile home, rent for a houseboat (including mooring charges), or payments for a licence or other permission to occupy your home. It is not essential to have a written agreement; it could be verbal. There are a number of situations in which you could be treated as not liable to pay rent. For example, you cannot get HB if:

- you live with, and pay rent to, your parents, a sister, brother, son or daughter (including in-laws, partners and step-relatives);
- you pay rent to someone, but your tenancy is not on a commercial basis. This rule often prevents students getting HB for accommodation owned by their parents. However, it is possible to get HB in these circumstances if you can prove that the tenancy is a commercial one. You need to provide evidence of regular rent payments or a tenancy agreement. Seek advice if you are in this position;
- your tenancy was contrived in order to try and get HB;
- you pay rent to an ex-partner with whom you used to share the home in which you now live, or your landlord is your child's parent.

The list above is not exhaustive.

Halls of residence

University-owned accommodation used to be ineligible for HB. From 1 August 2004, the Government removed this rule to widen access to both mature and disabled students. Part-time students living in university-owned accommodation, however, can only get HB if, were they full time, they would be eligible to claim HB as a lone parent, a disabled student, someone with a child and a full-time student partner, or if they are aged 60 or over. If you get income support (IS) or income-based jobseeker's allowance (JSA) as a part-time student, you can only get HB in a hall of residence if you also fall into one of these other full-time eligible groups.

Sometimes colleges manage accommodation that is owned by private companies, but which is intended to provide accommodation for students. This type of accommodation has always been eligible for HB.

During the summer vacation, you can get HB if it is necessary for you to remain in the hall of residence, providing your grant or loan covers the vacation period and you are expected to study throughout the year.

Students and housing benefit

Under 20

Even if you are studying full time, you can qualify for HB if:

- you are under 19 and not in higher education; *or*
- you are a child or 'qualifying young person' for child benefit purposes (see p88) – eg, you are under 20 and in full-time education or approved training. You must have started the course or training when you were under 19.[9]

You can claim HB whether or not you are entitled to IS or JSA as a full-time student. You must satisfy the basic HB rules outlined on p127. You can only get HB if you are living away from your parents. Your claim may be restricted to the 'single room rent' (see p135).[10]

Example

Robbie is 17 and studying electronics at NVQ Level 3. He shares a flat with friends. He can claim HB.

Bear in mind that you can get HB under this rule up until your 20th birthday but not beyond. If your course continues, check below to see if you are in one of the groups of students aged 19 or over who can claim HB. If not, ask your college if there is any discretionary financial assistance. Alternatively, you may be able to argue that HB should continue if you transfer to a part-time course.[11] (If you abandon or are dismissed from your full-time course, you stop being classed as a full-time student.) However, your student support is affected if you go part time, so get advice from your college if you are considering such a move.

Under 20 in full-time higher education

In this case you are treated exactly the same as a full-time student aged 19 or over. You are not eligible for HB unless you are in one of the groups listed on p132 who can claim HB.

'**Higher education**' includes teacher and youth worker training, foundation degree, first and postgraduate degree courses, HND and HNC courses, and courses at a higher level in preparation for a professional qualification.

Full-time students

If you are a full-time student 'attending or undertaking a full-time course of study', you cannot normally claim HB.[12] However, there are exceptions that allow some students to claim. If you are aged 19 or under check to see if you come under the rules outlined above.

You count as a student from the first day you attend or undertake the course. You stop counting as a student after the last day of the final academic term in which you are enrolled, or from the day you finally abandon your course or are dismissed from it.[13]

Who counts as a full-time student

If you attend a **further education** college and your course is government funded you will usually count as a part-time student as long as your course comprises 16 guided learning hours or less a week.[14] 'Guided learning hours' include all supervised study – eg, classes, lectures, tutorials and structured assessment periods. They do not include unstructured or unsupervised study time – eg, studying at home or in a library. A document called a 'learning agreement' is used to provide proof of course hours. It is important to use the official learning agreement. The hours on this document are calculated as an average figure and may differ from the hours on your timetable. Ask about your learning agreement at your college or check with your course tutor. The local authority uses your learning agreement to decide whether or not you are studying full time.

In Northern Ireland, the definition of a full-time course does not depend on the number of hours of guided learning, but on the institution's definition of 'full time'. A letter from the institution stating that your course is part time will be sufficient when applying for HB.

Students in **higher education** are counted as full-time students if the college or university says that the course is full time. Ask at your college, or check with the course tutor or the registry department for evidence of whether you are registered on a full- or part-time course.

A course could be full time even if you only attend a few lectures a week. You may be asked for a 'learning agreement' to show whether you are registered as part time or full time. You are not required to provide this and your registration document should be sufficient evidence.

Guidance states that postgraduates stop being treated as full-time students for HB purposes when their course ends. If you go on to undertake further research or are writing up a thesis, whether or not you are regarded as full time depends on how much time this is taking, rather than on whether the course is full time and whether you are still registered on the course.

Who can claim housing benefit

You can claim HB as a full-time student if you are in one of the following groups.[15]

- **IS/JSA/employment and support allowance (ESA) recipients.** If you are on IS income-based JSA, or income-related ESA, you receive maximum HB (see p134).
- **Lone parents.** If you are the lone parent of a child under 16 (or a qualifying young person – ie, under 20 and in full-time non-advanced education or approved training), you are eligible for HB. Lone parents can only get IS until their youngest child's 12th birthday (this will reduce gradually to age seven over the next two years. If your IS stops, make sure you notify the local authority to ensure your HB continues while your child stays on at school or college. **Note:** your entitlement to HB under this rule ends on your youngest child's 20th birthday or when you no longer have a child or qualifying young person living with you (eg, when s/he leaves school), even if you are part-way through your course.
- **Under-19-year-olds** who are not in higher education.
- **Children or 'qualifying young people'** for child benefit purposes (see p88) – eg, under-20-year-olds in full-time education or approved training who started the course or training when under 19.
- **Pensioners.** If you, or your partner, are aged 60 or over, you are eligible for HB for the duration of your course.
- **Disabled students.**
  - If you qualify for a disability premium or severe disability premium with your HB (eg, you get disability living allowance or long-term incapacity benefit (IB) or are registered blind), you are eligible for HB.
  - If you have had limited capability for work for the last 28 weeks. You should claim ESA to have your limited capability for work acknowledged. You can add together the weeks of limited capability for work on either side of a gap of up to 12 weeks.
  - If you get a disabled students' allowance because of deafness, you are eligible for HB from the date you apply for the allowance.[16] However, if you are still waiting to receive confirmation about the allowance, the local authority may put off making a decision on your HB claim, but should then fully backdate your benefit.[17]
- **Student couples** (of the same or opposite sex, where both members of the couple are students) with a child or qualifying young person. If you are a couple, your partner is also a full-time student and you have a dependent child

or qualifying young person, you are eligible for HB. Unlike IS and JSA, where you can only claim in the summer vacation, you can claim HB throughout the year. If you are claiming IS or income-based JSA, remember that when those benefits stop at the end of the summer vacation, you need to notify the local authority. You then receive a new assessment based on your student support income.

- **Responsible for a boarded child.** If you are single and caring for a child boarded out with you by the local authority or a voluntary organisation, you are eligible for HB for the duration of your course, or as long as this responsibility lasts.
- **Students' partners.** If you are part of a couple and your partner is not a student, s/he is entitled to make a claim for both of you.

Studying part time

If you are a part-time student, you can claim HB throughout your studies. You must satisfy all the basic rules (see p127). You are a part-time student if you do not count as a full-time student under the definition on p131. If you are a part-time student living in university-owned accommodation you can only get HB if you fall into one of the categories of full-time students eligible for HB, other than IS/JSA recipients – eg, you are a lone-parent or a disabled student.

---

3. **Amount of benefit**

The amount of housing benefit (HB) you get depends on the maximum rent that the local authority is allowed to pay and on your income compared with the amount the law says you need to live on. To work out your HB go through the following steps.

Step 1: capital

If your capital is over £16,000 you cannot get HB unless you are 60 or over. People aged 60 or over who get pension credit (PC) guarantee credit have all their capital ignored. Others 60 or over, including those who get PC savings credit but not guarantee credit, are still excluded from HB if their capital is over £16,000. Some kinds of capital are ignored.

If your capital is over £6,000 (£10,000 if you live in a care home), £1 for every £250 or part of £250 over this amount is added to your income. If you are 60 or over, £1 for every £500 or part of £500 over this amount is added to your income.

You usually have to submit three months' bank statements to the local authority and details of any savings accounts you hold.

Some students believe that they are unable to claim HB or will receive reduced benefit when they receive their student support at the beginning of each term because this payment can in itself be over £6,000 (especially if childcare costs are included), or it can increase their original savings to above this amount. However, your student support payments count as income divided over the year, not as capital (see Chapter 20).

Examples

Paul makes a claim for HB. He has £7,300 in savings. His income is initially assessed as £71 a week but tariff income on the £1,300 over the capital limit generates a further £6 a week in income. Paul is treated as having £77 a week income for benefit purposes.

Paul receives arrears of disability living allowance of £4,500 after an appeal. This money is treated as capital and disregarded for 52 weeks. Paul continues to qualify for HB and be treated as having £77 a week income.

Claire receives her student support payment of £4,625 in her bank account in September. She has a separate savings account, containing £4,000. The only capital that is taken into account is the £4,000. This does not affect her HB.

Step 2: maximum housing benefit

Your maximum HB is your 'eligible rent' (see below), minus any deductions made for your non-dependants (see Step 3). This might not be the actual amount of rent you are meant to pay – eg, if you pay services charges that cannot be covered by HB, or if the local authority decides your rent for HB purposes must be restricted. The latter might happen, for example, if your home is too big for the size of your family or too expensive, or you rent from a private landlord and your rent is higher than the 'local housing allowance'. See p135 for further information about rent restrictions, including the local housing allowance scheme.

Eligible rent

The amount of your rent that is eligible for HB might not be the same as the amount of rent you actually pay. HB does not cover some items included in rent, such as:

- water or sewerage charges;
- fuel charges – either the actual charge if specified in the rental agreement, or a fixed rate, is deducted;
- meal charges – if these are included in your rent, the local authority may deduct a fixed rate;
- service charges – some are included (eg, cleaning communal areas, provision of a laundry room, TV aerial and radio relay charges, including free-to-view TV but not an individual satellite dish or set-top box), and others are not (eg, sports facilities, TV rental).

In addition, unless you rent from a local authority, your eligible rent might be restricted if your rent is seen to be too high, or your accommodation is larger than is needed for a family of your size, or if the local housing allowance rules apply to you, your rent is higher than the 'local housing allowance'. See below for further information about the rent restriction rules.

If you rent from a local authority, your eligible rent is the same as the weekly rent actually due less any of the above ineligible charges. The same almost always applies if you rent from a housing association. If you pay rent monthly, convert it into weekly rent by multiplying by 12, dividing by 365 (or 366 in a leap year) and multiplying by 7.

Rent-free periods

If you have a regular rent-free period (eg, you get four weeks rent-free every year), you get no HB during your rent-free period. Your applicable amount, weekly income, non-dependant deductions, the set deductions for meals and fuel charges and the minimum amount payable (but not your eligible rent) are all adjusted. **Note:** this does not apply if your landlord has temporarily waived the rent in return for you doing repairs.

Restrictions on rent

Your eligible rent might be restricted if you are a private or a housing association tenant. There are two main sets of rules that can apply:
- the local reference rent rules;
- the local housing allowance rules.

Note: some people are exempt from these rules and a third (more generous) set of rent restriction rules can apply. This is the case, for example, if you have been renting the same property and getting HB since 1 January 1996, or if you live in certain types of hostel or supported accommodation.

If you claimed or moved home before 7 April 2008, the **local reference rent** rules will normally apply to you, and the local authority normally will refer your case to a rent officer. The rent officer provides figures which the local authority must then use to decide your eligible rent for HB purposes. The figures are as follows.
- A **single room rent**. This is the mid-point of local reasonable market rents for a single room – eg, in a flatshare or bedsit. It applies if you are under 25 and single, unless you have a non-dependant living with you (see p136), are a former care leaver under age 22 or get a severe disability premium.
- A **claim-related rent**. This is your actual rent, or a lower amount if your home has more rooms or is more expensive than you need according to set criteria.
- A **local reference rent**. This is the mid-point of reasonable market rents in your area for the same sized homes (or smaller if your home has 'too many' rooms) in a reasonable state of repair.

The local authority deducts meal charges (if appropriate) from the claim-related and local reference rents (not from the single room rent) but not other charges since the rent officer has already taken these into account. The maximum rent used in the HB calculation is the lowest of whichever of these figures the rent officer has provided, once meal charges are deducted.

To find out what the maximum rent will be for a tenancy before you sign for it, you can apply for a pre-tenancy determination to find out the rent figure that will be used to calculate your HB. Ask the local authority for a form and get the landlord to sign it. You should get a reply in about a week, though it depends on which authority you apply to – some are quicker than others.

There is no right of appeal against a rent officer's determinations. The local authority can ask for these to be re-determined on your behalf, but the re-determinations may reduce your maximum rent, so you need to consider your position carefully as you could end up with less HB. The rent officer should, however, take into account your individual circumstances – eg, your age and health.

Most private sector tenants who claim HB or move home on or after 7 April 2008 will come under the **local housing allowance** rules. People who are in one of 18 'Pathfinder' areas who piloted this scheme before 7 April 2008 may already come under the rules. Under the rules, the following apply.

- Your eligible rent is based on a standard 'local housing allowance', set by the rent officer depending on the area in which you live and the size of your household. The local housing allowance that is appropriate when your claim is assessed is used. Your claim is then normally reassessed annually.
- If you are a single claimant under 25, the local housing allowance is based on accommodation in which a tenant has exclusive use of one bedroom only and all or some of the other facilities are shared. This does not apply if you get a severe disability premium or have a non-dependant living with you.
- If your rent is lower than the local housing allowance (and therefore your HB is higher than your rent) your eligible rent will be the lower of either the rent you are liable to pay plus £15 (in which case you can keep the difference between the rent and the eligible rent) or the local housing allowance.

Note: more generous rules applied in the Pathfinder areas and if this applied to you, they may continue to apply for a transitional period.

Discretionary housing payments

If the local authority applies a rent reduction on your home and this is causing you hardship, it is worth applying to the local authority for discretionary housing payments. These are paid in exceptional circumstances to top up HB to the full amount of your rent. Discretionary housing payments are usually made for a temporary period and subject to regular review.

Step 3: non-dependants

Non-dependants are older sons and daughters or other adults living in your household. The Government expects these adults to contribute to your housing costs and a deduction is made from your eligible rent. The amount of the deduction depends on the income of the non-dependant. In Northern Ireland there are non-dependant deductions for rates as well as rent.

No non-dependant deduction is made if either you or your partner are registered blind or have regained your eyesight in the last 28 weeks, or if you are receiving attendance allowance or the care component of disability living allowance (DLA), or equivalent benefits paid because of an injury at work or a war injury.

No deductions are made for someone who is:
- staying in the household but her/his normal home is elsewhere;
- a full-time student during the course of study;
- a full-time student during the summer vacation (but there is a deduction if s/he starts to work more than 16 hours a week unless her/his student support covers the summer vacation);
- a full-time student at any time if you or your partner are aged 65 or over;
- a joint occupier/tenant;
- a resident landlord;
- a sub-tenant;
- the claimant's partner, or dependent child under 20 as long as child benefit is still being paid;
- aged under 18;
- in hospital for over 52 weeks;
- in prison;
- under 25 and receiving income support (IS), income-based jobseeker's allowance (JSA), or income-related employment and support allowance (ESA) without a work-related activity component or support component (this usually applies only in the first 13 weeks of an ESA claim);
- receiving a training allowance in connection with a youth training scheme under specific provisions;
- a live-in paid carer from a voluntary organisation;
- receiving pension credit (PC).

If your non-dependant is working, you should give the local authority evidence of her/his gross income. If you do not, the local authority might make the highest deduction whatever her/his income. This can be particularly hard where older sons/daughters still living at home refuse to give their parents their income details.

If you or your partner are 65 or over, the deduction is not made (or changed) until 26 weeks after the non-dependant moves in with you (or there has been a change in respect of her/him).

Step 4: getting a means-tested benefit

If you get IS, income-based JSA, income-related ESA or PC guarantee credit, HB is the amount worked out at Step 2 (maximum HB) – ie, your eligible rent (and in Northern Ireland, rates) less any amount for non-dependants. You do not need to continue with the rest of these steps.

Step 5: not getting a means-tested benefit

If you do not get IS, income-based JSA, income-related ESA or PC guarantee credit, you must compare your income with your weekly needs.

Step 6: work out your applicable amount

This is an amount for basic weekly needs. It is made up of:
- personal allowances; *and*
- premiums; *and*
- a work-related activity or support component, for those who have limited capability for work.

The applicable amount includes amounts for yourself and for your partner, if you have one. It also includes amounts for any dependent child(ren) or qualifying young people. The amounts for HB are the same as for IS (see pxvi), with the following differences.
- **Personal allowance:**
  - the child allowance is included in HB;
  - single people under 25 and lone parents under 18 who are entitled to main phase ESA get £60.50;
  - young couples get £94.95, unless both are under 18 and the claimant is not entitled to main phase ESA, in which case they get £72.35;
  - single people have a personal allowance of £124.05 if they are aged 60 to 64, or £143.80 if aged 65 or over;
  - couples get £189.35 if at least one is aged 60 to 64 and £215.50 if one or both is 65 or over.
- **Premiums:**
  - family premium, disabled child premium and enhanced disability premium for a child are included in HB. The family premium is increased by £10.50 if you have a child under one;
  - you do not get a disability premium if you have been assessed as having limited capability for work for ESA.
- **Components:**
  - instead of a disability premium, add a work-related activity component of £24 if you have claimed ESA and have limited capability for work, or a support component of £29 if you have limited capability for work-related activity.

Step 7: work out your weekly income

Chapter 20 explains how your loan or other income is taken into account and how to work out your weekly income. Income is generally calculated in the same way as for IS but with the following differences.

- Lone parents who are not claiming IS or income-based JSA receive a £25 earnings disregard.
- There is a maintenance disregard of £15 (although all maintenance is expected to be disregarded by the end of 2008).
- There is a 16/30 hours earnings disregard of £16.05 a week in certain circumstances.
- Claimants in receipt of widowed mother's/parent's allowance receive a £15 disregard.

Example

Caroline is a lone-parent student who earns £80.80 a week and receives £20 a week maintenance in addition to her student funds. She works 16 hours a week. She makes a claim for HB and has a total of £66.05 disregarded from her income (£10 for her student loan, plus £15 maintenance, £25 earnings and £16.05 for working 16 hours).

Step 8: calculate your housing benefit

If your income is *less than or the same as* your applicable amount, HB is the amount worked out at Step 2 (maximum HB) – ie, your eligible rent (and in Northern Ireland, rates) less any amounts for non-dependants.

If your income is *more than* your applicable amount, work out 65 per cent of the difference between the two. Your HB is the amount worked out at Step 2 (maximum HB – ie, your eligible rent less any amounts for non-dependants) minus 65 per cent of the difference between your income and applicable amount.

In Northern Ireland, 65 per cent of the difference is applied to the eligible rent and 20 per cent of the difference is applied to the eligible rates. If your HB does not cover your full rates charges, you may qualify for extra help – called rate relief. Your rate relief is your remaining rates charges once your HB for rates has been deducted, minus 12 per cent of the difference between your income and your applicable amount.

Examples

Maria is 18 and studying full time for a National Diploma in animal husbandry. She shares a private rented flat with a friend. They each pay £65 a week rent. Maria has an education maintenance allowance of £30 a week that she receives for 30 weeks. The rent officer uses the local housing allowance amount for a single room rent in Maria's area (£60 a week) to calculate her entitlement.

	£
Eligible rent	60.00
Applicable amount	47.95
Income:	0
(Education maintenance allowance disregarded)	
Weekly HB	**60.00**

Craig is a lone-parent father with two children. He is a second-year student, covered by the 'current system' rules. He is also a joint tenant with his friend Karl, who is not a student. Craig's share of the rent is £80. His income is his student support, child tax credit (CTC) and child benefit. He makes a claim for HB at the start of the academic year. Craig's benefit entitlement from September 2008 is calculated as follows:

	£
Eligible rent	80.00
Applicable amount:	
Personal allowance	60.50
Allowances for two children	105.18
Family premium	16.75
Total applicable amount	**182.43**

	£
Income:	
Student loan	£4,625
Less travel £295	
Less books £380	3,950
Divided by 43 weeks	
(1 September 2008 to 29 June 2009)	91.86
Less £10 disregard	81.86
(Special support grant disregarded in full)	
(Parents' learning allowance disregarded in full)	
CTC	90.58
Child benefit (£18.80 + £12.55)	31.35
Total income	**203.79**

	£
Craig's HB is worked out as follows:	
Income	203.79
Less applicable amount (£182.43)	21.36
65% x £21.36	13.88
Eligible rent (£80.00) – £13.88	66.12

Craig is entitled to **£66.12 HB a week**.

Summer 2009

Craig's student loan is only treated as income between 1 September 2008 and 28 June 2009. If Craig has no other income at this point he is entitled to claim IS and receive full help with his rent – ie, **£80 HB a week.**

Northern Ireland

If Craig were living in Northern Ireland, his HB for rent would be calculated in exactly the same way. If, in addition to his rent, he were liable to pay rates of £15 a week, his HB for rates would be calculated as follows:

	£
Income less applicable amount	21.36
20% x £21.36	4.27
12% x £21.36	2.56
HB for rates:	
Maximum rates (£15.00) – £4.27	10.73
Rate relief:	
Maximum rates (£15.00) – £10.73	4.27
Remaining rate liability (£4.27) – £2.56	1.71

Craig would be entitled to **£66.12 HB** for rent and **£10.73** for rates, plus rate relief of **£1.71.**

4. **Claiming housing benefit**

Unless you are allowed to claim by telephone, all claims for housing benefit (HB) must be in writing on a properly completed claim form. You can get a claim form from your local authority HB office. When you return it, check that you have provided all the documents and information required and ask for a receipt.

You can sometimes claim HB by telephone if your local authority has published a telephone number for this purpose. **Note:** even if you cannot claim by telephone, if you telephone to ask for a claim form and return it within one month, your claim is backdated to the date of your phone call.

If you are also claiming income support (IS), income-based jobseeker's allowance (JSA), incapacity benefit or pension credit (PC), you can claim HB at the same time. The Jobcentre Plus office may give you a form, usually an HCTB1 (HCTB1(LHA) if local housing allowance rules apply) or HCTB1(PC) if you are claiming PC. If you are claiming any of these benefits by telephone you can claim HB at the same time.

Providing you enclose all the required information, the local authority should make a decision on your claim within 14 days (see p142). You should not delay your claim because you do not have all the evidence required, but you must provide this within one month. The local authority can allow you longer than one month if it thinks this is reasonable.

If you post the claim form, keep a copy and obtain proof of posting. Claim forms are often lost. If you need to fill in another one, the local authority can backdate your HB if you can show the date of the original claim and provide evidence that you claimed earlier.

When your housing benefit starts

Your HB usually starts from the Monday after you make your claim. It can be backdated for up to 52 weeks if you ask for this and you have continuous 'good cause' for not claiming throughout the whole period. The Government is currently considering reducing the backdating period for HB to three months.

In deciding whether there is good cause to backdate a claim, a local authority must take account of how a reasonable person of your age, experience and state of health would have acted, or failed to act, in the circumstances.[18]

If you or your partner are 60 or over and not getting IS, income-based JSA or income-related ESA, you do not have to show good cause to get your claim backdated for 52 weeks.

Getting paid

HB is paid directly into your rent account if you are a local authority tenant, otherwise it is either paid to you by cheque, into your bank account or directly to your landlord. If the local housing allowance rules apply to you, your HB is usually paid to you and not to your landlord.

Unless budgeting is a problem for you it is generally better to have HB paid to yourself. This is because of the lengthy delays and administrative problems that can occur during the processing of HB. In some instances a huge amount of credit can be owed to claimants by the time they receive payment of HB, which means they would have had to have paid most of their rent before the HB is paid to them to prevent possession proceedings. It can also be difficult and time-consuming to get private landlords and housing associations to release the credit generated by a large back-payment of HB

By law, the local authority must make a decision on your claim, tell you what the decision is and pay you any HB to which you are entitled within 14 days of receiving your completed claim form with all the documentary evidence, or if that is not reasonably practicable, as soon as possible after that. However, in many areas there are long delays. If you are a private tenant, ask for an interim payment or payment on account, which is a standard amount paid at a reduced rate until your claim can be properly assessed. If the delay in HB is causing you to accrue rent arrears, it is worth getting advice on how much benefit you are entitled to so that you can budget for rent in the meantime. If your arrears build up and the landlord starts to take legal action and you qualify for free legal help, it may be worth asking a solicitor to issue a legal notice to the local authority to speed up the claim assessment. If you are a private or housing association tenant, local authorities are legally obliged to give you an interim payment of a reasonable amount unless it is obvious that you will not be entitled to HB or you have not supplied information requested.

5. **Overpayments**

If you are overpaid housing benefit (HB) you might have to repay it. An 'overpayment' is an amount of HB which has been paid, and to which the local authority later decides you were not entitled under the HB rules – eg, because of ignorance of or a mistake about the facts. Because it can take time to deal with a change in your circumstances, this can also lead to you being overpaid.

The local authority has discretion on whether or not to recover any amount of overpayment, no matter how it was caused and to offset any overpayment with the HB to which you were entitled. However, an overpayment is not recoverable at all if you can show that it was caused by an 'official error', you did not cause the official error and you could not reasonably have been expected to realise you were being overpaid. If you have provided all the appropriate information for the local authority to determine your entitlement to HB, there is a good chance that you can argue that the overpayment was caused by official error and you could not have been expected to know you were being overpaid. It is important to keep a record of any information you give to the local authority and obtain a receipt when handing in any document so you can prove exactly what information you have given, should you need to at a later date.

Seek advice if you think the local authority's decision to recover an overpayment is wrong. You can appeal against the decision. While your appeal is being decided, local authority guidance advises staff to freeze the recovery of the overpayment until the outcome of the appeal is known and this could help if you are facing hardship as a result of deductions from benefit. Even if the appeal is lost at a later date, the local authority has the discretion not to recover the money – eg, on grounds of hardship. See below for information about challenging a decision.

6. **Challenging a decision**

If you think a decision about your housing benefit (HB) is wrong (eg, because the decision maker got the facts or law wrong, or your circumstances have changed since the decision was made), there are a number of ways you can try to get the decision changed.

- You can seek a revision or a supersession of the decision. In some cases you have to show specific grounds. In others, you must apply within a strict time limit.
- You can appeal to an independent tribunal. There are strict time limits for appealing – usually one month from the date you are sent or given the decision. You can make a late appeal in limited circumstances.

If you are considering challenging a decision, you should seek advice as soon as possible.

Bear the following in mind.

- Students regularly receive incorrect HB assessments. This is because local authorities are often unfamiliar with the calculation of student income and take into account income that should be disregarded.
- New grants, including the special support grant, and bursaries were introduced from 2006. If the college or university bursary is for course-related costs or tuition fees, it should be disregarded in full when calculating HB. This bursary may be called the special support bursary in some circumstances. You should produce evidence of what the bursary is for when you claim HB.
- The special support grant and special support bursary should be disregarded when working out entitlement to HB. If you receive the wrong grant initially – eg, a maintenance grant instead of a special support grant, this can reduce your benefit entitlement. In this case, you should request the correct grant from the local authority then, if necessary, appeal the incorrect benefit decision (within the one-month time limit) requesting that the local HB office use its discretion to stockpile the appeal until the correct income is awarded. You need to give the new student support statement with the correct income to the HB department as soon as possible in order for benefit to be calculated correctly. Otherwise, it could be difficult to get the correct rate of benefit backdated as there is no provision for student income to be applied retrospectively.
- If you have missed the appeal deadline, it might be worth complaining to the relevant Ombudsman if you have lost benefit as the result of an incorrect assessment of student support. It may be possible to receive compensation for the HB you have lost.
- If there has been a series of errors in the assessment of your benefit you can complain to the local authority about the maladministration of the claim and then, in England, complain further to the local government Ombudsman. The Ombudsman scheme has been set up to look into complaints, try to put things right and award compensation, if appropriate. It is particularly useful if you are experiencing lengthy delays with local authority assessments and appeals. In Wales, the equivalent body is the Public Services Ombudsman for Wales, and in Northern Ireland, it is the Northern Ireland Ombudsman's Office. Contact details for all three organisations are in Appendix 2.

7. **Other benefits and tax credits**

If you are a full-time student and you get income support (IS), income-based jobseeker's allowance (JSA), income-related employment and support allowance (ESA) or pension credit (PC), you are also eligible for housing benefit (HB) if you pass the other conditions for HB. If your IS, income-based JSA or income-related ESA stops because you start full-time work or your earnings increase, you must reclaim HB directly from the local authority.

Child tax credit (CTC) and working tax credit (WTC) count in full as income when HB is worked out, unless you are 60 or over and not on IS/income-based JSA/income-related ESA. It is the actual amount you are paid that counts. If your CTC or WTC award is reduced because an overpayment of tax credits is being recovered, it is the reduced amount that counts for HB. If you are underpaid CTC or WTC and get a lump-sum repayment, it is treated as capital for HB but can be ignored for 52 weeks. It therefore only affects your HB if it takes your savings above the capital limit after this time. In either case, your HB is only affected from the time your payments of CTC or WTC change; there is no retrospective reassessment of HB.

Bear in mind that you should tell the local authority about any changes in income when they occur, including benefit and tax credit changes. Do not assume that the Department for Work and Pensions or HM Revenue and Customs passes on the information for you.

Notes

2. **Who is eligible**
1 Reg 55 HB Regs
2 Regs 53(1) and 55 HB Regs
3 Reg 7(16)(c)(viii) HB Regs
4 Reg 7(3) HB Regs
5 Reg 7(6)(d) HB Regs
6 Reg 7(6)(e) HB Regs
7 Reg 7(6)(a) HB Regs
8 Reg 7(6)(b) HB Regs
9 Reg 56(2)(h) HB Regs
10 Reg 13(4) HB Regs
11 para 2.41-2.42 C2 GM
12 Regs 53(1) and 56(1) HB Regs
13 Reg 53(1) and (2)(b) HB Regs
14 Reg 53(1) HB Regs
15 Reg 56(2) HB Regs
16 Reg 56(2)(i) HB Regs
17 para 2.30 C2 GM

4. **Claiming housing benefit**
18 Reg 83(12) HB Regs; R(S) 2/63(T)

Chapter 13

Incapacity benefit

This chapter covers:

Basic facts

– Incapacity benefit (IB) is an earnings-replacement benefit for people who are unable to work because of an incapacity or disability.

– It was abolished for new claims from 27 October 2008 and replaced by employment and support allowance, although existing claimants continue to receive it.

– It is not means tested, so most of the income you have does not affect the amount you receive.

– Contribution-based IB is payable to people who are unable to work, whether studying part time or full time, who have paid sufficient national insurance contributions.

– Youth-based IB is available to young people who have not built up sufficient national insurance contributions.

– Full-time students under 19 are not eligible for youth-based IB, but may still be eligible for contribution-based IB.

– Full-time students who have been unable to work because of an incapacity for at least 28 weeks become eligible for youth-based IB from the age of 19.

– Students incapable of work for 28 weeks who do not qualify for IB may be able to claim income support instead of, or in addition to, IB.

– Claims are administered by local Jobcentre Plus offices.

From 27 October 2008, you cannot usually make a new claim for IB. You must claim employment and support allowance instead (see Chapter 10).

1. **What is incapacity benefit**

Further information

This chapter gives an outline of the incapacity benefit rules and focuses on issues relevant to students. For more detailed information on the rules, see CPAG's *Welfare Benefits and Tax Credits Handbook*.

Incapacity benefit (IB) is an earnings-replacement benefit for people who are unable to work because of an incapacity. Incapacity is assessed by the Department for Work and Pensions (DWP) (or the Department for Social Development in Northern Ireland) under the 'own occupation test' or the 'personal capability assessment' (see p151). IB is not means tested, so most income you have does not affect the amount you receive. Pension payments can, however, reduce the amount.

There are two ways to qualify for IB.

Contribution-based IB. This is payable to people who are unable to work because of an incapacity and who have paid sufficient national insurance (NI) contributions.

Youth-based IB. This is payable to young people who have not had time to build up sufficient NI contributions. You must have become incapable of work while under the age of 20 or, in some circumstances, age 25 (see p149). You must have been incapable of work for 28 weeks before you can get IB. If you are aged under 19, you cannot claim IB if you are in full-time education.

IB is paid for the first 28 weeks at the short-term lower rate, then at the short-term higher rate. After 52 weeks it is paid at the long-term rate (see p152).

Note:
- Receipt of student support income does not affect your eligibility for IB, but as IB is a taxable social security benefit, you must declare it on your application for student support.
- Starting a full-time course can affect your entitlement to IB if the DWP decides as a result that you are capable of work (but see p151).

2. **Who is eligible**

To qualify for incapacity benefit (IB) you must:[1]
- be unable to work because of incapacity (see p151); *and*
- be under 60 if you are a woman or under 65 if you are a man. (You may qualify for short-term IB but cannot receive it for more than five years beyond pension age.)

You must also have made a claim for IB before 27 October 2008, unless your claim can be backdated (see p153). From this date, IB was replaced by employment and support allowance (ESA) and you will need to claim this instead.

In addition to the two mandatory conditions above, you must meet the relevant conditions below for either contribution-based IB or youth-based IB.

Contribution-based incapacity benefit

To qualify for contribution-based IB you must have paid or been credited with sufficient national insurance (NI) contributions.

Contribution-based IB is payable after three days of incapacity.

Youth-based incapacity benefit

In order to qualify for youth-based IB you must be at least 16 and have been under 20 (or 25 in some cases) when your period of incapacity for work started. You must also have been incapable of work for 196 consecutive days (28 weeks). You can serve the 28-week qualifying period before you reach 16 so your youth-based IB can start from your 16th birthday. Once you have qualified for IB on the grounds of youth, you can continue to receive it as long as you continue to meet the other conditions – eg, still being incapable of work.

If you are under 19 and studying in full-time education, you are not eligible to receive youth-based IB. See p148 for what is full-time education.

The amount to which you are entitled depends on the age at which you became incapable of work.

You must also meet the residence and presence conditions and not be a person subject to immigration control. You can get further advice from UKCISA (see Appendix 2).

Aged under 19 and in full-time education

Students in full-time education under age 19 are not eligible for youth-based IB, but may be eligible for contribution-based IB if they can qualify through their NI contributions record.[2]

You can get youth-based IB as soon as you reach your 19th birthday if you are still in full-time education. You must be incapable of work for 28 weeks before benefit can be paid, but these weeks can fall before your 19th birthday.

Students under age 19 in part-time education are eligible for youth-based IB. You can claim from the age of 16.

In either case, if you claim on or after 27 October 2008 you will have to claim contributory ESA instead (see Chapter 10) unless you are able to backdate your claim (see p153).

Full-time education

You are regarded as being in **'full-time education'** if you attend a course of education at a university, college or other educational establishment for 21 hours or more a week. The Department for Work and Pensions (DWP) (Department for Social Development in Northern Ireland) says that classes, lectures, seminars and periods of supervised study all count towards the 21 hours, but lunch breaks, private unsupervised study or work at home do not.[3] You continue to be regarded as being in full-time education during any temporary interruption of your studies.

When calculating the hours, instruction or tuition which is unsuitable for people of your age or sex who do not have a physical or mental disability must be ignored. So any extra classes or tuition you get because of your disability do not count towards the 21 hours.

The DWP normally requires written confirmation of a student's expected weekly hours of supervised study and classes. Evidence of such study can usually be satisfied by a letter from your faculty or department confirming the number of hours.

Aged 19

At age 19 students can receive youth-based IB regardless of whether they are studying full or part time. If you have already been incapable of work for 28 weeks when you reach your 19th birthday, you can claim and be paid youth-based IB straight away.

If you claim on or after 27 October 2008 you will have to claim contributory ESA instead (see Chapter 10) unless you are able to backdate your claim (see p153).

Aged 20 or over

If you already receive youth-based IB, you can continue to receive it after the age of 20. If you have not already claimed, you can do so at the end of a continuous period of 196 days (28 weeks) of incapacity that began before your 20th birthday. You have another three months after this 196-day period to make your claim. After that, you can only get IB if:

- you have paid sufficient NI contributions in order to receive contribution-based IB; *or*
- you are 25 or under and a former student. There is an age exception that allows certain people to claim up to age 25 when they have left their course (see below).

If you claim on or after 27 October 2008 you will have to claim contributory ESA instead (see Chapter 10) unless you are able to backdate your claim (see p153).

Age exception for under-25-year-olds

Most people who are 20 or over can usually only qualify for contribution-based IB and must have paid sufficient NI contributions. However, you may be able to qualify for youth-based IB if you meet *all* of the following conditions.[4]

- You were registered on a course of full-time education, or registered on vocational or work-based training, three months or more before your 20th birthday. Any course counts, from secondary school education to university undergraduate or postgraduate degrees. If you are studying part time because your disability prevents you doing a full-time course, you are regarded as studying full time for this rule. The law does not define what 'full time' means nor give a set number of hours. The DWP may ask you for evidence from the school, college or university.[5]

- You attended the course in the first academic term after registration, starting it at least three months before your 20th birthday.
- You finished or left the course sometime after the start of the last two complete tax years before the benefit year in which you claim IB. A tax year runs from 6 April and a benefit year runs from the first Sunday in January. (For example, if you claim IB in September 2008 your benefit year is January to December 2008 and you must, therefore, have finished the course at some point after 6 April 2005.) You are regarded as still attending the course while taking time off temporarily because of illness or a domestic emergency.
- You claim for a period no later than the end of a continuous period of 196 days (28 weeks) that started before your 25th birthday. You then have another three months to make your claim.

You can claim once you have left your course. Neither the law nor guidance is clear on whether you can get youth-based IB under this age exception if you are incapable of work but have gone on to do another course. It is possible that such claims could be successful.

If you claim on or after 27 October 2008 you will have to claim contributory ESA instead (see Chapter 10) unless you are able to backdate your claim (see p153).

Examples

In each of these examples the claim for IB must have been made before 26 October 2008. If the claim is made on or after 27 October 2008 the claim must be for contributory ESA instead unless the claim can be backdated (see p153).

Abby is 18 and has been taking A levels at college. She has a mental health problem and has had to give up her course. Abby is eligible for IB after she has been incapable of work for 28 weeks. If she starts another course after her 19th birthday, she can continue to get IB if the DWP still regards her as incapable of work.

Carter is 20 and has been on a full-time degree course. He has been injured in a road accident and has had to give up the course. He registered on the course when he was 18 and has attended for two academic years. He can claim IB under the age exception once he has been incapable of work for 28 weeks.

Carrie is 43 and has been getting IB for some years since she injured her back at work. She intends to begin a course leading to a qualification in accountancy. While on her course she can continue to get IB at the same rate as before, providing the DWP continues to treat her as incapable of work.

Assessing incapacity for work

Personal capability assessment

Incapacity for work is usually determined by the DWP under the '**personal capability assessment**'. Until the DWP assesses you, your incapacity is accepted on the basis of a certificate from your doctor.

Under the personal capability assessment, your ability to perform various physical or mental tasks is assessed. You must score at least 15 points via physical descriptors, or 10 points via mental health descriptors or 15 combined points (of which a minimum of six points must be obtained via mental health descriptors).[6] The personal capability assessment is compiled by the DWP's Medical Service.

You are exempt from the personal capability assessment if you are blind, get the highest rate care component of disability living allowance, are paraplegic or tetraplegic, and in some other circumstances. This does not always happen in practice. If this happens and you are refused benefit you should appeal.

Own occupation test

If you have a regular occupation, for the first 28 weeks of your incapacity for work you only have to qualify under the 'own occupation test'. After 28 weeks you are then expected to undergo a personal capability assessment.

The '**own occupation test**' is a test of whether you are incapable, because of a specific disease or bodily disablement, of doing work which you could reasonably be expected to do in the course of the occupation in which you were engaged.[7]

If you do not have a regular occupation when you fall ill, the personal capability assessment will apply immediately.

Linking period

If the incapacity is separated by periods of fitness of not more than eight weeks, the eight weeks are treated as part of the same spell of incapacity. If you are a 'welfare to work beneficiary' (ie, you are doing work or training in specified circumstances) the linking period can be up to 104 weeks.

Incapacity benefit and students

Studying part time or full time should not affect your entitlement to contribution-based IB.

Beginning studies, however, may prompt the DWP to reassess your incapacity if you are not exempt (see above), although this should not happen routinely. At the next assessment, your ability to perform set activities will be considered in the context of what you can do in a typical day, including your college or university routines. For example, you may be asked questions about:

13

- your ability to get around campus;
- your ability to get to and from lectures;
- how long you can sit comfortably to study;
- your ability to hold a pen to take notes or write essays;
- the support you need to produce assessed work and whether you need extra time.

The questions you are asked depend on which of the set activities (walking, sitting, manual dexterity, vision) are relevant to your condition. Attending a full-time course is not the same as full-time work – the number of hours of attendance plus the nature of the course should be considered, as well as whether you are doing the course for therapeutic reasons to help cope with your illness. The support you require from the college, other students and members of staff should also be considered, as well as any specialist equipment required to do the course and entitlement to disabled students' allowance.

3. **Amount of benefit**

Weekly rate from April 2008

Short-term lower rate (first 28 weeks)	£63.75 (£81.10 if pension age)
Short-term higher rate (weeks 29 to 52)	£75.40 (£84.50 if pension age)
Long-term rate (after 52 weeks)	£84.50 + £17.75 if under 35 or £8.90 if under 45 at the start of your incapacity

You can also claim extra benefit for an adult dependant provided s/he does not earn too much. If you have a child, an adult dependant is someone who looks after her/him – eg a spouse or civil partner, or unmarried/same-sex partner. If you do not have a child, an adult dependant is a spouse or civil partner aged 60 or over.

If your entitlement to IB started on or after 6 April 2001, it can be reduced if you receive certain kinds of pension income (eg, occupational pensions and certain health insurance policies). This does not apply if you are entitled to the highest rate disability living allowance care component.

4. **Claiming incapacity benefit**

There are three different forms to use depending on your route into incapacity benefit (IB).

- Claim on Form IB(Y)1 if you are under 20 or claiming under the age exception for under-25-year-olds.

- If you have worked and built up a national insurance contribution record, claim on Form SC1.
- If you are working for an employer when you fall ill and earning £90 or more a week, your employer should pay you statutory sick pay for the first 28 weeks of incapacity. After that, claim IB on Form SSP1, which you can get from your employer, or employment and support allowance (ESA) if it is on or after 27 October 2008.

Unless you are employed when you fall ill, you should normally start your claim by telephoning a Department for Work and Pensions 'contact centre'. Your Jobcentre Plus office has this number. Alternatively, you can submit a short electronic form at www.dwp.gov.uk/eservice to start your claim. The DWP then phones you to complete a full claim form. If you cannot, or do not want to, start your claim by phone or online, the DWP should accept a paper claim form, which you can get from your local DWP or Jobcentre Plus office or the Jobcentre plus website. You need to send in medical certificates from your GP until your incapacity for work is assessed. If you have to serve a 28-week qualifying period before you can get IB, ask your doctor for a backdated medical certificate and send this in with your claim. Ask for your claim to be backdated. Claims can normally only be backdated for three months (see below), but you have less time to wait to qualify for benefit.

All new claimants are likely to be required to attend a work-focused interview after the first eight weeks of the claim. This is intended to ensure you maintain contact with the job market and eventually return to work.

You are usually required to complete Form IB50, listing all aspects of your physical and/or mental incapacity. The DWP usually decides whether you pass the personal capability assessment based on this information. If it is not satisfied with the information on this form you will probably be required to attend a medical examination.

IB can normally only be backdated for a maximum of three months. Although you do not have to give a reason for a late claim, you must have met all the conditions of entitlement at the time the backdating is to take effect. This means that new claims for IB can be made up to 26 January 2009, so long as the date of claim began before ESA was introduced on 27 October 2008. Claims after this date will be treated as claims for ESA.[8]

Getting paid

IB is usually paid into your bank (or similar) account. Which account it goes into is up to you. If you do not want your benefit to go into an account that is already overdrawn, give the DWP details of an alternative account if you have access to, or can open, one.

If you are overpaid IB, you might have to repay it.

5. **Challenging a decision**

If you think a decision about your incapacity benefit (IB) is wrong (eg, because the decision maker got the facts or law wrong, or your circumstances have changed since the decision was made), there are a number of ways you can try to get the decision changed.

- You can seek a revision or a supersession of the decision. In some cases you have to show specific grounds. In others, you must apply within a strict time limit.
- You can appeal to an independent tribunal. There are strict time limits for appealing – usually one month from the date you are sent or given the decision. You can make a late appeal only in limited circumstances.

If you are considering challenging a decision, you should seek advice as soon as possible.

If the Department for Work and Pensions (DWP) disputes your entitlement because it says you are not incapable of work, you can apply for a revision or supersession of the decision or you can appeal against it. It is worth getting medical evidence from any consultant, counsellor or psychiatrist that you are (or were) seeing, as the DWP (and the tribunal) has to take into account any medical evidence you provide, as well as the report produced by the DWP's Medical Service. You should point out if the medical examination seemed rushed, or you were not given sufficient opportunity to discuss your disabilities or feel you were interrupted by the doctor.

If you are a disabled student receiving the disabled students' allowance, it is sometimes useful to insert a copy of the disabled students' allowance report when appealing if it outlines your medical problems, the difficulties you have with studying and the support you require.

While you are waiting for the appeal to be heard, you might be able to claim income support, but it might be paid at a reduced rate.

7. **Other benefits and tax credits**

You cannot get incapacity benefit (IB) if you are getting statutory sick pay from an employer. This runs out after 28 weeks, after which you can claim IB at the short-term higher rate.

If you get IB and live with your parents, they cannot continue to get child benefit or child tax credit (CTC) for you. Before 6 April 2004 the rules allowed parents to get CTC for young people getting IB. If you got IB before 6 April 2004 and your parents got CTC for you under the old rules, they can keep getting CTC until you leave full-time non-advanced education or approved training or reach age 20, whichever is the sooner.[9]

IB counts as income for means-tested benefits. The lower rate of short-term IB is ignored in the tax credits calculation if you get CTC or working tax credit, but other rates are taken into account.

The advantage of receiving IB while studying full time is that it is a non-means-tested benefit and can be paid in addition to any student support funding you receive, providing you continue to meet the eligibility requirements. It can also help you to qualify for a special support grant instead of a maintenance grant as part of your student support funding if you have been receiving it for at least 28 weeks. Make sure you provide evidence of your IB when applying for student support.

Once you have been incapable of work for 28 weeks, you may qualify for means-tested benefits as a full-time student – eg, income support (IS) or housing benefit (HB) if you were not already eligible. After 52 weeks of incapacity you satisfy the criteria for a disability premium to be paid as part of the means-tested benefits applicable amount, making it easier to qualify for some and/or a higher rate of benefits. If IB is awarded, you should inform your local Jobcentre Plus if you get IS, and your local authority HB office if you get HB or council tax benefit.

Notes

2. **Who is eligible**
   1 s30A and Sch 12 para 1 SSCBA 1992
   2 s30A(2A)(e) SSCB 1992; reg 17 SS(IB) Regs
   3 paras 57131 and 57132 DMG
   4 Reg 15 SS(IB) Regs
   5 para 56024 Vol 10 DMG
   6 s171C SSCBA 1992; reg 25 and Sch SS(IFW) Regs
   7 s171B SSCBA 1992

4. **Claiming incapacity benefit**
   8 Regs 2 and 4 ESA(TP) Regs

7. **Other benefits and tax credits**
   9 Reg 3(1) CTC Regs

Chapter 14

Income support

This chapter covers:
1. What is income support (p157)
2. Who is eligible (p157)
3. Amount of benefit (p168)
4. Claiming income support (p173)
5. Challenging a decision (p174)
6. Other benefits and tax credits (p175)

Basic facts

– Income support (IS) is basic financial support for people under 60 who are not required to be available for work.

– A full-time student under 20 on a non-advanced course (known as 'relevant education') can claim if, for example, s/he is a parent, an orphan, has a disability, or is estranged or separated from her/his parents. Nineteen-year-olds must have started their courses before turning 19.

– Other full-time students can claim in some circumstances.

– A part-time student can claim if s/he is a lone parent, a carer or pregnant, or is incapable of work or has a disability, and in some other circumstances.

– IS was abolished for most new claims on the grounds of incapacity or disability from 27 October 2008, although existing claimants receiving IS on these grounds will continue to do so. From 27 October 2008, people who are long-term sick or disabled should claim income-related employment and support allowance instead.

– IS is a means-tested benefit. The amount you get is usually affected by your grant, loan and other income.

– IS can help with the cost of mortgage payments, loans for repairs and improvements, and some other housing costs.

– IS claims are administered by the Department for Work and Pensions via Jobcentre Plus.

1. **What is income support**

Further information

This chapter gives an outline of the income support rules and focuses on issues relevant to students. For more detailed information on the rules, see CPAG's *Welfare Benefits and Tax Credits Handbook*.

Income support (IS) is paid to people under 60 who are on a low income and are not required to be available for work – eg, because of sickness or disability, or childcare or other caring responsibilities. It is also paid to people in some other circumstances – eg, under-20-year-olds who are studying full time and who are estranged from their parents, or have no parents. From 27 October 2008 disabled students making a new claim must claim income-related employment and support allowance instead (see Chapter 10). You do not have to have paid national insurance contributions to qualify for IS. The amount you get is affected by your income, including some elements of student support. Even if you are entitled to IS, therefore, the amount may be reduced because of your student income. Chapter 20 explains how your income affects your benefit.

2. **Who is eligible**

To qualify for income support (IS), you must satisfy the basic rules of entitlement. If you are studying full time, you must also satisfy additional rules. For information on whether you can qualify while you are in 'relevant education' or a full-time student, see pp159 and 163.

Basic rules

You can qualify for IS if:[1]
- you fit into one of the groups of people who can claim IS (see p158);
- neither you nor your partner count as in full-time paid work. For you, this is 16 hours or more a week. For your partner, this is 24 hours or more a week;
- you are not entitled to contribution-based jobseeker's allowance (JSA), and neither you nor your partner are entitled to income-based JSA;
- your partner is not entitled to pension credit;
- you are aged at least 16 and are under 60;
- your income is less than your 'applicable amount';
- your savings and other capital are worth £16,000 or less;[2]
- you satisfy presence and residence conditions. You might be able to claim during a temporary absence abroad;

- you are not subject to immigration control for benefit purposes (although there are limited exceptions).

See Chapter 20 for how your income (including student income) and capital affect your benefit. **Note:** your student support payments count as income, *not* capital.

Groups of people who can claim income support

To qualify for IS, you must satisfy all the basic rules and fit into one of the groups of people who can claim. If you are a full-time student, see p163. If you are in 'relevant education', see p160.

If you are studying part time, you must be:[3]

- aged 16 to 24 and on a training course being provided by the Learning and Skills Council for England or the National Assembly for Wales. This does not apply if you are a child or 'qualifying young person' for child benefit purposes (see Chapter 8);
- incapable of work. Note that unlike for full-time students (see p163), part-time students can claim IS as soon as they are incapable of work – they do not need to wait for 28 weeks (but see p159);
- disabled and your working hours or earnings are reduced because of this (but see p159);
- registered blind (but see p159);
- working while living in a care home, Abbeyfield home or independent hospital;
- a lone parent responsible for a child under 16 (12, after 24 November 2008) – see p159;
- someone who is:
  - fostering children under 16; *or*
  - on unpaid parental leave or paternity leave; *or*
  - looking after a child under 16 temporarily while her/his partner is out of the UK, or the child's parents (or the person who usually looks after her/him) are ill or temporarily away; *or*
  - looking after your partner or child (or qualifying young person) who is temporarily ill;
- pregnant, from 11 weeks before the birth (or earlier if incapable of work because of pregnancy), or you have had a baby not more than 15 weeks ago;
- a carer receiving carer's allowance, or you care for someone who gets (or who has claimed) attendance allowance or the middle or highest rate care component of disability living allowance;
- attending a court or tribunal as a JP, juror, witness or party to the proceedings;
- remanded in custody pending trial or sentence;
- a refugee learning English in order to obtain employment, in your first year in Great Britain;

- subject to immigration control, but entitled to the urgent cases rate of IS;
- involved in a trade dispute, or you have recently returned to work following one.

If you do not fit into one of the above groups but your partner does, s/he might be able to claim IS instead of you.

Changes for disabled students

From 27 October 2008, if you are incapable of work, disabled or registered blind you cannot make a new claim for IS and must instead claim income-related employment and support allowance (ESA). See Chapter 10.

Changes for lone parents

From 24 November 2008, you can only make a new claim for IS as a lone parent if your youngest child is under age 12. From October 2009, this age limit will decrease to age 10 and, from October 2010, it will decrease to seven.

Draft regulations indicate that if you are on a course of education when the rules change, so that you are no longer eligible for IS as a lone parent, the rule change will not take effect until you have finished your course of education. You should seek advice if you are affected by the changes.

The changes do not affect foster parents.

If you are a lone parent, and your child is above the age at which you can count as a lone parent for IS, but is under 20 and in 'relevant education' (see p160) or on approved training, you can claim IS during the summer vacation.[4] You must be one in one of the groups who are eligible for IS (see p158). If you are not in one of these groups, you can claim JSA in the summer vacation instead (see Chapter 15).

Overseas students

Most overseas students cannot claim IS because they are subject to immigration control for benefit purposes. Even if you are entitled to IS, a successful claim for benefit could affect your right to stay in the UK and it is best to get immigration advice before making a claim. If you are not eligible for benefit, but there are no restrictions on your partner, either as a student or as a 'person subject to immigration control', s/he may be able to claim instead. However, if s/he receives benefit and you are a 'person subject to immigration control', this may affect your right to remain in the UK under the immigration rules. You should get advice from UKCISA (see Appendix 2).

Studying and claiming income support

The general rule is that you cannot qualify for IS if you are studying full time. If you are already claiming IS, your entitlement may be affected if you start full-time study. There are, however, exceptions to the rules. If you are:

- under 20 and in 'relevant education', see p160;

- a 'full-time student', see p163.

To see if you can claim IS while studying part time, see p166.

Under 20 and in relevant education

You cannot usually qualify for IS if you are in **'relevant education'**.[5] You count as in relevant education if you are a 'qualifying young person' for child benefit purposes (ie, you are under 20 and in full-time non-advanced education or approved training.[6] You must have started the education or training before you were 19.

Note:
- You can continue to count as in relevant education for a period after your education or training ends (see p163).
- There is not a 'relevant education' rule for housing benefit (HB) or council tax benefit (CTB) purposes, so you might be able to claim HB and CTB even if you cannot claim IS (see Chapters 12 and 23).

Definitions

'Non-advanced education' is usually study at Level 3 or below[7] – eg, NVQs up to Level 3, GNVQs up to intermediate level, and GCSE, AS and A levels. In effect, this definition covers any course that is not 'a course of advanced education'. See p164 for what counts as advanced education.

A course is **'full time'** if you attend for more than 12 hours a week.[8] This includes time spent during term time receiving tuition, undertaking supervised study, examinations or practical work. Meal breaks and unsupervised study on or off the premises are ignored.

If you are in advanced education (see p164), you may be able to claim IS as a 'full-time student' (see p163).

Who can claim income support

If you are in relevant education you qualify for IS if:[9]
- you are a parent of a child under 16 for whom you are treated as responsible and who lives in the same household as you; *or*
- you are disabled – ie,
  - you qualify for the IS disability premium or severe disability premium as part of your applicable amount (see p169); *or*
  - you have been treated as incapable of work for a continuous period of at least 28 weeks (two or more periods of incapacity separated by a break of no more than eight weeks count as one continuous period); *or*
- you have no parent and no one acting as your parent (eg, a foster parent); *or*
- you have to live away from your parents (or someone acting in their place) because:

– you are 'estranged'; *or*
– you are in physical or moral danger. The danger does not have to be caused by your parents. Therefore, a young person who is a refugee and cannot rejoin her/his parents can claim IS while at school;[10] *or*
– there is a serious risk to your physical or mental health.

Estrangement implies emotional disharmony, where you have no desire to have any prolonged contact with your parents or they feel similarly towards you.[11] It is possible to be estranged even if your parents are providing you with some financial support or you still have some contact with them. If you are in care, it is possible to be estranged from your local authority. If so, you could qualify for IS if you live away from the accommodation provided by the local authority;[12] *or*

• you live apart from your parents (or anyone acting as your parent) and they cannot support you financially because they are:
  – in prison; *or*
  – prohibited from coming to Great Britain because they do not have leave to enter under UK immigration laws; *or*
  – chronically sick, or mentally or physically disabled. This covers people who are substantially and permanently disabled or who could qualify for an IS disability premium or higher pensioner premium, or have an armed forces grant for car costs because of disability;[13] *or*

• you have left local authority care and are living away from your parents (or anyone acting as your parent) by necessity (but see p162); *or*

• you are a person from abroad with limited leave to remain in the UK without recourse to public funds and your funds from abroad are temporarily disrupted, but are likely to resume. You can get a reduced, 'urgent cases' rate of IS for a maximum of six weeks. Note that this provision is rarely used, so seek advice if your claim is refused; *or*

• you are a refugee who is learning English in order to obtain employment. You must be on a course of more than 15 hours a week and, at the time the course started, you must have been in Great Britain for a year or less. You can get IS for a maximum of nine months.

Note: a person acting in place of your parents includes a local authority or voluntary organisation if you are being cared for by them, or foster parents, but only until you leave care.[14] It does not include a person who is your sponsor under the immigration laws.[15] If you are not in any of the above groups, you cannot get IS. Instead:

• you may have to rely on any statutory support to which you are entitled and any discretionary support your college or school may offer you (see Chapter 1 for more details);

• your parents (or a person acting in their place) may be able to claim child benefit and child tax credit (CTC) for you.

In some circumstances, you may count as both a person who can claim IS while in relevant education and as a person for whom someone else can claim child benefit and CTC. You should seek advice about how you would be better off financially.

Example

Clara is 17. She has been living with her mother and stepfather. Her mother is in hospital as a result of domestic violence from Clara's stepfather. Clara has moved out of her family home because she is at risk of physical danger. She is able to claim IS.

Care leavers

Since 1 October 2001 (in England and Wales) and 22 November 2002 (in Northern Ireland), some 16- and 17-year-olds who were formerly looked after by a local authority receive financial and other support from the local authority and cannot qualify for IS. You cannot usually qualify for IS if:[16]

- you were looked after by a local authority for at least 13 weeks after the age of 14, ending after you turned 16; *or*
- you are not subject to a care order, but you were in hospital or detained in a remand centre, or a young offenders or similar institution when you turned 16 and immediately before that you were looked after by a local authority for at least 13 weeks since your 14th birthday.

There are exceptions to the rules, including if you are a lone parent, a disabled student, or unable to work because of illness or disability (although in the latter two cases, you cannot make a new claim after 27 October 2008 and should apply for income-related ESA instead – see Chapter 10).

The local authority is responsible for providing funding for accommodation, practical life skills, education and training, employment, financial support, specific support needs and contingency plans for support if independent living breaks down.

Care leavers aged 18 and over are treated like any other claimant and you may be able to make a claim for IS if you fall into one of the other categories listed in this section. The local authority still has a duty to assist you with your expenses associated with education and training until you have completed the agreed programme of education and training, set out in a 'Pathway Plan'.[17]

Example

Brandon is 17 and lives in England. In May 2003, when he was 14, he was taken into foster care after his mother died. He has now left foster care and lives in a housing association flat. He cannot claim IS because since October 2001 he has been looked after by a local authority for over 13 weeks. It is his local authority's responsibility to provide for his living and housing costs to a level equivalent to what he would receive if he were claiming IS or HB.

When you turn 20

If you turn 20, you no longer count as in relevant education, even if you are still studying. However, you may then count as a full-time student. You can only receive IS if you are in one of the categories of full-time students who can claim (see p165). This may mean you cannot qualify for IS from your 20th birthday even if you qualify up to that date.

When relevant education ends

When your course or training ends, you continue to count as in relevant education:
- if you are enrolled on another course; *or*
- until the latest of the following:
  - the 31 August after your 16th birthday;
  - if you are under 18, the end of your 'extension period' (see p90);
  - the first Sunday on or after your 'terminal date' (see p90); *or*
- until you turn 20, if this is earlier than any of the above.

Once you have left relevant education (or you turn 20) you might be able to qualify for IS or JSA if you satisfy the rules for getting these benefits (see below and Chapter 15).

Full-time students

If you are a full-time student you cannot usually qualify for IS for the duration of your course, including vacations.[18] See p165 for exceptions to this rule. See p166 if you are studying part time and p167 if you give up or change your course. See Chapter 25 if you take time out from studies.

In general, students are expected to receive student support (eg, student loans and supplementary grants) to support them while in full-time education. See Chapters 1 to 6 for details of student support.

Who counts as a full-time student

You count as a full-time student if you are not a 'qualifying young person' for child benefit purposes (see p88) and:[19]
- you are under 19 and on a full-time course of advanced education (see p164); *or*
- you are 19 or over but under pension age (60 for women, 65 for men) and on a full-time course of study. If your course is full time, you are treated as a full-time student regardless of the level of the course, unless you are aged under 20 and can still be treated as in 'relevant education' (see p89). See p164 for what counts as a full-time course; *or*

- you are on a sandwich course (see below).

You are treated as a student until either the last day of your course or until you abandon or are dismissed from it.[20] The 'last day of the course' is the date on which the last day of the final academic year is officially scheduled to fall according to the term dates fixed by the college.[21] If you are unsure when your course is scheduled to end, ask the college or university for a copy of its official term dates.

Note: if you are 19 and in relevant education, you do not count as a full-time student. Instead, the rules on p163 apply.

Definitions

A '**course of advanced education**' means:[22]

- a course leading to a postgraduate degree or comparable qualification, a first degree or comparable qualification, a diploma of higher education, a Higher National Diploma or Higher National Certificate of either the Business and Technology Education Council or the National Vocational Education Council, or a teaching qualification; *or*
- any other full-time course which is a course of a standard above advanced GNVQ or equivalent, ordinary National Diploma, a National Diploma or National Certificate of either the Business and Technology Education Council or the National Vocational Education Council, or a General Certificate of Education (advanced level).

A '**sandwich course**'[23] (excluding a course of initial teacher training) is one that consists of alternate periods of study at your education institution and periods of industrial, professional or commercial placement, or work experience. Taking the course as a whole, you must attend periods of study at your institution for an average of not less than 18 weeks a year. If your periods of full-time study and work experience alternate within any week of your course, the days of study are aggregated with any weeks of full-time study to determine the number of weeks of full-time study in each year. If your course includes the study of one or more modern languages for at least half of your study time, any period during which you are working while living in the country whose language is part of your course is counted as a period of work experience.

Full-time courses

Whether your course is full time depends on the country in which you are studying and on who is funding your education. Your course counts as full time if:

- it is funded by the Learning and Skills Council (LSC) in England or the National Assembly for Wales and involves more than 16 'guided learning hours' a week.[24]

  Courses include academic and vocational qualifications, basic literacy, numeracy and ICT skills, English as a second language programmes, access to higher education courses and courses developing independent living skills for people with learning difficulties.

'**Guided learning hours**' include all supervised study – eg, classes, lectures, tutorials and structured assessment periods. They do not include unstructured or unsupervised study time – eg, studying at home or in a library. You should be given a 'learning agreement' by your education provider stating the number of guided learning hours you are undertaking. This is used to provide proof of your course hours. On this document the hours are calculated as an average figure and may differ from those on your timetable. The Jobcentre Plus office uses your learning agreement to decide whether you are studying full time; *or*

- it is *not* funded by the LSC or the Welsh Assembly and it is a 'full-time course of study' (see below) – eg, you are on a full-time course of higher education.

There is no definition of a '**full-time course of study**' in the IS rules. Whether your course counts as full time depends on how it is defined by the college or university. A course could be full time even if you only have to attend for a few hours a week. Definitions are often based on local custom and practice within education institutions, or determined by the demands of course validating bodies, or by the fact that full-time courses can attract more resources. The education establishment's definition is not final, but if you want to challenge it you have to produce a good argument showing why it should not be accepted.[25] If your course is only for a few hours each week, you should argue that it is not full time. However, a course could be full time even though you only have to attend a few lectures a week. You should check how your course is described by the education institution and how you are registered on it.

Full-time students who can claim income support

Even if you are a full-time student, you can qualify for IS if you are:[26]

- a **lone parent** who is responsible for a child under 16 (12, from 24 November 2008 who lives in your household. Once your only or youngest child turns 16 (12, from 24 November 2008), you cannot claim IS unless you fit into one of the other groups of full-time students who can claim. Check to see if you can qualify for JSA instead (see Chapter 15);
- **fostering** a child under 16 through a local authority or voluntary organisation and are not a member of a couple;
- a **disabled student** – ie:
  - you qualify for the IS disability premium or severe disability premium as part of your 'applicable amount' (see p169); *or*
  - you qualify for a disabled students' allowance because you are deaf; *or*
  - you have been treated as incapable of work for a continuous period of at least 28 weeks. Two or more periods of incapacity separated by a break of no more than eight weeks count as one continuous period. See Chapter 13 for further information about incapacity for work;

- **a person from abroad** with limited leave to remain in the UK without recourse to public funds and your funds from abroad are temporarily disrupted, but are likely to resume. You can get a reduced, 'urgent cases' rate of IS for a maximum of six weeks. For example, you could claim IS if you are an international student who is funded by a government scholarship and those funds cannot be paid because of a natural disaster (eg, an earthquake). Note that this provision is rarely used, so seek advice if your claim is refused;
- **a refugee who is learning English** in order to obtain employment. You must be on a course of more than 15 hours a week and, at the time the course started, you must have been in Great Britain for a year or less. You can get IS for a maximum of nine months;
- a member of a **couple who are both full-time students**, and you or your partner are responsible for a child or 'qualifying young person'. You can only claim IS under this rule during the summer vacation. You must fit into one of the groups of people who can claim IS as a part-time student (see below). If you cannot qualify for IS, check whether you qualify for JSA instead;
- **you are on the Adult Learning Option scheme.**

If you are a full-time student who cannot claim IS, check to see if you can claim JSA, ESA or pension credit (PC) instead. If you have a partner who is not a full-time student, s/he might be able to claim IS, JSA or PC for you. Remember that your student support income is taken into account in working out how much IS, JSA or PC s/he can get.

Part-time students

You count as a part-time student if you are studying, but are not in 'relevant education' (see p89) or a full-time student (see p163). In the latter case, you should check with the education institution to see how you are registered and whether your course counts as part time. You can qualify for IS while a part-time student if you satisfy all the basic rules of entitlement (see p157) and you fit into one of the groups of people who can claim IS (see p158).

What counts as part time

Generally, it is your college or university that determines whether you count as a part-time or full-time student, rather than the actual number of hours that you study or attend lectures. However, if your course is funded or partly funded by the LSC or the Welsh Assembly, you count as on a part-time course if it involves up to 16 guided learning hours a week. This should be set out in a 'learning agreement' provided by your college.

If you are currently studying part time on a course you previously attended full time, or if you are attending a modular or similar course (see p167) on a part-time basis, the Department for Work and Pensions may say that you are attending a full-time course and should, therefore, be treated as a full-time student. It may be possible to challenge this interpretation.[27] You should seek specialist advice if you are in this situation.

Health-related courses

If you attend a health-related course for which you are entitled to receive an NHS bursary, you are treated as attending a full-time course.

Modular courses

A '**modular course**' is one that is made up of two or more modules and the institution requires you to do a certain number successfully to complete the course.[28] If you are attending or undertaking part of a modular course that is full time, you are treated as a full-time student for the duration of the modules from the day those modules begin until the last day of registration on those modules (or earlier if you abandon the course or are dismissed from it).[29] This includes all vacations during the modules on which you are registered and, except for the final module, the vacation immediately following the modules. It also includes periods when you are attending the course to do re-sits of any modules you have undertaken on a full-time basis. This is the case even if you are registered part time with the institution while you are doing these re-sits. You should seek advice from your students' union or institution's student services about the student support to which you might be entitled while you are re-sitting.

Because the rules provide no definition of a full-time course (unless it is funded by the LSC or the Welsh Assembly) you may be able to argue that you are not attending a full-time course.[30] If you are in any doubt, you should seek advice.

If the modular course allows you to undertake some modules on a part-time basis, you are not excluded from IS while you are studying part time. Remember, however, that you must not be studying on any modules that you have previously done on a full-time basis.

See the example on p187 for further details.

Giving up or changing your course

If you are in any of the circumstances below, your entitlement to any student support you receive might be affected and you should seek specialist advice.

- If you abandon your course or are dismissed from it, you can claim IS from the day after that date provided you satisfy the other rules of entitlement.
- If you complete one course and start a different one, you are not treated as a student during any period between the courses.[31]
- If you are on a sandwich course (see p164), or your course includes a compulsory or optional period on placement, you count as a full-time student during the sandwich or placement period even if you have been unable to find a placement or your placement comes to an end prematurely.[32]

- If you attend a course at an education institution which provides training or instruction to enable you to take examinations set and marked by an entirely different and unconnected body (ie, a professional institution) and you abandon or take time out from it because you fail the examinations set by the other body (or you finish the course at the education institution but fail the exams), you may be able to argue that you are not a student from the date you left the course at your education institution even if you intend to re-sit the examinations set by the other body at a later date.[33]

If you are taking time out of your course for any other reason, see Chapter 25.

You may also retain entitlement to some student support on a statutory or discretionary basis – eg, through student loans or hardship funds. You should seek specialist advice.

Changing from full-time to part-time attendance

If you have to change from full-time to part-time attendance on a full-time course for personal reasons, you may be able to argue that you have abandoned your full-time course and are registered on a part-time course and, therefore, you are not a full-time student.[34] If, because of exam failure or any other reason, you change to a different course, or your college requires you to change the level of course (eg, from A level to GCSE) and this involves a change from full-time to part-time study, you should argue that you are a part-time student (see p166).[35] However, changing your attendance may affect your entitlement to any student support you may be receiving. You should seek advice on this before acting.

3. **Amount of benefit**

Income support (IS) is a means-tested benefit that tops up your income to a level that is set by the Government. The amount you get depends on your basic weekly needs (your 'applicable amount' – see p169) and on how much income and capital you have (see Chapter 20). Some students may find, therefore, that they can only receive IS for part of any year (eg, during the summer vacation).

The amount of IS you get depends on your circumstances and the circumstances of your partner. The following steps show how to work out the amount of IS to which you are entitled.

Note: benefit rates are increased in April each year, but it is usually possible to find out what the new rates will be from the beginning of December. Check the Department for Work and Pensions (DWP) (or the Department for Social Development in Northern Ireland) website, or see CPAG's *Welfare Rights Bulletin*.

Step 1: capital

If your capital is over £16,000, you cannot get IS. Some kinds of capital are ignored. Note that student support grants and loans count as income, not as capital.

Step 2: work out your applicable amount

This is an amount for your basic weekly needs. It is made up of:

- a personal allowance;
- premiums for any special needs – eg, if you have been incapable of work for a period, are disabled or are caring for a disabled person;
- housing costs (see p170), principally for mortgage interest payments.

See pxv for the current rates.

Allowance and premiums for children

If you claim IS and are getting child tax credit (CTC), IS does not include allowances and premiums for your children. CTC does not count as income for IS, nor does child benefit.

If you were getting IS on 5 April 2004 and this included allowances and premiums for your children but you were not yet entitled to CTC, you will be transferred onto CTC sometime in the future. Until then, you continue to get allowances and premiums for your children as part of your IS. A change of circumstances, such as starting a full-time course, may trigger the transfer. You should seek advice about whether you might be better off financially if you claim CTC now rather than wait until you are transferred.

Step 3: work out your weekly income

Chapter 20 explains how your loan, grant or other income is taken into account and how to work out your weekly income.

Step 4: deduct weekly income from applicable amount

If your income is *less than* your applicable amount, IS equals the difference between the two.

If your income is *the same as or more than* your applicable amount, you cannot get IS. You can claim again if your income drops – eg, during the summer vacation when your student loan and adult dependants' grant are no longer treated as income.

Example

Karen is aged 35, a full-time, first-year undergraduate student and a lone parent of Penny, aged two. She gets a full loan to pay for her tuition fees of £3,145, a full special support grant of £2,835 per year, a full student loan of £4,625 per year, a parents' learning allowance of £1,470 per year and £55 a week childcare grant. Her only other income is £18.80 a week child benefit and £50.54 a week CTC.

During the academic year September 2008 to June 2009

Step 1	Karen has no savings or capital.	
Step 2	Her applicable amount is:	
	Personal allowance for herself	£60.50
Step 3	Her weekly income during the period of study is:	
	Student loan	
	(The loan for tuition fees, special support grant, parents' learning allowance, childcare grant, CTC and child benefit are disregarded. Her loan, less certain disregards, is divided over the 43 weeks of the academic year. See Chapter 20.)	£81.86
Step 4	Karen's income is above her applicable amount so she cannot get IS.	

During the summer vacation June 2009 to September 2009

Step 2	Karen's applicable amount will be based on the same elements as above, but note that the rates will increase from April 2009. Based on April 2008 rates, her applicable amount is:	
	Personal allowance for herself	£60.50
Step 3	Her weekly student income from the end of June 2009 to the beginning of September 2009 is nil. This is because her loan for living costs only counts as income during the academic year. Child benefit and CTC continue to be disregarded.	
Step 4	Based on April 2008 rates, her weekly IS is £60.50. Karen should reclaim IS at the end of June.	

Housing costs

If you own or are buying your home, your IS applicable amount can include help with a variety of housing costs.[36] Normally, help only starts once you have been getting IS for a period, although there are some exceptions. For help with rent, you need to claim housing benefit (HB – see Chapter 12). This is only a brief outline of some of the rules.

Your applicable amount can include help with:
- mortgages and other loans for house purchase;
- loans used to pay for specified types of repairs and improvements or to meet a service charge for these; *and*
- other housing costs – eg, ground rent, payments under co-ownership schemes and service charges.

IS does *not* include amounts for insurance or any endowment premiums.

The amount you get for loans is based on a standard interest rate so it could be higher or lower than what you actually pay. If you have a 'non-dependant' living with you (eg, an adult child or a parent) a deduction is usually made because s/he is assumed to be making a contribution towards your housing costs. Payment is usually made directly to your mortgage lender. It is important to note that:

- if your loans amount to more than £100,000, your housing costs might not be met in full;
- the amount you are paid might be restricted if:
  - the DWP (or the Housing Executive in Northern Ireland) decides that your costs are excessive (eg, if your home is bigger than you need); *or*
  - you took out or increased your loan while on IS, jobseeker's allowance (JSA) or pension credit (PC), or during a period between claims (see below).

Buying a house while on benefit

You cannot usually get IS to help you pay the cost of a loan to buy a home if you became liable for it, or increased it, while on IS, JSA or PC, or during a period of up to 26 weeks between claims. There are exceptions to the rules. These include where:

- you are replacing one mortgage with another. However, you cannot usually get help with any increase (but see below);
- you took out or increased the loan to buy a home more suitable for the needs of a disabled person, or to provide separate bedrooms for a son and daughter aged 10 or over;
- you buy a home and immediately beforehand you were in rented accommodation and getting HB. You can only get IS for housing costs up to the amount of HB you were entitled to, plus any other housing costs you were already getting.

The waiting periods

Help with housing costs is not usually included in your IS applicable amount until you have been entitled to (or treated as entitled to) IS or JSA for a number of weeks – known as a waiting period. The length of your waiting period depends on when you agreed to pay your loan or other housing costs. If your partner is 60 or over, there is no waiting period.

If you agreed to pay your home or repair loan or other housing costs:

- before 2 October 1995, you get nothing for the first eight weeks, 50 per cent for the next 18 weeks, then full housing costs after you have been entitled to (or treated as entitled to) IS or JSA for 26 weeks;
- after 1 October 1995, you get nothing for the first 39 weeks, then full housing costs after you have been entitled to (or treated as entitled to) IS or JSA for 39 weeks. There are some exceptions to this rule.

Your income (eg, your student income) may mean that you cannot qualify for IS until housing costs are included in your applicable amount because your income is higher than your personal allowances and premiums. In this case, there are special rules that allow you to be treated as entitled to IS during your waiting period.[37] This helps you qualify for IS at the end of your waiting period. If you are a lone parent or a carer, you must make a claim for IS first, get refused, then claim again once your waiting period is over. You can also be treated as entitled to IS during periods when you are getting incapacity benefit, statutory sick pay, contribution-based JSA, or national insurance credits for unemployment or incapacity.

The rules are complicated and you should seek specialist advice if you are in this situation.

Example

Sally is a full-time student and a lone parent. She claims IS in October 2008. Her IS applicable amount is made up of a personal allowance only. Because she took out a mortgage to buy her home in 2003, housing costs cannot be included until her waiting period of 39 weeks has passed. This means her claim is refused because her student and other income that must be taken into account is higher than her personal allowance. However, because she can be treated as entitled to IS for 39 weeks, when she claims again after 39 weeks, her applicable amount is now made up of a personal allowance and housing costs. Because her income is now lower than her applicable amount, she qualifies for IS.

Living away from home

Housing costs are usually only paid for the home in which you live. There are a number of exceptions, including some specifically for full-time students – eg, if you have moved somewhere to study, but your normal home is elsewhere.

If you have to live away from your normal home because you are a full-time student or are on a training course:

- you can get housing costs for both homes indefinitely if you are one of a couple and it is unavoidable for you to live in two separate homes.[38] It must be reasonable for you to get housing costs for both; *or*
- you can get housing costs for the home for which you pay if you are a single person or lone parent and have to pay for either your normal home or your term-time accommodation, but not both.[39]

Otherwise, in some circumstances you can get housing costs for your normal home for up to 52 weeks if you are away temporarily and are unlikely to be away for longer than this (or in exceptional circumstances, substantially longer than this). This applies if you are a full-time student living away from your partner who cannot get housing costs for both of your homes, or a single claimant or lone parent who is liable to pay housing costs on both a term-time and a home address.[40] It also applies in other situations, including if you are in hospital, a care home or prison.

4. **Claiming income support**

If you think you might be entitled to income support (IS), you should claim as soon as you can. There are only very limited situations where backdating is allowed.

You can make initial contact about claiming by telephone or letter. You may also be able to start a claim online at www.dwp.gov.uk/eservice. The date of your initial contact is important because it usually determines the date from which you can be paid IS.

Normally, you must start your claim by telephoning a 'contact centre'. Your local Jobcentre Plus office has the number and it may also be displayed in local advice centres and libraries. The centre takes basic information, then calls you back to go through the details of your claim. The date of a work-focused interview is set, unless it is agreed you do not need to attend one. You are then sent a statement recording the information you gave over the telephone, which you are asked to sign, and details of the evidence and information you should bring with you to the interview (or forward to the Department for Work and Pensions (DWP)). The signed statement comprises your official claim.

It is best to start your claim in this way if you can. However, if you cannot, or do not want to, use the telephone to start your claim, the Jobcentre Plus office can still deal with your claim in other ways. You might, for example, be invited for a face-to-face interview or, in some cases, an old-style claim form can be accepted.

You should request an old-style claim form if you need one to make your claim – eg, if you are a disabled student and need the help of an adviser. Old-style claim forms are available from Jobcentre Plus offices and online at www.jobcentreplus.gov.uk. In Northern Ireland you can get the form from the Department for Social Development (DSD) website at www.dsdni.gov.uk. They might be available at your student services department or at local advice centres. If you obtain a claim form, it is still important to telephone the DWP (or DSD) or JobCentre Plus office to let them know that you want to claim IS. If you do not, you could lose benefit. You should complete the form and send or take it to the DWP (or DSD) or Jobcentre Plus office within one month of your initial contact.

Whenever you call the DWP (or DSD), you need to provide your national insurance number. You also need this number, as well as that of your partner, when you claim, as well as any other information required on the claim form. If you are a disabled student who needs to qualify on the grounds of your incapacity for work, you must usually also fill in Form SC1. This should not be necessary if you qualify as a disabled student for another reason – eg, because you are receiving disability living allowance.

If you are a member of a couple, either of you can make the claim, but whoever claims must be eligible in her/his own right.

Getting paid

Payment is usually made directly into your bank (or similar) account. Which account it goes into is up to you. If you do not want your benefit to go into an account that is overdrawn, give the DWP or DSD details of an alternative account if you have access to, or can open, one.

If you are overpaid IS, you might have to repay it.

5. Challenging a decision

If you think a decision about your income support (IS) is wrong (eg, because the decision maker got the facts or law wrong, or your circumstances have changed since the decision was made), there are a number of ways you can try to get the decision changed.

- You can seek a revision or a supersession of the decision. In some cases, you have to show specific grounds. In others, you must apply within a strict time limit.
- You can appeal to an independent tribunal. There are strict time limits for appealing – usually one month from the date you are sent or given the decision. You can make a late appeal in limited circumstances.

If you are considering challenging a decision, you should seek advice as soon as possible.

If your claim for IS is unsuccessful, consider whether you can challenge the decision. You should bear the following in mind.

- As student claims are not necessarily commonplace and the rules about how student income is treated are complex, it is always worth checking a decision with a student adviser in your students' union or institution.
- If the decision maker says you are a full-time student, but you disagree, you should get advice to see if there are grounds for challenging the decision.
- Claims for IS are sometimes refused because the Department for Work and Pensions (or Department for Social Development in Northern Ireland) miscalculates student income or takes the wrong types of student income into account.
- You might not currently be entitled to IS, but would be once you or a member of your family become entitled to a 'qualifying benefit' – eg, disability living allowance or carer's allowance. In this case, you need to claim. Your initial claim will be refused. However, if you claim again once the qualifying benefit is awarded, your IS will be backdated to the date of your original claim, or the date on which the qualifying benefit was first payable (if later). Alternatively, you might be entitled to a higher rate of IS once the 'qualifying benefit' is awarded. In this case, you need to ask for a revision or a supersession of your IS

award. Your IS should then be increased from the date the qualifying benefit was first payable.

Note: you may find that you can qualify for IS in the summer vacation (even if you cannot qualify during term time) because of the way your grant and loan are divided throughout the year. In this case, you need to claim again as soon as you think you might qualify.

6. **Other benefits and tax credits**

Income support (IS) tops up any other income you have to the level of your basic requirements (your applicable amount), so most other benefits are taken into account as income when working out the amount of your IS. This means they reduce your IS pound for pound. Disability living allowance, attendance allowance, guardian's allowance, housing benefit (HB) and council tax benefit (CTB) are, however, always disregarded as income.

If you get IS, and you have rent (and, in Northern Ireland, rates) or council tax to pay, you are eligible as a student for HB and CTB.

Child tax credit (CTC) is ignored as income when assessing IS. Child benefit is ignored unless you still have amounts for children in your IS and you do not get CTC. In this case, £10.50 a week of your child benefit is disregarded if you have a child under one.

Even though getting a benefit may reduce your IS, it can still be worth claiming. Getting another benefit may, for instance, mean you qualify for premiums, and therefore a higher rate of IS. For example, getting carer's allowance means you qualify for a carer premium – so you may be better off overall.

You cannot claim employment and support allowance and IS at the same time.

Passported benefits

If you are entitled to IS you are also entitled to:
- free prescriptions;
- free dental treatment;
- free sight tests;
- vouchers for glasses;
- Healthy Start food and vitamins;
- education benefits, such as free school meals;

See Chapter 11 for information about health benefits. You may also qualify for social fund payments (see Chapter 17).

Notes

2. Who is eligible

1 s124 SSCBA 1992
2 Regs 45 and 53 IS Regs
3 Reg 4ZA and Sch 1B IS Regs
4 Social Security (Lone Parents and Miscellaneous Amendments) Regulations 2008
5 s124(1)(d) SSCBA 1992
6 s142 SSCBA 1992; regs 2-7 CB Regs; reg 12 IS Regs
7 Reg 1(3) CB Regs, definition of 'advanced education'
8 Reg 1(3) CB Regs, definition of 'full-time education'
9 Reg 13(2)(a)-(e) IS Regs
10 R(IS) 9/94
11 R(SB) 2/87
12 CIS/11441/1995
13 Reg 13(3)(b) IS Regs
14 CIS/11766/1996
15 R(IS) 9/94
16 C(LC)A 2000; Children (Leaving Care) (England) Regulations 2001 No.2874; Children (Leaving Care) (Wales) Regulations 2001 No.2189; Children (Leaving Care) Act (Northern Ireland) 2002
17 ss23C, 24, 24A or 24B CA 1989
18 Reg 4ZA(2) IS Regs
19 Reg 61(1) IS Regs, definition of 'full-time student'
20 Regs 2(1) and 61(1) IS Regs, definition of 'period of study'
21 Reg 61(1) IS Regs, definition of 'last day of the course'
22 Reg 61(1) IS Regs
23 Reg 61(1) IS Regs
24 Reg 61(1) IS Regs
25 R(SB) 40/83; R(SB) 41/83
26 Reg 4ZA(3) and Sch 1B IS Regs
27 CIS/152/1994; R(IS) 15/98; CJSA/836/1998; R(IS) 1/00
28 Reg 61(4) IS Regs
29 Reg 61(2)(a) and (3) IS Regs
30 R(IS) 15/98; R(IS) 7/99; CJSA/836/1998; R(IS) 1/00
31 R(IS) 1/96
32 CIS/368/1992; R(IS) 6/97
33 R(JSA) 2/02
34 paras 30230–33 DMG
35 CIS/152/1994; R(IS) 15/98

3. Amount of benefit

36 Sch 3 IS Regs
37 Sch 3 para 14 IS Regs
38 Sch 3 para 3(6)(b) IS Regs
39 Sch 3 para 3(3) IS Regs
40 Sch 3 para 3(11)(viii) and (12) IS Regs

Chapter 15

Jobseeker's allowance

This chapter covers:
1. What is jobseeker's allowance (below)
2. Who is eligible (p178)
3. Amount of benefit (p188)
4. Claiming jobseeker's allowance (p190)
5. Challenging a decision (p191)
6. Other benefits and tax credits (p192)

Basic facts
– Jobseeker's allowance (JSA) is basic financial support for people who are required to be available for, and look for, work.
– Full-time students cannot normally claim.
– Student couples with children can claim in the summer vacation.
– Lone parents can claim in the long vacation if they are not eligible for income support.
– Part-time students can claim if they are available for, and actively seeking, work.
– There are two main types of JSA. Contribution-based JSA is paid if you have sufficient national insurance contributions; income-based JSA is means tested, so the amount you get is usually affected by your grant, loan and other income.
– JSA claims are administered by Jobcentre Plus.

1. What is jobseeker's allowance

Further information
This chapter gives an outline of the jobseeker's allowance rules and focuses on issues relevant to students. For more detailed information on the rules, see CPAG's *Welfare Benefits and Tax Credits Handbook*.

Jobseeker's allowance (JSA) is a benefit for people of working age (under 60 for women, under 65 for men) who are not in full-time paid work and who are expected to 'sign on' as available for and actively seeking work.

Full-time students cannot normally qualify for JSA, but there are exceptions. Part-time students can claim if they satisfy the rules for entitlement.

There are two main types of JSA. You can qualify for **contribution-based JSA** if you have paid (or been credited with) sufficient national insurance contributions. It is paid for 26 weeks and in addition to any student income or other income you might have, although certain pension payments of more than £50 a week reduce the amount you get. You can qualify for **income-based JSA** if you satisfy the means test. The amount you get is affected by your income, including some elements of student support. So even if you are entitled to income-based JSA, the amount may be reduced. Chapter 20 explains how your income affects your benefit.

A third type of JSA, **joint-claim JSA**, is very similar to income-based JSA. It is paid to some couples who have to make a joint-claim for JSA (see p190). In this *Handbook*, references to income-based JSA include references to joint-claim JSA unless otherwise stated.

2. **Who is eligible**

To qualify for jobseeker's allowance (JSA), you must satisfy the basic rules of entitlement. If you are studying full time, you must also satisfy additional rules. For information on whether you can qualify while you are in 'relevant education' or a full-time student, see pp180 and 181.

Basic rules

You can qualify for jobseeker's allowance (JSA) if:[1]
- you do not count as in full-time paid work, and if you are claiming income-based JSA, nor does your partner. For you, this is 16 hours or more a week. For your partner this is 24 hours a week;
- you are capable of work. However, you can continue to get JSA for up to two weeks if you are sick;
- you satisfy what are known as the 'labour market conditions' – ie, you:
  - are available for work. You must be willing and able to take up work immediately (although some people are allowed some notice). You must be prepared to work at least 40 hours a week. People with caring responsibilities (including for a child under 16) and disabled people can restrict their hours to less than 40 a week;
  - are actively seeking work;
  - have a current jobseeker's agreement. This sets out the hours you have agreed to work, the type of work you are looking for and any restrictions on, for example, hours, travel and pay;
- you are under pension age (60 for women, 65 for men);

- you are not getting income support (IS);
- you are present in Great Britain (although JSA can be paid in other countries in some circumstances); *and*
- you meet the conditions for either contribution-based JSA or income-based JSA, or both (see below). If you meet the conditions for both, you can get contribution-based JSA topped up by income-based JSA.

Overseas students

Most overseas students cannot claim JSA because they are subject to immigration control for benefit purposes. Even if you are entitled, a successful claim for benefit could affect your right to stay in the UK and it is best to get immigration advice before making a claim. If you are not eligible for benefit, but there are no restrictions on your partner, either as a student or as a 'person subject to immigration control', s/he may be able to claim instead of you. However, if s/he receives benefit and you are a 'person subject to immigration control', this may affect your right to remain in the UK under the immigration rules. You should get advice from UKCISA (see Appendix 2).

Contribution-based jobseeker's allowance

As well as satisfying all the basic rules above, to qualify for contribution-based JSA, you must:[2]
- have paid (or been credited with) sufficient national insurance contributions; *and*
- not have earnings above a specified amount. The specified amount is your rate of contribution-based JSA, plus one penny.

You need to have paid contributions of 25 times the lower earnings limit in one of the two complete tax years (6 April to 5 April) before the start of the benefit year (which runs from the first Sunday in January) in which you claim. You also need to have paid or been credited with contributions on earnings of 50 times the lower earnings limit in these years.

For example, you would qualify if you claimed JSA in 2008 and paid contributions on earnings of £4,100 in the tax year April 2005 to April 2006 and £4,200 in the tax year April 2006 to April 2007.

Income-based jobseeker's allowance

As well as satisfying all the basic rules above, to qualify for income-based JSA:[3]
- you must be aged 18 or over. You can still get income-based JSA if you are aged 16 or 17, but there are extra rules (see p188);
- neither you nor your partner are getting IS or pension credit (PC);
- you must satisfy residence conditions;
- you must not be subject to immigration control for benefit purposes (although there are some limited exceptions);

- you must have income of less than your 'applicable amount' (see p189);
- you must have savings and capital worth £16,000 or less.

See Chapter 20 for how income (including student income) and capital affect your benefit. **Note:** your student support payments count as income, *not* capital.

Studying and claiming jobseeker's allowance

The general rule is that you cannot qualify for JSA if you are studying full time. If you are already claiming JSA, your entitlement might be affected if you start studying full time. There are exceptions to the rules. If you are:
- under 20 and in 'relevant education', see below;
- a full-time student, see p181.

To see if you can claim JSA while studying part time, see p184.

Under 20 in relevant education

You cannot qualify for JSA if you are in what is known as 'relevant education'.[4] You count as in relevant education if you are a child or 'qualifying young person' for child benefit purposes (see p88). The rules are the same as for IS (see p160). However, unlike for IS, so long as you do not count as a full-time student (see p181), you are *not* treated as in relevant education if:[5]
- you are on the full-time education and training option of the New Deal; *or*
- you are on a non-advanced course, or one that does not count as a full-time course under the rules for full-time students. Your course might count as full time, even if you are studying for 12 hours or less, if the educational establishment defines your course as full time; *and*
  - you previously ceased relevant education and it is after your 'terminal date' (see p90); *and*
  - you got JSA, incapacity benefit (IB) or IS on the grounds that you were incapable of work, or were on a modern apprenticeship scheme or other similar training:
    - for at least three months before the start of the course; *or*
    - for three out of the last six months before the start of the course, if you were working the rest of the time.

If you cannot get JSA, you may have to rely on any statutory support to which you are entitled and any discretionary support your college or school may offer you (see Chapter 1 for more details). You may be able to claim IS if you fit into one of the groups who can claim while in relevant education (see p160). Alternatively, your parents (or a person acting in their place) may be able to claim child benefit and child tax credit for you.

Full-time students

If you are a full-time student, you cannot usually qualify for JSA for the duration of your course, including vacations, because you are treated as unavailable for work, even if you are available.[6] See p182 for exceptions to this rule. See p184 if you are studying part time and p187 if you give up or change your course. See Chapter 25 if you take time out from studies.

In general, students are expected to receive student support (eg, student loans and supplementary grants) to support them while in full-time education. See Chapters 1 to 6 for details of student support.

Who counts as a full-time student

You count as a full-time student if you are not a 'qualifying young person' for child benefit purposes (see p88) and:[7]

- you are under 19 and on a full-time course of advanced education; *or*
- you are 19 or over but under pension age (60 for women, 65 for men) and on a full-time course of study. If your course is full time, you are treated as a full-time student regardless of the level of the course, unless you are aged under 20 and can still be treated as in 'relevant education' (see p160).

You may also count as a full-time student while you are on a sandwich course (see p164).

For what counts as a course of advanced education, see p164, and as a full-time course of study, see p164. The rules are the same as for IS.

Note: if you are 19 and in relevant education, you do not count as a full-time student. Instead, the rules on p180 apply.

When you count as a full-time student

You count as a full-time student during your '**period of study**'. This is the whole of your course from the first day you attend or undertake the course until either the last day of your course, including short and long vacations, or until you abandon or are dismissed from it.[8] It includes a period of study in connection with the course after you have stopped doing the course itself. The Department for Work and Pensions (DWP) says it does not include freshers' week unless your course actually starts that week.[9]

You do not count as a student between courses. For example, you can claim JSA in the summer between completing an undergraduate degree and starting a postgraduate course.

If you are a postgraduate writing up your thesis at the end of your course, you may have difficulty getting JSA if this is regarded as 'a period of study undertaken by the student in connection with the course'.[10] However, the DWP says you are *not* a full-time student during the period after the end of the course when you are expected to complete any course work.[11] If you do claim, remember that to qualify for JSA you must be both available for and actively seeking work. If you say you are not prepared to fit your thesis around a job should one come up, the Jobcentre Plus office may decide that you are not available for work.

Full-time students who can claim jobseeker's allowance

Even if you are a full-time student, you can qualify for JSA if you are:

- one of a couple, both of you are full-time students and either or both of you are responsible for a child aged under 16 (or a 'qualifying young person' aged under 20 – see p88). This exception only applies during the summer vacation. The person who claims must be available for work and meet all the other basic rules for JSA;[12] *or*
- a lone parent with a dependent child aged under 16 (or a 'qualifying young person' aged under 20 – see p88). You must be available for work and meet the other basic rules for JSA. You may be able to claim IS instead, depending on the age of your youngest child;[13] *or*
- aged 25 or over and on a full-time, 'qualifying course', approved in advance by an employment officer at the Jobcentre Plus office. See p183 for further information; *or*
- a full-time student on an employment-related course approved in advance by an employment officer at the Jobcentre Plus office (for one period of up to two weeks in any 12 months);[14] *or*
- attending a compulsory residential course as part of an Open University course (for up to one week for each course);[15] *or*
- attending a residential training programme run by the Venture Trust (for one programme only for a maximum of four weeks in any 12-month period);[16] *or*
- a full-time student who has suspended your studies because of illness or caring responsibilities, and you have either recovered from your illness or ceased caring and are waiting to return to your course.[17] You can qualify for JSA for up to a year. See Chapter 25 for further information.

If you are a full-time student who cannot claim JSA, check to see if you can claim IS, employment and support allowance (ESA) or PC instead. If you have a partner who is not a full-time student, s/he may be able to claim IS, ESA, JSA or PC for you. Remember that your student support income is taken into account when working out how much IS, ESA, JSA or PC s/he can get.

Examples

Kiera and Mike are a couple and are both studying full time on degree courses. They have a seven-year-old son. Kiera signs on for JSA during the summer vacation, claiming benefit for herself and Mike. They also get housing benefit (HB), child tax credit (CTC) and child benefit throughout the year.

Marvin is unemployed and looking for work. His partner, Claudette, is studying full time for a degree. They have two children so get CTC and child benefit. Marvin can claim JSA, but the amount he receives is affected by Claudette's student loan for living costs and maintenance grant. Her parents' learning allowance is ignored. Marvin may also receive HB and council tax benefit.

In some situations, you can take a full-time '**qualifying course**' and continue to get JSA. While you are on the course, you are treated as available for and actively seeking work. You can get JSA while attending a 'qualifying course' if you:[18]

- are aged 25 or over; *and*
- have been 'receiving benefit' (see below) for at least two years at the time the course starts; *and*
- have been given approval to attend the course by an employment officer at the Jobcentre Plus office; *and*
- satisfy the conditions for being treated as available for and actively seeking work (see below).

Definitions

A '**qualifying course**' is a course of further or higher education which is employment-related and lasts no more than 12 consecutive months.[19] A higher level course can also be a qualifying course if your employment officer agrees.

'**Receiving benefit**' means getting JSA or IS as an unemployed person, or national insurance credits for unemployment or because you are 60 or over.[20] It also means getting IS as an asylum seeker, but only if you have been accepted as having refugee status or have been granted exceptional leave to remain in the UK, and you were getting IS as an asylum seeker, or were subsequently paid backdated IS, at some time in the 12 weeks before you were first entitled to JSA, which includes the date that your course starts.

While on a qualifying course, you are treated as being available for work in any week:[21]

- that falls entirely or partly in term time, so long as you provide written evidence within five days of it being requested confirming that you are attending and making satisfactory progress on the course. This must be signed by you and by the college or educational establishment; *or*
- in which you are taking exams relating to the course; *or*
- that falls entirely in a vacation if you are willing and able to take up any 'casual employment' immediately. 'Casual employment' means employment you can leave without giving notice or, if you must give notice, which you can leave before the end of the vacation.

While on a qualifying course, if you are treated as being available for work, you are also treated as actively seeking work.[22] If this is in any week which falls entirely in a vacation, you must take such steps as can reasonably be expected in order to have the best prospects of getting casual employment.

Studying part time

You count as a part-time student if you are studying, but you are not in 'relevant education' (see p160) or a full-time student (see p181). In the latter case, you should check with the education institution to see how you are registered and whether your course counts as part time. See p166 for further information about what counts as part time. The rules are the same as for IS.

You can qualify for JSA while studying part time if you meet the labour market conditions (ie, you are available for work, actively seeking work and you have a valid jobseeker's agreement). If you have agreed restrictions with the DWP on the hours that you are available for work there are special rules that can help you claim JSA and study part time (see p185).

Examples

Tina is attending a further education college and studying for A levels funded by the Learning and Skills Council. She has 15 hours a week of classes. She is a part-time student.

Parminda is studying for a degree in social science at a university in Wales. The university describes the course as part time and, therefore, the course is counted as part time for JSA purposes.

Studying and availability for work

When you claim JSA you may have agreed which hours of the day and which days of the week you are available for work. This 'pattern of availability' is set out in your jobseeker's agreement. You are allowed to do this so long as the hours you choose still give you a reasonable chance of getting work and do not considerably reduce your prospects of getting work.

If the hours you study are completely different to the hours you have agreed to be available for work, you should have no problem. But if there is some overlap, or if you have agreed to be available for work at any time of day and on any day of the week, the Jobcentre Plus office must be satisfied that you are available for work despite your course. It expects you to:[23]

- arrange the hours of the course to fit round a job;
- be prepared to give up the course if a job comes up;
- be ready to take time off the course to attend a job interview; *and*
- be ready to start work immediately.

Deciding if you are available for and actively seeking work

Guidance tells Jobcentre Plus office decision makers to look at various factors when deciding whether you are genuinely available for work while studying part time. These are:[24]

- what you are doing to look for work;
- whether your course will help you get work. Bear in mind that if you say the course is necessary to get the kind of job you want, the Jobcentre Plus office may assume you are not prepared to give it up to do another kind of job and decide that you are not available for work. It is important that you stress how the course will improve your general employability skills, such as communication, IT, team work or organisational skills;
- whether you can be contacted about a possible job if you are studying away from home. Some colleges offer a central phone number you can give. You should check this with student services;
- whether you gave up work or training to do the course;
- your hours of attendance on the course;
- whether it is possible to change the hours if necessary;
- whether if you missed some attendance you could still complete the course;
- how much you paid for the course and whether any fee could be refunded if you gave up the course. The Jobcentre Plus office is likely to assume that you would not be prepared to give up the course to take a job if you have paid a significant amount in course fees;
- whether any grant would need to be repaid if you gave up your course.

The guidance for decision makers states that where a number of claimants are following the same course some may be able to show that they are available, but others may not.[25] The decision maker should not operate a blanket policy of treating all students on the same course as not being available. Equally, you cannot assume that you will be treated as available just because other people on your course are getting JSA. Each claim should be considered individually. The decision maker assumes that you may be less willing to leave a course if you are near the end of the course, or as the chance of obtaining a qualification approaches.[26] When you claim JSA, you are given a student questionnaire (Form ES567S, *Attending a Training or Education Course*) to complete, asking about such factors.

Once you have qualified for JSA, you must continue to be available for and actively seeking work. When you 'sign on' you must show what steps you have taken to look for work – eg, checking job advertisements or applying for jobs. If you do not look for work each week, or you turn down a job or an interview, you could lose your JSA under a sanction, which could be for up to 26 weeks. If this happens you can appeal. You might be able to get the sanction period reduced or have it overturned. You should seek advice and ask for a hardship payment in the meantime.

If you have restricted your availability for work

Special rules allow your course of study to be ignored when deciding whether you are available for work. These apply if you are a part-time student, and:[27]

- you have been allowed to restrict the total hours you are available for work:
  - because of your physical or mental condition, caring responsibilities or because you are working short time; *or*
  - to at least 40 hours a week; *and*
- the hours of your course are within your 'pattern of availability' (see p184) and you are willing and able to rearrange these to take up a job at times that fall within this pattern; *and*
- you got JSA, incapacity benefit (IB) or IS on the grounds that you were incapable of work, or were on a training course under specific provisions:
  - for at least three months before the start of the course; *or*
  - for three out of the last six months before the start of the course, if you were working the rest of the time.

The three-month and six-month periods can only begin after you have reached your 'terminal date' (see p90).

Note: you still have to be available for and actively seeking work during the rest of the week when you are not on your course.

Health-related courses

If you attend a health-related course for which you are entitled to receive an NHS bursary, you are treated as attending a full-time course.

Modular courses

A **'modular course'** is one made up of two or more modules and the institution requires you to do a certain number successfully to complete the course.[28] If you are attending or undertaking part of a modular course that is full time according to the rules described above, you are treated as a full-time student for the duration of the modules from the day those modules begin until the last day of registration on those modules (or earlier if you abandon the course or are dismissed from it).[29] This includes all vacations during the modules on which you are registered and, except for the final module, the vacation immediately following the modules. It also includes periods when you are attending the course to do re-sits of any modules you have undertaken on a full-time basis. This is the case even if you are registered part time with the institution while you are doing these re-sits. You should seek advice from your students' union or institution's student services about the student support to which you may be entitled while you are re-sitting.

Because the rules provide no definition of a full-time course (unless it is funded by the Learning and Skills Council or the Welsh Assembly), you may be able to argue that you are not attending a full-time course.[30] If you are in any doubt, you should seek advice.

If the modular course allows you to undertake some modules on a part-time basis, you are not excluded from JSA while you are studying part time. Remember, however, that you must not be studying any modules that you have previously studied on a full-time basis.

Example

Carlton is 42 and single. He started a BSc undergraduate degree in October 2008. He registers for six modules in year one on a full-time basis. For this academic year, until 31 August 2009, Carlton is treated as a full-time student for JSA and cannot claim.

At the end of year one, he fails a module. For year two, he registers on a part-time basis to re-take his failed module and to take two new modules. Although he is registered with the university on a part-time basis, for JSA purposes from 1 September 2009 to 31 August 2010 he is still classed as a full-time student because he is undertaking a module he has previously done on a full-time basis. He cannot claim JSA during this period.

During year three, he registers with his university on a part-time basis to study three new modules. From 1 September 2010 to 31 August 2011 he will be counted as a part-time student for JSA. As long as he meets the conditions for receiving JSA (eg, being available for and actively seeking work), he may claim.

Giving up or changing your course

If you are in any of the circumstances below, your entitlement to any student support you may receive might be affected and you should seek specialist advice.

- If you abandon your course or are dismissed from it you can claim JSA from the day after that date so long as you satisfy the other rules of entitlement.
- If you complete one course and start a different one, you are not treated as a student during any period between the courses.[31]
- If you are on a sandwich course (see p164), or your course includes a compulsory or optional period on placement, you count as a full-time student during the sandwich or placement period even if you have been unable to find a placement, or your placement comes to an end prematurely.[32]
- If you attend a course at an education institution which provides training or instruction to enable you to take examinations set and marked by an entirely different and unconnected body (ie, a professional institution) and you abandon or take time out from it because you fail the examinations set by the other body (or you finish the course at the education institution but fail the exams), you may be able to argue that you are not a student from the date you left the course at your education institution even if you intend to re-sit the examinations set by the other body at a later date.[33]

If you are taking time out of your course for any other reason, see Chapter 25.

You may also retain entitlement to some student support on a statutory or discretionary basis – eg, through student loans or hardship funds. You should seek specialist advice.

Changing from full-time to part-time attendance

If you have to change from full-time to part-time attendance on a full-time course for personal reasons, you may be able to argue that you have abandoned your full-time course and are registered on a part-time course and, therefore, that you are not a full-time student.[34] If, because of exam failure or any other reason, you change to a different course, or your college requires you to change the level of course (eg, from A level to GCSE) and this involves a change from full-time to part-time study, you should argue that you are a part-time student (see p184).[35] However, changing your attendance may affect your entitlement to any student support you may be receiving. You should seek advice on this before acting.

16/17-year-olds

You can usually only get JSA if you are aged 18 or over. If you are under 18 you can get income-based JSA in some circumstances, provided you meet all the other rules of entitlement. The situations in which you can qualify for JSA include the following.

- You are in severe hardship. All your circumstances should be considered. Payments are discretionary and usually for just eight weeks at a time.
- You come within one of the groups of people who can claim IS (see p158). In this case, you may be able to choose whether to claim JSA or IS.
- You are a part of a couple with a child.
- You are married (or in a civil partnership) and your partner is aged 18 or over. JSA is paid for a limited period after you leave education or training.
- You are married (or in a civil partnership) and your partner is under 18 and:
  – registered for work or training; *or*
  – long-term sick or disabled; *or*
  – a student who can claim IS; *or*
  – a carer who can claim IS.
  JSA can be paid for a limited period after you leave education or training.

3. Amount of benefit

The amount of jobseeker's allowance (JSA) you get depends on whether you are claiming contribution-based JSA or income-based JSA.

Contribution-based jobseeker's allowance

Contribution-based JSA is paid at different weekly rates, depending on your age.

You may get less money if you have part-time earnings or an occupational or personal pension, but the amount is not affected by a student loan or grant. Contribution-based JSA is only paid for up to 26 weeks. You can claim income-based JSA to top-up your contribution-based JSA or after your contribution-based JSA runs out if you satisfy the means test.

Income-based jobseeker's allowance

Income-based JSA is a means-tested benefit that tops up your income to a level set by the Government. The amount you get depends on your basic weekly needs and those of your partner (your 'applicable amount') and on how much income and capital you have (see Chapter 20). Some students may find, therefore, that they can only receive JSA for part of any year (eg, during the summer vacation).

Your applicable amount is made up of:
- a personal allowance;
- premiums for any special needs – eg, if you are disabled or are caring for a disabled person;
- housing costs (see p170), principally for mortgage interest payments.

The total of these is called your 'applicable amount'. If you have no other income (the student loan and some grants count as income), you are paid your full applicable amount. Otherwise, any income you do have is topped up with income-based JSA to the level of your applicable amount. If your weekly income is above your applicable amount, you are not entitled to income-based JSA. See Chapter 20 for how to work out your weekly income. The rules are the same as for income support (IS), except for some couples, when the following applies.
- If only one of you is under 18, you get the higher £94.95 personal allowance if the younger partner is responsible for a child or is eligible for both income-based JSA or severe hardship payments *and* IS or income-related employment and support allowance (ESA).
- If both of you are under 18, you get the higher £72.35 personal allowance if:
  - you are responsible for a child; *or*
  - you were both single, both of you would be eligible for income-based JSA or your partner would be eligible for IS or income-related ESA; *or*
  - you are both eligible for severe hardship payments, or one of you is and the other is eligible for income-based JSA, IS or income-related ESA; *or*
  - you are married or civil partners and one of you is registered with the Careers Service, or both of you are eligible for income-based JSA.
- Joint-claim couples can get a disability premium (at the couple rate) if one has had limited capability for work for 364 days (196 days if terminally ill). You need to claim ESA to establish limited capability for work even if you might not get it.

4. **Claiming jobseeker's allowance**

If you think you might be entitled to jobseeker's allowance (JSA), you should claim as soon as you can. There are only very limited situations where backdating is allowed.

You can make initial contact about claiming by telephone or letter. You may also be able to start a claim online at www.dwp.gov.uk/eservice. The date of your initial contact is important because it usually determines the date from when you can be paid JSA.

You must usually start your claim by telephoning a 'contact centre'. Your local Jobcentre Plus office has the number and it may also be displayed in local advice centres and libraries. The centre takes basic information, then calls you back to go through the details of your claim. The date of an interview is set. You will be sent a statement recording the information you gave over the telephone, which you are asked to sign, and details of the evidence and information you should bring with you to the interview. The signed statement comprises your official claim.

It is best for you to start your claim in this way if you can. However, if you cannot or you do not want to use the telephone to start your claim, the Jobcentre Plus office can still deal with your claim in other ways. You might, for example, be invited for a face-to-face interview or, in some cases, an old-style claim form can be accepted. JSA claim forms are only available from Jobcentre Plus offices.

Whenever you call the Department for Work and Pensions (or Department for Social Development), you need to provide your national insurance number. You also need this number, as well as that of your partner, when you claim, as well as other information required on the claim form.

Showing you are available for and actively seeking work

When you claim JSA, you may be given a form to complete about the work for which you are available and how you are actively seeking work. The information you give forms the basis of your jobseeker's agreement. You may also be asked to fill in a student questionnaire. When completing the forms, remember that even though you are a student, you are expected to be available for and actively seeking work. In your answers you should make sure that you do not cast doubt on your willingness to work. If you are a part-time student, you may be asked to get a 'learning agreement' from your college to show that you are studying part time.

Couples

If you are a full-time student but your partner is not, s/he can claim JSA for both of you if s/he is eligible for JSA. In some cases, you both need to claim JSA (known as '**joint-claim JSA**'), but only your partner may need to continue to 'sign on' and look for work. Similarly, your partner can get JSA for both of you if you are not yet a full-time student, but you have applied for, or been accepted on a course. You *must* make a joint claim if:

- neither of you has dependent children; *and*
- at least one of you is 18 or over; *and*
- at least one of you was born after 28 October 1947.

Getting paid

Jobseeker's allowance is usually paid directly into your bank (or similar) account. Which account it goes into is up to you. If you do not want your benefit to go into an account that is overdrawn, give the DWP (or DSD) details of an alternative account if you have access to, or can open, one.

If you are overpaid JSA, you might have to repay it.

5. **Challenging a decision**

If you think a decision about your jobseeker's allowance (JSA) is wrong (eg, because the decision maker got the facts or law wrong, or your circumstances have changed since the decision was made), there are a number of ways you can try to get the decision changed.

- You can seek a revision or a supersession of the decision. In some cases you have to show specific grounds. In others, you must apply within a strict time limit.
- You can appeal to an independent tribunal. There are strict time limits for appealing – usually one month from the date you are sent or given the decision. You can make a late appeal in limited circumstances.

If you are considering challenging a decision, you should seek advice as soon as possible.

If your claim for JSA is unsuccessful, consider whether you can challenge the decision. You should bear the following in mind.

- As student claims are not necessarily commonplace and the rules about how student income is treated are complex, it is always worth checking a decision with a student adviser in your students' union or institution.
- If the decision maker says you are a full-time student, but you disagree, you should get advice to see if there are grounds for challenging the decision.
- Claims for JSA are sometimes refused because the Department for Work and Pensions (or Department for Social Development) miscalculates student income or takes the wrong types of student income into account.
- If your JSA is not paid because you are sanctioned – eg, if the decision maker says you gave up a job voluntarily or were dismissed for misconduct, it is always worth getting advice about challenging the decision. Even if a tribunal

agrees that a sanction should be applied, it can reduce the length of the sanction period. However, getting advice is important because a tribunal can also *increase* the period of a sanction.

- You might not currently be entitled to JSA, but would be once you or a member of your family become entitled to a 'qualifying benefit' – eg, disability living allowance or carer's allowance. In this case, you need to claim. Your initial claim will be refused. However, if you claim again once the qualifying benefit is awarded, your JSA will be backdated to the date of your original claim, or the date on which the qualifying benefit was first payable (if later). Alternatively, you might be entitled to a higher rate of JSA once the 'qualifying benefit' is awarded. In this case, you need to ask for a revision or a supersession of your JSA award. Your JSA should then be increased from the date the qualifying benefit was first payable.

Note: you may find that you can qualify for JSA in the summer vacation (even if you cannot qualify during term time) – eg, if you have children or because of the way your grant and loan are divided throughout the year. In this case, you need to claim again as soon as you think you might qualify.

6. **Other benefits and tax credits**

You cannot get income support (IS) and jobseeker's allowance (JSA) at the same time. If you are eligible for both, you need to choose which to claim. In general, the amounts of income-based JSA and IS are the same, but you are not expected to be available for work to qualify for IS.

Income-based JSA tops up any other income you have to the level of your basic requirements (your applicable amount), so most other benefits are taken into account as income when working out the amount. This means they reduce your JSA pound for pound. Disability living allowance, attendance allowance, guardian's allowance, housing benefit (HB) and council tax benefit (CTB) are, however, always disregarded as income.

If you get income-based JSA, you are also eligible for HB and CTB if you meet the other qualifying criteria for these benefits.

Child tax credit (CTC) is ignored as income when assessing JSA. Child benefit is ignored unless you still have amounts for children in your income-based JSA and you do not get CTC. In this case, £10.50 a week of your child benefit is disregarded if you have a child under one.

Even though getting a benefit may reduce your income-based JSA, it can still be worth claiming. Getting another benefit may, for instance, mean you qualify for premiums and, therefore, a higher rate. For example, if your partner gets carer's allowance, you qualify for a carer's premium – so you may be better off overall.

Passported benefits

If you are entitled to income-based JSA, you are also entitled to:
- free prescriptions;
- free dental treatment;
- free sight tests;
- vouchers for glasses;
- Healthy Start food and vitamins;
- education benefits, such as free school meals.

See Chapter 11 for information about health benefits. You may also qualify for social fund payments (see Chapter 17).

Contribution-based JSA does not give you automatic access to these benefits, but you may qualify for health benefits on low-income grounds (see Chapter 11).

Notes

2. Who is eligible
1 s1 JSA 1995
2 s2 JSA 1995
3 ss3 and 13 JSA 1995
4 s1(2)(g) JSA 1995; reg 54 JSA Regs
5 Reg 54(3) JSA Regs
6 Reg 15(1)(a) JSA Regs
7 Reg 1(3) JSA Regs, definition of 'full-time student'
8 Regs 1(3A) and 4 JSA Regs
9 para 30221 Vol 6 DMG
10 Reg 4(b) JSA Regs
11 Para 30238 DMG
12 Reg 15(3)(a) JSA Regs
13 Reg 15(3)(b) JSA Regs
14 Reg 14(1)(a) JSA Regs
15 Reg 14(1)(f) JSA Regs
16 Reg 14(1)(k) JSA Regs
17 Reg 1(3D) and (3E) JSA Regs
18 Reg 17A(2), (3) and (5) JSA Regs
19 Reg 17A(7) and (8) JSA Regs
20 Reg 17A(7), (7A) and (7B) JSA Regs
21 Reg 17A(3) and (7) JSA Regs
22 Reg 21A JSA Regs
23 paras 21239–41 DMG
24 para 21242 Vol 4 DMG
25 para 21243 DMG
26 para 21244 DMG
27 Reg 11 JSA Regs
28 Reg 1(3C) JSA Regs
29 Reg 1(3A)(a) and (3B) JSA Regs
30 R(IS) 15/98; R(IS) 7/99; CJSA/836/1998; R(IS) 1/00
31 R(IS) 1/96
32 CIS/368/1992; R(IS) 6/97
33 R(JSA) 2/02
34 paras 30230–33 DMG
35 CIS/152/1994; R(IS) 15/98

Chapter 16

Maternity, paternity and adoption benefits

This chapter looks at:
1. What are maternity, paternity and adoption benefits (below)
2. Who is eligible (p195)
3. Amount of benefit (p197)
4. Claiming maternity, paternity and adoption benefits (p197)
5. Challenging a decision (p198)
6. Other benefits and tax credits (p199)

Basic facts

– Women having a baby can claim statutory maternity pay (SMP) if they have an employer, or maternity allowance (MA) if they have recently worked or been self-employed.
– The mother's (or adopter's) partner can claim statutory paternity pay (SPP).
– Someone adopting a child can claim statutory adoption pay (SAP) or SPP.
– Part-time and full-time students are eligible for these benefits.
– SMP, SPP and SAP are administered by employers. Claims for MA are administered by the Department for Work and Pensions.

1. **What are maternity, paternity and adoption benefits**

Further information
This chapter gives an outline of the rules for maternity, paternity and adoption benefits and focuses on issues relevant to students. For more detailed information on the rules, see CPAG's *Welfare Benefits and tax Credits Handbook*

Statutory maternity pay

You can get statutory maternity pay (SMP) if you are pregnant and within the 11 weeks before your expected week of childbirth, or if you have just had a baby. You must have an employer and earn at least £90 a week on average. SMP is paid for 39 weeks.

Maternity allowance

Maternity allowance (MA) is a benefit for women who have recently worked, either in an employed or self-employed capacity. It is paid for up to 39 weeks.

Statutory paternity pay

Statutory paternity pay (SPP) is a benefit for people whose partners are having a baby or adopting a child. It is payable for two weeks if you are taking leave from work to care for your partner or for the child. Unmarried and same-sex partners can claim SPP.

Statutory adoption pay

Statutory adoption pay (SAP) is a benefit for people who are adopting a child and earning an average of at least £90 a week from employment. It is paid for a maximum of 39 weeks. If a couple (including same-sex couples) are adopting a child, one can claim SAP and the other can claim SPP for two weeks.

Future changes

The Government intends to increase the payment period for SMP, SAP and MA from 39 weeks to 52 weeks and to introduce 'additional SPP', paid during the year after the birth or adoption for a period of up to six months. The exact date when these changes will be implemented is not yet known, but it is unlikely they will affect you if your baby is due before April 2010.

2. **Who is eligible**

Students are eligible for maternity, paternity and adoption benefits if they meet the basic conditions. What follows is a brief outline of the qualifying conditions.

Statutory maternity pay

You can get statutory maternity pay (SMP) if:
- you are pregnant (and are within the 11 weeks before your expected week of childbirth) or have recently had a baby;[1] *and*
- you have worked for the same employer for 26 weeks ending with the 15th week before your expected week of childbirth;[2] *and*
- you have ceased work for the employer who pays you SMP; *and*
- your average gross earnings are at least £90 a week;[3] *and*

- you give your employer the correct notice (at least 28 days before you expect a payment to start or, if this is not practicable, as soon as practicable after that date).

You must provide evidence of the expected date of birth – eg, by providing a Form MAT B1, within three weeks after the start of the maternity pay period.

Maternity allowance

You can get maternity allowance if you cannot get SMP and:
- you are pregnant (and within the 11 weeks before your expected week of childbirth) or have recently had a baby;[4]
- you have worked, in either an employed or self-employed capacity, for at least 26 weeks out of the 66 weeks before your expected week of childbirth;[5] *and*
- your average earnings are at least £30 a week.[6]

Statutory paternity pay

You can get statutory paternity pay (SPP) if:[7]
- in either the 15th week before the expected week of childbirth or the week in which the adopter is told of being matched with a child, you have been employed by the same employer for at least 26 weeks, and you continue in that job up to the day the baby is born or the day the child is placed for adoption; *and*
- your average gross earnings are at least £90 a week; *and*
- you give your employer the correct notice and information (at least 28 days before your pay period is due to start, or if this is not practicable, as soon as practicable after that date); *and*
- you are not working for the employer who pays you SPP; *and*
- you do not work for any other employer.

In addition, for claims based on birth:
- you are the child's father or partner of the child's mother and you will be caring for the child or supporting the mother; *and*
- you are the child's father and you will have responsibility for his/her upbringing *or* your partner is the child's mother and, apart from the mother's responsibility, you will have the main responsibility for the child's upbringing.

In addition, for claims based on adoption:
- your partner or you and your partner are adopting a child; *and*
- the person adopting the child is doing so under UK law; *and*
- you have (or expect to have) the main responsibility for the upbringing of the child (along with the other adopter); *and*
- you intend to care for the child or to support the person adopting the child; *and*

- you have not elected to receive statutory adoption pay (SAP).

You can use Form SC3 (for claims based on birth) or SC4 (for claims based on adoption) to provide the necessary information to your employer. You can obtain these from your employer or from HM Revenue and Customs.

You cannot get both SPP (adoption) and SAP at the same time, although one member of a couple can claim SAP while the other claims SPP (adoption).

Statutory adoption pay

You can get SAP if:[8]
- you are adopting a child; *and*
- the child has been placed with both you and your co-adopter and your co-adopter is not claiming SAP; *and*
- you have not elected to receive SPP; *and*
- you have worked for the same employer for 26 weeks, ending with the week in which you are told you have been matched with a child for adoption; *and*
- your average gross earnings are at least £90 a week; *and*
- you have ceased work for the employer who pays you SAP; *and*
- you give your employer the correct notice and information at least 28 days before you expect a payment to start, or if this is not practicable, as soon as possible after that date.

3. Amount of benefit

Rates from April 2008

Statutory maternity pay	First six weeks: 90% of average weekly earnings
	Following 33 weeks: £117.18 (or 90% of earnings if less)[9]
Maternity allowance	For 39 weeks: £117.18 (or 90% of earnings if less)
Statutory paternity pay	For two weeks: £117.18 (or 90% of earnings if less)
Statutory adoption pay	For 39 weeks: £117.18 (or 90% of earnings if less)[10]

4. Claiming maternity, paternity and adoption benefits

You claim statutory maternity pay (SMP), statutory paternity pay (SPP) and statutory adoption pay (SAP) from your employer. You must provide appropriate notice and information. For SMP you must provide evidence of the expected date of birth. You can use Form MAT B1, issued by your doctor or midwife. For SPP you can use Form SC3 for SPP (birth) and Form SC4 for SPP (adoption) to give the required information to your employer. These forms are produced by HM Revenue and Customs and are available from www.hmrc.gov.uk.

You claim maternity allowance (MA) from your local Jobcentre Plus office on Form MA1.

Getting paid

Your employer usually pays SMP, SPP or SAP in the same way as your normal wages or salary.

MA is usually paid directly into your bank (or similar) account. Which account it goes into is up to you. If you do not want your benefit to go into an account that is overdrawn, give the Department for Work and Pensions details of an alternative account if you have access to, or can open, one.

If you are overpaid MA, you might have to repay it. If your employer attempts to recover SMP, SPP or SAP it says you were not entitled to, you should seek advice.

5. Challenging a decision

If you think a decision about your maternity allowance is wrong (eg, because the decision maker got the facts or law wrong, or your circumstances have changed since the decision was made), there are a number of ways that you can try to get the decision changed.

- You can seek a revision or supersession of the decision. In some cases you have to show specific grounds. In others you must apply within a strict time limit.
- You can appeal to an independent tribunal. There are strict time limits for appealing – usually one month from the date you are sent or given the decision. You can make a late appeal in limited circumstances.

If you are considering challenging a decision, you should seek advice as soon as possible.

If you disagree with your employer's decision on your entitlement to statutory maternity pay (SMP), statutory paternity pay (SPP) or statutory adoption pay (SAP), or your employer fails to make a decision, you can ask HM Revenue and Customs (the Revenue) to make a formal decision on your entitlement. You should normally apply on Form SMP 14 (for SMP), SPP 14 (for SPP) and SAP 14 (for SAP).

If either you or your employer are unhappy with the decision you can appeal to the tax appeal commissioner.[11] Your appeal should reach the Revenue within 30 days of the date the decision was issued.[12]

6. **Other benefits and tax credits**

There are a number of other benefits you may be able to get when you have a baby, including the following:

- When the baby is born, you can get child benefit (see Chapter 8).
- You can also claim child tax credit (CTC) or increase your existing award. Tell HM Revenue and Customs within three months of the birth. See Chapter 18 for further details.
- If you are under 19 (or under age 20 if you started the course before your 19th birthday) and in full-time non-advanced education, you count as in relevant education and you are eligible for income support (IS) as a parent (father or mother). See Chapter 14 for further details.
- If you are a lone parent, you are eligible for IS and housing benefit (HB) as a full-time student. If your baby has not yet been born (or your child has not yet been placed with you for adoption), you may still qualify for IS and HB on another ground – eg, if you have been incapable of work for at least 28 weeks. See Chapter 12 for further details.
- If you get a qualifying benefit (including IS and CTC at a rate above the family element), you can claim a Sure Start maternity grant from the social fund within three months of the birth (see p201). If you are waiting for a decision on your qualifying benefit, make sure you still claim the maternity grant within three months of the birth and tell the Department for Work and Pensions that you are waiting for the decision on the qualifying benefit. See Chapter 17 for more details.

Notes

2. **Who is eligible**
1 s164(2)(c) SSCBA 1992
2 s164(2)(a) SSCBA 1992
3 s164(2)(b) SSCBA 1992
4 s35 SSCBA 1992
5 s35(1)(b) SSCBA 1992
6 ss35(1)(c) and 35A(4) SSCBA 1992
7 ss171ZA(2) and (3), 171ZB(2) and (3), 171ZC, and 171ZE(4) and (7) SSCBA 1992; regs 4 and 11 SPPSAP(G) Regs; reg 4(2)(b) and (c) Paternity and Adoption Leave Regulations 2002, No.2788
8 s171ZL(2)–(4) and (6) SSCBA 1992; regs 23 and 24 SPPSAP(G) Regs

3. **Amount of benefit**
9 s166 SS CBA 1992
10 Regs 2 and 3 Statutory Paternity Pay and Statutory Adoption Pay (Weekly Rates) Regulations 2002, No. 2818

5. **Challenging a decision**
11 S11(2)(a) SSCA(TF)A 1999
12 S12(1) SSCA(TF)A 1999

Chapter 17

The social fund

This chapter looks at:

Basic facts

– To get help from the social fund (except crisis loans) you must receive a qualifying benefit (eg, income support or child tax credit at a rate higher than the family element).

– Both part-time and full-time students can qualify if they satisfy the rules of entitlement.

– If you are in receipt of a qualifying benefit it does not matter how much student support income you get – this has already been taken into account in working out your qualifying benefit.

– Full-time students under 20 who are on a non-advanced course or are in approved training cannot get a crisis loan unless they are eligible for income support, pension credit or income-based jobseeker's allowance.

– Other full-time students can claim a crisis loan, but if they do not get income support, pension credit or income-based jobseeker's allowance they can only claim for expenses arising out of a disaster.

– The social fund has two parts, comprising regulated and discretionary payments.

– The social fund is administered by local Jobcentre Plus offices.

1. **What is the social fund**

The social fund comprises two types of payments.[1]
- **Regulated social fund** payments, made up of:
  - Sure Start maternity grants;
  - funeral payments;
  - cold weather payments;
  - winter fuel payments.
- **Discretionary social fund** payments, made up of:
  - community care grants;
  - budgeting loans;
  - crisis loans.

You are entitled to regulated social fund payments if you satisfy the qualifying conditions.

The discretionary part of the social fund has a fixed budget.[2] There is no legal entitlement to a payment and no right of appeal to an independent tribunal if you are refused. Even though you might meet all the criteria for a payment, you may not get one. If you are turned down, you should ask for a review. If you are refused again, you can ask for a further review by social fund inspectors.[3]

2. **Sure Start maternity grants**

A Sure Start maternity grant is a grant of £500 to help with the costs of a new baby.[4]

To qualify you or your partner must have:[5]
- been awarded:
  - income support; *or*
  - income-based jobseeker's allowance; *or*
  - child tax credit at a rate above the family element (£1,090 a year when you have a child under one, otherwise £545); *or*
  - income-related employment and support allowance; *or*
  - working tax credit including a disability or severe disability element; *or*
  - pension credit (guarantee or savings credit); *and*
- received health and welfare advice from a health professional.

In addition:

- you or a member of your family must be pregnant or have given birth in the last three months (including where the baby was stillborn); *or*
- you or your partner must have adopted a child aged under 12 months.

Note: you can also qualify if you and your spouse have been granted a parental order allowing you to have a child by a surrogate mother.

You claim on Form SF100, which you can get from the local Jobcentre Plus office or from www.jobcentreplus.gov.uk. You must make your claim up to 11 weeks before the birth or within three months after the birth (or adoption, residence order or parental order).[6]

If you are waiting to hear about a claim for one of the qualifying benefits, the Department for Work and Pensions may defer making a decision until the claim for the qualifying benefit is decided. If your maternity grant application is refused in these circumstances, you must re-claim within three months of the decision awarding the qualifying benefit. If you claim before your baby is born you must submit a maternity certificate (MATB1) or another medical note showing your expected date of childbirth. If you claim after the child is born you must show a maternity, birth or adoption certificate.

3. **Funeral payments**

A funeral payment can be made to help with burial or cremation costs. To qualify you must accept responsibility for the funeral expenses[7] and must have been awarded:[8]

- income support; *or*
- income-based jobseeker's allowance; *or*
- child tax credit at a rate above the family element (£1,090 a year when you have a child under one, otherwise £545); *or*
- income-related employment and support allowance; *or*
- working tax credit including a disability or severe disability element; *or*
- pension credit (guarantee or savings credit); *or*
- housing benefit; *or*
- council tax benefit; *or*
- second adult rebate where you are the second adult.

You qualify for a payment if you were the partner of the deceased, or the deceased was a child for whom you were responsible. You may also qualify if you were the parent, son or daughter of the deceased, or a close relative or friend of hers/his. In this case you must show that it is reasonable for you to accept responsibility for the funeral expenses. The rules on this are complicated and there are exceptions, so you should seek advice if you are refused a payment.[9]

You must claim on Form SF200 (which you can get from your local Jobcentre Plus office or download from the Department for Work and Pensions (DWP) website) at the local DWP office. You must claim within three months of the funeral.[10] If you are waiting to hear about a claim for one of the qualifying benefits, the DWP may defer making a decision on your claim until the claim for the qualifying benefit is decided. If your funeral payment application is refused in these circumstances, you must re-claim within three months of the decision awarding the qualifying benefit.

4. **Cold weather payments**

Cold weather payments are made to help you with heating costs during periods of cold weather.

A period of cold weather is a period of seven consecutive days during which the average daily temperature is equal to or below 0 degrees Celsius. A payment of £8.50 is made for each week of cold weather – this has been increased temporarily to £25 for the period between 1 November 2008 and 31 March 2009. There is no need to apply as the Department for Work and Pensions (DWP) should automatically select those people who are eligible and send out payments.[11]

To qualify for a cold weather payment, you must have been awarded income support (IS), income-based jobseeker's allowance (JSA) or pension credit (PC) guarantee or savings credit for at least one day in the period of cold weather. Unless you are entitled to PC:[12]

- your IS or income-based JSA must include a disability, severe disability, enhanced disability, disabled child, pensioner or higher pensioner premium; *or*
- you must be responsible for a child under five; *or*
- you must get child tax credit which includes a disability or severe disability element.

There are no time limits for claiming a cold weather payment as you do not have to submit a claim. If, however, you think you have missed out on a payment you should have received, contact your local Jobcentre Plus office.

5. **Winter fuel payments**

Winter fuel payments are made to people aged 60 or over who are ordinarily resident in Great Britain and who were aged 60 or over by the third Monday in September (the qualifying week). You cannot get a payment if you are receiving pension credit or income-based jobseeker's allowance and have been in residential care for 12 weeks or more. There are other situations when you might not get a payment or where you might get a reduced payment. Seek advice if you think you have been wrongly refused a winter fuel payment or if you have been paid less than the amount to which you think you are entitled.

Rates from April 2008

Aged 60–79 (in the qualifying week)	£250
Aged 80 or over (in the qualifying week)	£400

Note that the amounts above are temporary increases for winter 2008/09 and may decrease in future years. Payments should be made automatically without having to make a claim if you are in receipt of certain social security benefits or if you received a payment in the previous year. Otherwise, you should contact the Winter Fuel Helpline on 08459 151 515 or textphone 0845 605 613 to make a claim.

6. **Community care grants**

Community care grants (CCGs) are non-repayable grants intended to help you live independently in the community. There is no ceiling on the amount for which you can apply. You can claim for items such as:
- removal expenses, furniture and household equipment;
- redecoration and refurbishment;
- bedding, clothing and footware;
- domestic appliances, such as heaters and washing machines;
- items needed because of a disability;
- expenses for setting up home if, for example, you have been homeless or living in temporary accommodation.

You must need the CCG for a specific purpose – eg, to ease or prevent exceptional pressure on you and your family, to assist with continued independent living in the community, or to help with certain travel expenses (eg, to visit someone who is ill or attend a relative's funeral).[13]
    In order to qualify for a CCG you must usually be in receipt of a qualifying benefit when your application is treated as made.[14] The qualifying benefits are:
- income support;
- income-based jobseeker's allowance; *or*
- pension credit (guarantee or savings credit).

It is expected that income-related employment and support allowance will also be a qualifying benefit.

You should apply to the Jobcentre Plus office on Form SF300. If you are moving out of care or temporary accommodation, you need to apply to the office covering the area to which you are moving.

7. **Budgeting loans**

You can get a budgeting loan (BL) to help you pay for certain items that are difficult to budget for when on benefits for a long period. These are:[15]
- furniture and household equipment;
- clothing and footwear;
- removal expenses;
- rent in advance;
- home improvements, maintenance and security;
- travelling expenses;
- job-seeking expenses or expenses on starting work;
- repaying hire purchase loans and other debts for any of the above expenses.

Budgeting loans are interest-free loans of between £100 and £1,500. You must be able to afford to repay the loan.[16] The amount you can get depends on the size of your family and the amount of outstanding BL debt you may already have. To qualify, you must have been getting one of these benefits for at least 26 weeks before your application is decided:[17]
- income support;
- income-based jobseeker's allowance;
- pension credit (guarantee or savings credit).

It is expected that income-related employment and support allowance will also be a qualifying benefit.

You should apply to the local Jobcentre Plus office on Form SF500. You should always apply for a community care grant (CCG) first, if you are eligible, rather than a BL because you do not have to re-pay a CCG. Your application for a BL will not be normally considered as an application for a CCG even though both benefits can pay for the same items. If you are refused a CCG, you can always apply for a BL at a later date.

You can re-apply for a BL at any time for the same or different items.

You should always consider the repayment terms of the BL before taking up the loan because set amounts are deducted from weekly benefit and these could cause you hardship. You can ask for repayments to be reduced if this is the case. You are not charged interest on a BL, so it may be a preferable to other types of loans.

8. Crisis loans

Crisis loans are intended to help with expenses in an emergency or after a disaster. They are interest-free loans paid only if you have no other money to meet your immediate needs. If your college has a hardship fund to which you can apply, you should apply to this first. You are likely to be refused a crisis loan if the hardship fund could help instead.

You may get a crisis loan, for example, if you have lost money that you needed to live on, if your regular income has not been paid and you are in hardship, if there has been a disaster like a fire or flood that has caused damage, or if you need to pay fuel reconnection charges. A crisis loan has to be the only way of preventing serious damage or risk to your health and safety, or that of a member of your family.

Claim on Form SF401 at your local Jobcentre Plus office. In some areas Jobcentre Plus prefers you to claim by telephone, but should not turn you away if you wish to claim in person at a local office.

Under 20 in non-advanced education or approved training

If you are under 20 and in full-time non-advanced education or approved training and you began your course before your 19th birthday, you can claim a crisis loan if you are eligible for income support (IS) or income-based jobseeker's allowance (JSA).[18] It is expected that income-related employment and support allowance (ESA) will also be a qualifying benefit. If you are not eligible for these benefits, you cannot get a crisis loan.

Other full-time students

If you are under 19 and in full-time advanced education or you are older and in full-time education (advanced or non-advanced) and you are eligible for IS, income-based JSA or pension credit, you can claim a crisis loan as normal. It is expected that income-related ESA will also be a qualifying benefit. If you are not eligible for one of these benefits, you can only get a crisis loan to alleviate the consequences of a disaster, not in any other circumstances.[19]

9. Challenging a decision

Regulated social fund decisions are made on behalf of the Secretary of State and can be challenged by revision, supersession and appeal, the rules of which are the same as for most other benefits. See the benefit chapters in this *Handbook* for information about challenging a decision.

Discretionary social fund decisions cannot be appealed, but you can apply for a review within 28 days of the date the decision was issued to you.[20] A decision must be reviewed if it is based on a mistake of the law or material fact, or (in the case of community care grants and crisis loans) if there has been a change of circumstances since the decision was issued, or (in the case of budgeting loans) there has been a change in the district budget.[21]

Challenging repayment terms

You cannot request a review of repayment terms or the decision to recover a loan but you can ask the Department for Work and Pensions to reschedule the loan by lowering weekly repayments if the repayment terms are causing you hardship or if there has been a change in your financial circumstances.[22]

Notes

1. What is the social fund
1 s138 SSCBA 1992
2 s168 SSAA 1992
3 s38 SSA 1998; SF Dirs 31-39; s66 SSAA 1992

2. Sure Start maternity grants
4 Reg 5(2) SFM&FE Regs
5 Reg 5(1)(a) and (b) SFM&FE Regs
6 Reg 19 and Sch 4 para 8 SS(C&P) Regs

3. Funeral payments
7 Reg 7(7) SFM&FE Regs
8 Reg 7(3) and (4) SFM&FE Regs
9 Regs 7(8) and 8 SFM&FE Regs
10 Sch 4 para 9 SS(C&P) Regs

4. Cold weather payments
11 Regs 1(2), 1A and 2(1) and (2), and Schs 1 and 2 Social Fund Cold Weather Payments (General) Regulations 1988, No.1724
12 Regs 1, 1A and 2 and Schs 1 and 2 Social Fund Cold Weather Payments (General) Regulations 1988 No.1724

5. Community care grants
13 SF Dir 4
14 SF Dir 25

7. Budgeting loans
15 SF Dir 2
16 SF Dirs 10, 11 and 50-53
17 SF Dir 8(1)(a)

8. Crisis loans
18 SF Dir 15
19 SF Dir 16(a)

9. Challenging a decision
20 Reg 2(1)(a) and (2)(a) SF(AR) Regs
21 SF Dir 31
22 s38(13) SSA 1998

Chapter 18

Child tax credit

This chapter covers:
1. What is child tax credit (below)
2. Who is eligible (p209)
3. Amount of child tax credit (p210)
4. Claiming child tax credit (p213)
5. Challenging a decision (p214)
6. Other benefits and tax credits (p215)

Basic facts

– Child tax credit (CTC) is paid to families with children.
– Both part-time and full-time students with a child can qualify if they satisfy the rules of entitlement.
– The amount of CTC you get is affected by your income, but most student support is ignored when working this out.
– Tax credit claims are administered by HM Revenue and Customs.

1. **What is child tax credit**

Further information

This chapter gives an outline of the child tax credit rules and focuses on issues relevant to students. For more detailed information on the rules, see CPAG's *Welfare Benefits and Tax Credits Handbook*.

Child tax credit (CTC) is paid to people on low incomes with children. It is paid whether or not you are working. CTC is administered by HM Revenue and Customs (the Revenue). Claims are assessed on an annual basis, usually based on your income and that of your partner (of either sex) over the previous tax year.

Being a student does not affect your entitlement to CTC. You can qualify for CTC so long as you satisfy the rules of entitlement.

More information about tax credits is available on the Revenue's website. A tax credit calculator is available at www.taxcredits.inlandrevenue.gov.uk/Qualify/

DIQHousehold.aspx. The Revenue also runs a helpline on 0845 300 3900 (England and Wales) and 0845 603 2000 (Northern Ireland); textphone 0845 300 3909 (England and Wales) and 0845 607 6078 (Northern Ireland).

Changes to social security benefits

If you claim income support (IS) or income-based jobseeker's allowance (JSA) and are getting CTC, IS and income-based JSA do not include allowances and premiums for your children. Instead, you get financial support for your children in your CTC. You can get CTC in addition to IS and JSA and to child benefit.

However, if you were getting IS or income-based JSA on 5 April 2004 and this included allowances and premiums for your children but you were not yet entitled to CTC, you will be transferred to CTC sometime in the future. Until then, you continue to get allowances and premiums for your children in your IS or income-based JSA. A change of circumstances, such as starting a full-time course, may trigger the transfer.

2. **Who is eligible**

You can qualify for child tax credit (CTC) if:[1]
- you (and your partner) are 16 or over; *and*
- you are a lone parent and have at least one child or qualifying young person for whom you are responsible (see below); *and*
- you satisfy presence and residence conditions; *and*
- you are not subject to immigration control for tax credits purposes. You can get further advice from UKCISA (see Appendix 2); *and*
- you have a low income (see p212).

You count as responsible for a child or qualifying young person if:
- s/he normally lives with you; *or*
- you have the main responsibility for her/him. This only applies if you and another person – eg, your child's other parent, make competing claims for the same child.

Someone counts as a child until 1 September following her/his 16th birthday, whether or not s/he is in education.[2] Someone counts as a '**qualifying young person**' if s/he is:[3]
- under 20 and in full-time non-advanced education or approved training, or has been enrolled or accepted to undertake it. This does not apply if s/he is undertaking the education or training because of her/his employment. The education or training must have begun (or s/he must have been enrolled or accepted to undertake it) before s/he reached 19; *or*
- under 18, has ceased full-time education or approved training and it is not more than 20 weeks since s/he did so. For this rule to apply, s/he must notify

HM Revenue and Customs that s/he has registered for work or training with the Careers or Connexions service.

Students and child tax credit

You are not excluded from claiming CTC simply because you are a student. Indeed, the student support system was changed so that financial support for your dependent child(ren) would be provided via CTC.

Students funded through the NHS student support system in England and Wales are still able to claim both dependants' grant and CTC, but this arrangement remains under review and may change in future years.

When calculating how much CTC you can get, student loans and most other student income is disregarded. See Chapter 21 for how income affects tax credits.

3. Amount of child tax credit

The amount of child tax credit (CTC) you get depends on:
- your maximum CTC. This is made up of a combination of 'elements' (see below);
- how much income you have. If you have a partner, your joint income is taken into account. See p212 and Chapter 21 for further information; *and*
- the threshold that applies to you (see below).

The elements and threshold can be increased every April.

Maximum child tax credit

Your maximum CTC is calculated by adding together all the elements that apply to you.[4] The elements and rates for 2008/09 are shown in the table below. Note that HM Revenue and Customs (the Revenue) works out your entitlement by using daily rates of the elements for which you qualify.

	Maximum annual amount	Weekly equivalent
Family element (one per family)	£545	£10.50
Baby element (one per child under one year old)	£545	£10.50
Child element (one per child)	£2,085	£40.04
Disabled child element (one per child in receipt of disability living allowance or registered blind)	£2,540	£48.72
Severely disabled child element (one per child in receipt of the highest rate care component of disability living allowance)	£1,020	£19.60

Calculating child tax credit

You automatically qualify for maximum CTC if you are on income support, income-based jobseeker's allowance or pension credit. In all other cases, to work out the amount of your CTC, the Revenue compares your income with your threshold. If you qualify for CTC on its own, the threshold is £15,575. However, if you qualify for CTC and working tax credit (WTC), the threshold is £6,420.

If your income is the same as or lower than the threshold, you get maximum CTC. If your income is higher than the threshold, maximum CTC is reduced by 39 per cent of the excess.[5]

If you qualify for WTC (see Chapter 19) as well as CTC, the elements are tapered away in the following order:
* WTC elements (other than the childcare element); *then*
* WTC childcare element; *then*
* CTC child elements (other than the family element – including the baby element if relevant).

The family element of CTC (including the baby element) is not reduced unless your annual income is higher than £50,000. At this point, the family element is tapered away at a rate £1 for every £15 of income you have over £50,000 (6.67 per cent).

Examples

Mhairi has two children, James aged two and Meena aged four. Meena has asthma and gets the lowest rate care component of disability living allowance. Mhairi's maximum CTC for the tax year April 2008 to April 2009 includes two child elements, a family element and a disabled child element (for Meena). Whether she gets the maximum CTC or a reduced amount depends on her income.

Agnes applies for CTC in May 2008. She has a four-year-old daughter, Lizzie. Agnes' income for tax credits purposes in the tax year 2007/08 was £16,575, £1,000 over the threshold. Her income in 2008/09 will be only slightly higher, so the previous year's income is used to estimate her tax credits.

Agnes' estimated entitlement to CTC for the tax year 6 April 2008 to 5 March 2009 is calculated as follows:

Maximum CTC	£
Child element	2,085
Family element	545
Total	**2,630**

Compare income to threshold: £16,575 – £15,575 = £1,000.
Apply 39 per cent to the excess: 39 per cent x £1,000 = £390.

Deduct excess from maximum CTC: £2,630 – £390 = £2,240. This is roughly £43.07 a week.

Treatment of income

How income affects tax credits is covered in Chapter 21. It is important to remember that:

- most student income is fully disregarded when calculating entitlement to tax credits;
- income is calculated annually over a complete tax year (from 6 April to 5 April);
- the amount of income used to calculate CTC is worked out by comparing income in the current tax year with that in the previous tax year. Then, if income has:[6]
  - gone down, CTC is calculated using current year income;
  - stayed the same or has increased by £25,000 or less, CTC is calculated using previous year's income;
  - increased by more than £25,000, CTC is calculated using the current year's income, but deducting £25,000.

Examples

Antonio is a mature student. He is a lone parent with one child, Eva. In the tax year 2007/08 he was working full time and got a good salary. He starts university in September 2008 and now his only income apart from child benefit is his student loan, special support grant, parents' learning allowance and childcare grant. He claims and is awarded CTC. The amount he is awarded is equivalent to the family element (*pro rata* from three months before his claim) based on his earnings in 2007/08. Antonio phones the Tax Credit Helpline and gives details of his student support. The Revenue reassesses his CTC. Because his current year's income is less than that in the previous year, and is below the threshold, he is awarded maximum CTC.

Dosh is a lone parent and has a daughter, Sylvie, who is one. Dosh was getting IS before she became a student. She now gets a student loan, a special support grant, a parents' learning allowance and has part-time earnings of £5,000. She claims CTC and is awarded maximum CTC based on the IS she was getting in 2007/08. As regards her income for 2008/09, her student support is disregarded for the tax credit calculation, but her part-time earnings are taken into account. However, although her actual income in 2008/09 has gone up since the previous year, the increase is less than £25,000. Her CTC award is therefore still based on the previous year's income and Dosh is still entitled to maximum CTC.

4. **Claiming child tax credit**

Your first claim for tax credits must be made in writing on Form TC600. You use the same form for both child tax credit (CTC) and working tax credit (WTC). If you are a member of a couple, you must make a joint claim with your partner. It is very important to claim in time. A claim for tax credits can be backdated for a maximum of three months.[7] Unlike for means-tested benefits, you do not have to show any reasons for your delay.

Forms are available directly from the Tax Credit Office and from HM Revenue and Customs (the Revenue) enquiry centres, Jobcentre Plus offices, some money advice centres, Citizens Advice Bureaux, or institutions' finance offices or student services departments.

There is no section on the claim form to list student income, so it should be included in 'other'. You should only enter that part of student income that is taken into account for tax credits; disregarded income should not be listed on the form. Thus, only dependants' allowances paid by local authorities, certain bursaries or grants, or any career development loan paid for living costs should be entered as income. All other student income, including loans, grants, bursaries, childcare grants, travel, books and equipment grants, and all discretionary funds, should be ignored and not entered. See Chapter 21 for what student income is disregarded. If you are unsure of what to include, you should contact your students' union or association, or your institution's student adviser.

You should send the completed form to the Tax Credit Office. It can also be sent if necessary to any Jobcentre Plus office, Department for Work and Pensions office or Revenue enquiry centre.[8] You might be able to claim online on the Revenue website. However, at the time of writing, this service had been suspended.

Renewal awards

At the end of the tax year in which you claimed CTC, you (and your partner if you are a member of a couple), receive a 'final notice' from the Revenue asking you to confirm that your income and/or your household circumstances are as stated for the tax year just passed. The deadline is 31 July. The Revenue then makes a final decision, based on your actual income during the tax year. It decides whether you were entitled to CTC and, if so, the amount of your award. This is known as the 'end of year review'. The Revenue uses this information to renew your award for the next tax year.

Getting paid

CTC is usually paid directly into the bank account (or similar account) of whoever is deemed to be the main carer of your child(ren). Which account it goes into is up to you. If you do not want your benefit to go into an account that is overdrawn, give the Revenue details of an alternative account if you have access to, or can open, one.

If you are overpaid CTC, you might have to repay it. See below if you want to challenge a decision.

5. **Challenging a decision**

If you think a decision about your child tax credit, is wrong (eg, because the decision maker got the facts or law wrong, or your circumstances have changed since the decision was made), there are a number of ways you can try to get the decision changed.

- You can seek a revision of the decision if your circumstances have changed or HM Revenue and Customs (the Revenue) has reasonable grounds for believing you are entitled to tax credits at a different rate or there has been an official error.
- You can appeal to an independent tribunal. There are strict time limits for appealing – normally 30 days from the date on the decision letter. You can make a late appeal in limited circumstances.

If you are considering challenging a decision, you should seek advice as soon as possible.

Disputing recovery of an overpayment

A big source of difficulty is tax credits overpayments. All tax credit overpayments are recoverable and there is no right of appeal against a decision to recover an overpayment. However, the Revenue should use its discretion when deciding whether to recover the overpayment. Factors such as hardship and official error must be taken into account. It is always worth disputing whether an overpayment should be recovered, as the Revenue suspends recovery while it considers the situation. You should do this on Form TC846.

If an overpayment is recovered, this is usually done by reducing ongoing tax credits payments. There are maximum amounts by which payments can be reduced. These are:

- 10 per cent, if you get a maximum award;
- 100 per cent, if you only get the family element of child tax credit;
- 25 per cent, in all other cases.

Note: there *is* a right of appeal against the decision about entitlement to tax credits – ie, whether you have been overpaid.

6. **Other benefits and tax credits**

Child tax credit (CTC) does not count as income when calculating your entitlement to income support (IS), jobseeker's allowance (JSA) and pension credit (PC), but working tax credit (WTC) does. CTC (unless you are on IS or income-based JSA or are 60 or over) and WTC are taken into account as income for housing benefit and council tax benefit. If you get arrears of CTC, these count as capital and can be disregarded for a year for means-tested benefit purposes. This is also the case for arrears of WTC, except for PC purposes.

If you are entitled to CTC, you may also qualify for:
- health benefits (see Chapter 11). You do not have to satisfy the income test for these if your gross annual income is £15,050 or less;
- education benefits, such as free school meals. You do not have to satisfy the income test if you are getting CTC (but not WTC) and your gross annual income is £15,575 or less.

You may also be entitled to a Sure Start maternity grant and a social fund funeral expenses payment if you are awarded CTC at a rate which exceeds the family element.

Notes

2. **Who is eligible**
1 ss3(3) and (7), 8 and 42 TCA 2002; regs 3–5 CTC Regs; reg 3 TC(R) Regs; reg 3 TC(I) Regs
2 s8(3) TCA 2002; regs 2 and 4 CTC Regs
3 s8(4) TCA 2002; regs 2 and 5 CTC Regs

3. **Amount of child tax credit**
4 s9 TCA 2002; reg 7 CTC Regs
5 Reg 8 TC(ITDR) Regs
6 s7(3) TCA 2002

4. **Claiming child tax credit**
7 Reg 7 TC(CN) Regs
8 Regs 2 and 5 TC(CN) Regs

Chapter 19

Working tax credit

This chapter covers:

Basic facts

- Working tax credit (WTC) is paid to top up low wages.
- Both part-time and full-time students can qualify if they satisfy the rules of entitlement.
- WTC includes an amount to help you with childcare costs.
- The amount you get is affected by your income, but most student support is ignored when working this out.
- Tax credits claims are administered by HM Revenue and Customs.

1. What is working tax credit

Further information

This chapter gives an outline of the working tax credit rules and focuses on issues relevant to students. For more detailed information on the rules, see CPAG's *Welfare Benefits and Tax Credits Handbook*.

Working tax credit (WTC) is paid to people in low-paid work to top up wages and help with expenses, including childcare costs, associated with being in work. WTC is administered by HM Revenue and Customs (the Revenue). Claims are assessed on an annual basis, usually based on your income and that of your partner (of either sex) over the previous tax year.

Being a student does not affect your entitlement to WTC. You can qualify for WTC so long as you satisfy the rules of entitlement. Note, however, that you cannot receive both the higher education childcare grant (or NHS childcare allowance) and the WTC childcare element.

More information about tax credits is available on the Revenue's website. A tax credit calculator is available at www.taxcredits.inlandrevenue.gov.uk/Qualify/ DIQHousehold.aspx. The Revenue also runs a helpline on 0845 300 3900 (England and Wales) and 0845 603 2000 (Northern Ireland); textphone 0845 300 3909 (England and Wales) and 0845 607 6078 (Northern Ireland).

2. **Who is eligible**

You qualify for working tax credit (WTC) if:[1]
- you (and your partner) are 16 or over; *and*
- you (or your partner) are in full-time paid work, that is:
  - you (or your partner) are responsible for a child or qualifying young person and you work at least 16 hours a week; *or*
  - you have a disability which puts you at a disadvantage in getting a job, you qualify for a WTC disability element and work at least 16 hours a week. You qualify for a disability element if you get or have been getting specific benefits; *or*
  - you are 25 or over and work 30 hours a week; *or*
  - you (or your partner) are 50 or over, have been claiming a qualifying benefit – eg, income support, jobseeker's allowance or incapacity benefit, for at least six months and now work more than 16 hours a week; *and*
- you satisfy presence and residence tests; *and*
- you are not subject to immigration control for tax credits purposes. Further advice is available from UKCISA (see Appendix 2); *and*
- you are not claiming employment and support allowance; *and*
- you have a low income (see p220).

You must be actually working, or have accepted an offer of work which is expected to start within seven days. The work must be expected to last for at least four weeks.

Note: in some cases you can be treated as if you are in full-time paid work when you are not, or as if you are not in full-time paid work even if you are. In particular, you are treated as in full-time paid work for the four weeks immediately after you stop working at least 16 hours a week, so long as you counted as being in full-time paid work before stopping. If you are unsure whether you count as in full-time paid work, seek advice.

Students and working tax credit

You are not excluded from claiming WTC simply because you are a student. However, you must count as being in full-time paid work. So if, for example, you do sufficient hours of paid work (16 or 30 as the case may be) in addition to your studies or during the holidays, you can qualify for WTC. Remember that the work must be expected to last for four weeks.

Any work you do in studying for a degree or other qualification does not count as full-time paid work – any grant or loan you receive is for your maintenance and not paid in return for work done on the course. You are also not in full-time paid work if you are a student nurse because the NHS bursary and other grants or loans you get are not payments for work done on the course and do not count as income for tax credit purposes.[2] However, if you are paid in return for the work you do – eg, you are paid by an employer during a work placement, and you work sufficient hours, you could argue that you are in full-time paid work. There are a number of situations when you do not count as in full-time paid work even if you are – eg, if you are on a government training scheme being paid a training allowance.

When calculating how much WTC you can get, student loans and most other student income are disregarded. See Chapter 21 for how income affects tax credits.

Examples

Sian is aged 26. She does not work during the academic year but in the summer vacation she gets a job for 30 hours a week and expects to work for nine weeks. Sian qualifies for WTC. Whether any WTC is payable depends on the level of her wages and other income.

Katherine and Spencer have a four-year-old child at nursery school. Katherine is a student and Spencer works 20 hours a week. Katherine works 16 hours a week during the summer only. They qualify for WTC throughout the year. During the summer they can get a 30-hour element included in their WTC and they can also get a childcare element (for help with nursery charges), but only if Katherine is not in receipt of the childcare grant.

3. **Amount of working tax credit**

The amount of working tax credit (WTC) you get depends on:
- your maximum WTC. This is made up of a combination of 'elements' (see p219);
- how much income you have. If you have a partner, your joint income is taken into account. See p220 and Chapter 21 for further information; *and*
- the threshold that applies to you (see p219).

The elements and threshold can be increased every April.

Maximum working tax credit

Your maximum WTC is calculated by adding together all the elements that apply to you.[3] The elements and rates for 2008/09 are shown in the table on p219. Note that HM Revenue and Customs (the Revenue) works out your entitlement by using daily rates of the elements for which you qualify.

	Maximum annual amount	Weekly equivalent
Basic element	£1,800	£34.58
Lone parent or couple element	£1,770	£33.95
30-hour element	£735	£14.14
Disability element	£2,405	£46.13
Severe disability element	£1,020	£19.60
50+ return to work element (16–29 hours)	£1,235	£23.73
50+ return to work element (30+ hours)	£1,840	£35.35
Childcare element (one child)		Max £140.00
Childcare element (two or more children)		Max £240.00

Childcare costs

The childcare element of WTC is 80 per cent of the weekly 'relevant childcare charges' you pay for your child(ren). The maximum weekly amount payable is 80 per cent of £175 (£140 a week) if you have one child, or 80 per cent of £300 (£240 a week) if you have two or more children.[4]

You qualify for a childcare element if you incur 'relevant childcare charges' and:[5]

- you are a lone parent and in full-time paid work (see p217); or
- you are a member of a couple and:
  - you are both in full-time paid work (see p217); or
  - one of you is in full-time paid work (see p217) and the other is incapacitated, in hospital or in prison.

You can only get a childcare element to help meet the cost of 'relevant childcare charges'. This means the childcare must be provided by, for example, a registered childminder, a nursery, an after-school club or a local authority daycare service.

Note: you cannot get a higher education (HE) childcare grant or NHS childcare allowance if you have chosen to get a WTC childcare element.[6] The HE childcare grant pays a higher percentage of childcare costs (85 per cent) and it can be paid year-round, so it is usually better to apply for this.

Calculating working tax credit

To work out the amount of your WTC, the Revenue compares your income to your threshold. If you qualify for WTC, either on its own or with child tax credit (CTC), the threshold is £6,420. See p211 for information about how the threshold is applied if you also qualify for CTC.

If your income is the same as, or lower than, the threshold, you get maximum WTC. If your income is higher than the threshold, maximum WTC is reduced by 39 per cent of the excess.[7]

Note: you automatically qualify for maximum WTC if you are on income support (IS), income-based jobseeker's allowance (JSA) or pension credit. In practice, however, there are not many situations when you can claim IS or income-based JSA at the same time as WTC.

Example
Steph is 37. She is a part-time student, but also works 31 hours a week. She qualifies for WTC. Steph's maximum WTC includes a basic element and a 30-hour element.

Treatment of income

How income affects tax credits is covered in Chapter 21. It is important to remember that:

- most student income is fully disregarded when calculating entitlement to tax credits;
- income is calculated annually over a complete tax year (from 6 April to 5 April);
- the amount of income used to calculate WTC is worked out by comparing income in the current tax year with that in the previous tax year. If income has:[8]
  - gone down, WTC is calculated using current year's income;
  - stayed the same or has increased by £25,000 or less, WTC is calculated using previous year's income;
  - increased by more than £25,000, WTC is calculated using current year's income but deducting £25,000.

Examples
Chrystal is a student. Her partner, Jerome, is working 35 hours a week. In the tax year 2007/08 Jerome was working part time and earned £9,000. In 2008/09, he will earn £22,000. Their only other income (both in the previous and current year) is Chrystal's student support. They claim and are awarded WTC. The Revenue calculates their award based on Jerome's earnings in 2007/08. This is because although their income has gone up, the increase is less than £25,000.

Note that if their circumstances do not change, they are unlikely to qualify for WTC in 2009/10. This is because the calculation will then be based on their income in 2008/09.

Naveed is 36 and is the lone parent of one child aged 15. He is a part-time student. He also works 21 hours a week. He qualifies for both CTC and WTC. His income for tax credits purposes in the tax year 2007/08 was £18,000. His income in 2008/09 will be about £18,700 so the previous year's income is used to estimate his tax credits, as this is not more than £25,000 higher than last year.

Naveed's estimated entitlement to CTC and WTC for the tax year 6 April 2008 to 5 March 2009 is calculated as follows.

	£
CTC family element	545
CTC child element	2,045
WTC basic element	1,800
WTC lone parent element	1,770
Total	**6,160**

Compare income to threshold: £18,000–£6,420 = £11,580
Apply 39 per cent to the excess: 39% x £11,580 = £4516.20
Deduct excess from maximum WTC: £6,160–£4,516.20 = £1,643.80. This is roughly £31.61 a week.

4. **Claiming working tax credit**

For further information about claiming working tax credit (WTC) and about renewal awards, see p213. The rules are the same as for child tax credit.

Getting paid

WTC (other than the childcare element) is usually paid directly into your bank (or similar) account. WTC childcare element is paid into the account of whoever is deemed to be the main carer of your child(ren). Which account it goes into is up to you. If you do not want your benefit to go into an account that is overdrawn, give HM Revenue and Customs details of an alternative account if you have access to, or can open, one.

If you are overpaid WTC, you might have to repay it. See below if you want to challenge a decision.

5. **Challenging a decision**

If you think a decision about your working tax credit, is wrong (eg, because the decision maker got the facts or law wrong, or your circumstances have changed since the decision was made), there are a number of ways you can try to get the decision changed.

- You can seek a revision of the decision if your circumstances have changed or HM Revenue and Customs has reasonable grounds for believing you are entitled to tax credits at a different rate or there has been an official error.

- You can appeal to an independent tribunal. There are strict time limits for appealing – normally 30 days from the date you are sent or given the decision. You can make a late appeal in limited circumstances.

If you are considering challenging a decision, you should seek advice as soon as possible.

A big source of difficulty is tax credits overpayments. See p214 for information. The issues are the same as for child tax credit.

6. **Tax credits and benefits**

See p215 for information. The issues are the same as for child tax credit (CTC).

If you are entitled to working tax credit (WTC), you may also qualify for health benefits (see Chapter 11). You do not have to satisfy the income test for these if your gross annual income is £15,050 or less and your WTC includes a disability or a severe disability element, or you get CTC as well as WTC.

You may also be entitled to a Sure Start maternity grant and a social fund funeral expenses payment if your WTC award includes the disability or severe disability element.

Notes

2. Who is eligible
1 ss3(3) and (7), 10 and 42 TCA 2002 and regs 4-8 WTC(EMR) Regs; reg 3 TC(R) Regs; reg 3 TC(I) Regs
2 R(FIS) 1/83; R(FIS) 1/86; para 02403 TCTM, 'Student nurses'

3. Amount of working tax credit
3 s11 TCA 2002; regs 3 and 20 and Sch 2 WTC(EMR) Regs
4 Reg 20(3) WTC(EMR) Regs
5 Regs 13 and 14 WTC(EMR) Regs
6 Reg 43(3) E(SS) Regs
7 Reg 7 TC(ITDR) Regs
8 s7(3) TCA 2002

Part 3

Treatment of student income

Chapter 20

How income affects means-tested benefits

This chapter covers:
1. Working out your income (p226)
2. Grants and loans (p227)
3. Dividing income throughout the year (p232)
4. Hardship funds and other payments (p238)
5. Earnings (p239)
6. Benefits and tax credits (p240)
7. Maintenance (p241)
8. Savings and capital (p241)

This chapter explains how your weekly income affects your entitlement to means-tested benefits – income support (IS), income-based jobseeker's allowance (JSA), income-related employment and support allowance (ESA), housing benefit (HB) and council tax benefit (CTB). It explains how much of your student support is taken into account and how much can be disregarded, and considers how other types of income, such as earnings, are treated. It applies to both full- and part-time students.

If you, or your partner if you have one, are aged 60 or over and not getting IS, income-based JSA or income-related ESA, your student support is ignored as income for HB and CTB.

The way your income is assessed for tax credits and health benefits is different (see Chapters 21 and 22).

Basic facts
– Student loans for living costs are normally divided over 42 or 43 weeks from the beginning of September to the end of June (for students starting their course in the autumn) and taken into account as income for means-tested benefits during that period. If your income is too high you will not get IS, income-based JSA or income-related ESA over those weeks, and your HB or CTB will be reduced.
– Student loans for living costs are normally *not* taken into account as income for means-tested benefits from around the end of June until the beginning of September. You may

be able to get IS or more HB during these months even if your income was too high during the academic year.

– Some student support does not affect the amount of IS/JSA/ESA or HB/CTB you receive.

1. Working out your income

The way that student income is taken into account for income support (IS), income-based jobseeker's allowance, income-related employment and support allowance, housing benefit (HB) and council tax benefit is essentially the same. Chapters 14 and 12 take you through the IS and HB assessments step by step. This chapter explains how much weekly income counts in those assessments.

Calculating income for means-tested benefits

Step 1   **Add together annual income from grants and loans.**
Add together the annual amount of any student grants and/or loans, ignoring elements that are wholly disregarded.

Step 2   **Apply annual disregards.**
From the total annual grants and loans, deduct disregarded amounts for books, equipment and travel.

Step 3   **Divide income into weekly amount.**
Divide the annual amount of grants and loans by the number of benefit weeks in the period over which the grant and loan are counted as income for benefit purposes.

Step 4   **Deduct any weekly disregard.**
If you have a student loan, deduct £10 a week – this is the weekly disregard. If you have a regular hardship fund payment for living costs, deduct £20 a week, or £10 a week if you are also eligible to receive a student loan.

Step 5   **Add other income to weekly amount of grant and loan.**
Add together any other weekly income – eg, from hardship funds (p238), career development loans (p239), earnings (p239), tariff income from capital (p241), benefits and tax credits (p240) – ignoring any amount that is disregarded. This total, added to the weekly grant and loan total in Step 4, is the amount of income used in the benefit assessment.

If you want to work out benefit entitlement during the long vacation, p232 explains when the long vacation starts and finishes for benefit purposes – ie, when your student loan or grant counts as nil income. You should then total up on a weekly basis any other income that you have over the vacation.

2. **Grants and loans**

Student loan for fees

Loans for fees are disregarded.[1]

Student loan for living costs

You should include in the student loan:
- the maximum loan for which you are eligible. This is taken into account as your income whether or not you apply for it.[2] This means that students cannot choose to apply for maximum income support (IS) or income-related employment and support allowance (ESA) rather than applying for a loan. You will simply be treated as though you had taken out the full loan and your benefit will be reduced accordingly;
- the assessed contribution from a parent or partner, whether or not you receive it. For IS or income-related ESA, however, if you are a lone parent or a disabled student, you should only include contributions that are actually paid;[3]
- any payments for extra weeks' attendance.

You should deduct from the annual student loan the following disregarded amounts:[4]
- £380 for books and equipment;
- £295 for travel.

There is a further disregard of £10 a week that applies once the student loan has been divided into the relevant weekly amount (see p232).

Career development loans

How career development loans are treated depends on what they are paid for. Disregard any amounts paid for:
- tuition fees;
- course costs.

Any amounts paid for living costs are treated as income. This amount should be divided over the period for which the loan is paid.[5]

Professional studies loans

Loans paid to postgraduate students by banks for vocational study are treated in the same way as career development loans (see above).

Grants

In general, grants intended for living costs are taken into account as income, and grants for other costs are disregarded. For the way that hardship funds are treated, see p238.

If you are a full-time undergraduate assessed for support in England and receive a special support grant – eg, if you are a lone parent (see Chapter 2), this is disregarded as it is paid for course-related costs.[6] If you receive a maintenance grant – eg, if you are the partner of a jobseeker's allowance (JSA) or IS claimant, this is taken into account in full as it is paid for living costs.

If you are *not* eligible for a student loan, deduct from your grant the following disregarded amounts:

- £380 for books and equipment;
- £295 for travel.

Grants in higher education

The following higher education (HE) grants are completely **disregarded**:

- grant for tuition fees;[7]
- HE grant for full-time undergraduate students under the 'old system' in England and Wales;[8]
- special support grant for full-time undergraduate students in England, Wales and Northern Ireland;[9]
- childcare grant;
- disabled students' allowance;[10]
- Welsh Assembly learning grant for 'old system' students;
- Welsh individual learning account payments;[11]
- parents' learning allowance;
- travel expenses;[12]
- course costs grant for part-time undergraduate students;[13]
- institutional bursaries paid for anything other than living costs.[14]

The following grants are **taken into account**:

- maintenance grant for full-time undergraduate students assessed in England;
- Assembly learning grant for 'current system' students in Wales;
- maintenance bursary for full-time undergraduate students assessed in Northern Ireland;
- care leavers' vacation grant;
- adult dependant's grant
- NHS dependant's grant;[15]
- lone parents' grant;
- nursing and midwifery bursary;
- social work bursary;
- teaching incentive bursaries;[16]
- health professional course bursaries – eg, physiotherapy, occupational therapy, radiography, speech and language therapy, or podiatry (or dietetics in Northern Ireland);
- institutional bursaries paid for living costs.

Postgraduate grants

Postgraduate maintenance grants and dependants' grants awarded by a research council are taken into account in the same way as for undergraduates (see p228). You should **ignore** the following:

- disabled students' allowance;
- grants for tuition fees;
- grants for residential study away from your normal home;
- grants intended to meet the costs of books and equipment.

Grants in further education

The following further education (FE) grants are **disregarded**:

- education maintenance allowance;[17]
- Care to Learn grants paid for childcare costs;
- sixth-form childcare bursaries;
- childcare bursaries paid through the Learner Support Fund;
- residential bursaries paid through the Learner Support Fund (IS/JSA only);
- Welsh Assembly learning grant;
- the Northern Irish FE grant;
- additional grant allowances for disabled students;
- the first £675 per year (equivalent to the travel, books and equipment disregard) of the adult learning grant may be disregarded for housing benefit and council tax benefit at the discretion of the local authority.[18] **Note:** you cannot receive both an adult learning grant and JSA.[19]

The following grants are **taken into account** in full:

- the adult learning grant, subject to the standard disregard for travel, books and equipment;
- the maintenance element only of FE and advanced FE awards in Northern Ireland, subject to the standard disregard for travel, books and equipment.

Discretionary funds

Discretionary funds paid by colleges and universities for course or living costs may be called hardship funds, the Access to Learning Fund, Financial Contingency Fund or Learner Support Fund. If these funds are paid for course costs, they should be disregarded. If they are paid for living costs, they should be treated as capital if paid in a lump sum,[20] or as income if paid regularly.[21] Secondary shortage subject scheme payments are treated in the same way as other discretionary funds.

Grants and loans checklist

Student support	Treatment
Further education income	
Adult learning grant	Disregarded are: – £380 a year books and equipment; – £295 a year travel **Note:** you cannot receive both an adult learning grant and JSA.
Care to Learn or sixth-form childcare bursary	Disregarded
Education maintenance allowance	Disregarded
Learner Support Fund/Financial Contingency Fund/hardship funds	Taken into account if paid for basic living costs regularly, disregarded if paid for other items
Northern Ireland FE bursaries	Disregarded are: – £380 a year books and equipment; – £295 a year travel
Welsh Assembly learning grant for further education	Disregarded
Undergraduate income	
Access to Learning Fund grant	Taken into account if paid for basic living costs (as capital if not regular payments), disregarded if paid for other items
Adult dependant's grant	Taken into account in full
Care leavers' vacation grant (Northern Ireland)	Taken into account in full
Childcare grant	Disregarded
Disabled students' allowance	Disregarded
Financial Contingency Fund grant	Taken into account if paid for basic living costs (as capital if not regular payments), disregarded if paid for other items
HE grant (full-time undergraduates in 'old system')	Disregarded
HE special support grant (full-time undergraduates in 'current system')	Disregarded
HE maintenance grant (full-time undergraduates in 'current system')	Taken into account in full
Course costs grant (part-time undergraduates)	Usually disregarded (as it is less than the general books/equipment and travel disregards)
Hardship funds	Taken into account if paid for basic living costs (as capital if not regular payments), disregarded if paid for other items

NHS bursary/nursing and midwifery bursary	Taken in account, except: – £380 a year books and equipment; – £295 a year travel
NHS dependant's grant	Taken into account
Parents' learning allowance	Disregarded
Social work bursary	Disregard any element for non-living costs such as travel or tuition fee costs; take into account the remainder in full
Student loan for fees	Disregarded
Student loan for living costs	Disregarded are: – £380 a year books and equipment; – £295 a year travel; – £10 a week; – amount of student's contribution to loan disregarded as non-loan income; – partner's contribution disregarded from her/his income
Travelling expenses	Disregarded
Welsh Assembly learning grant (full-time undergraduates in 'old system')	Disregarded
Welsh Assembly learning grant (full-time undergraduates in 'current system')	Taken into account in full

Postgraduate income

Research council tuition fees	Disregarded
Research council maintenance grant	Disregarded are: – £380 a year books and equipment; – £295 a year travel
Research supplementary grants	As for undergraduate income
Social work bursaries	Taken into account in full
Teaching training salaries	Taken into account in full

Other

Career development loan	Disregarded: tuition and course cost payments Taken into account: payments for living costs
Professional study loan	Disregarded: tuition and course cost payments Taken into account: payments for living costs
Institutional bursaries	Disregarded: tuition and course costs Taken into account: payments for living costs

3. **Dividing income throughout the year**

The annual amount of your loan and grant is divided over the number of weeks in, usually, a standard academic year to arrive at the weekly amount that is used in the calculation of income support (IS), income-based jobseeker's allowance (JSA), income-related employment and support allowance (ESA), housing benefit (HB) and council tax benefit (CTB). Rules specify exactly the weeks over which the loan and grant are taken into account.

If your loan covers extra weeks of study beyond the usual academic year, that part of the loan is just included in with the rest of the loan. It does not extend the number of weeks over which your loan is taken into account for benefit purposes.

Student loans for living costs

For autumn term starters, student loans are normally divided over 42 or 43 weeks from the beginning of September to the end of June. During this period your student loan is taken into account as your income in the assessment of IS, income-based JSA, income-related ESA, HB and CTB. If your income is too high, you will not be eligible for these benefits. However, your student loan is not taken into account from around the end of June to the beginning of September. Because your income goes down in these months (unless you have other income – eg, earnings), you may be able to get benefit during the summer. It is important, therefore, to make a claim from the end of June even if you were refused benefit at the start of the academic year. Make your claim in mid-June or earlier so that your benefit can start as soon as you are entitled.

Courses starting in the autumn term lasting more than a year

The student loan is divided over the number of weeks starting from the first day of the first benefit week in September until the last day of the last benefit week in June.[22] In 2008/09 this is 42 weeks if your benefit week starts on a Thursday or Friday, or 43 weeks if it starts on any other weekday. The day that starts the 'benefit week' is the same as the payday for that benefit. For HB and CTB this is a Monday.[23] For IS it is usually the day after your pay day, for JSA it is the day after your 'signing-on' day, and for ESA it depends on your national insurance number.

This is the period over which your loan is taken into account as income in the benefit assessment, unless you do not count as a student at all. For example, at the start of your first year, you do not count as being a student until you actually start attending or undertaking the course. In other words, in the first year, the loan is still divided over 42/43 weeks, but the weekly amount arrived at is ignored as income until you start your course.

In the final year of study, the loan is divided over the number of benefit weeks starting from the first day of the first benefit week in September until the end of the benefit week on or before the last day of the final academic term.[24]

Example: first year, 'current system', higher education student in England
Agnes is in her first year at an institution in England. She has one child aged two and is claiming HB as a lone parent. She gets a loan of £3,145 for her fees, a student loan for living costs of £6,475 for studying in London. She also gets a special support grant of £2,835, a parents' learning allowance of £1,470 and a childcare grant of £100 a week, all of which are disregarded for IS and HB.

Her first term begins on Monday 6 October 2008. Her IS benefit week starts on a Monday. Her student loan is divided over the weeks from Monday 1 September 2008 until Sunday 28 June 2009 (43 weeks). However, as she is a first year student, her loan is not taken into account until she starts her course on Monday 6 October. So, from Monday 1 September until Sunday 5 October 2008, her student loan income will not be taken into account for benefit purposes. From Monday 6 October 2008 to Sunday 28 June 2009 her student loan income is £121.51 for benefit purposes. From Monday 29 June until Sunday 6 September 2009 her student loan income is nil again for benefit purposes.

	£
The weekly loan income taken into account is:	
Loan	6,475.00
Less disregards for books and equipment (£380) and travel (£295)	5,800.00
Divided by 43 weeks	134.88
Less £10 weekly loan disregard	124.88

£124.88 is taken into account as weekly income from her loan between 6 October 2008 and 28 June 2009. She also receives £50.54 a week child tax credit and £18.80 child benefit, which brings her weekly income for HB purposes to £194.22.

Her IS applicable amount is £60.50 and her HB applicable amount is £113.09 a week. From Monday 6 October 2008 to Sunday 28 June 2009 she is not entitled to IS because her income is higher than the IS applicable amount. From Monday 29 June until Sunday 6 September 2009 her weekly income from her loan and grants is nil. Agnes should claim again on 29 June 2009.

Example: final year, 'current system' higher education student in Northern Ireland
Graham is in his final year. He is claiming IS as a disabled student studying at an institution in Northern Ireland. He gets a student loan of £4,625. His parents are assessed to make a contribution of £890 towards his living costs, but this year they are refusing to pay. His parental contribution is not taken into account because he is a disabled student.

His first term started on Tuesday 16 September 2008 and his final term ends on Friday 12 June 2009. His IS benefit week starts on a Tuesday. His student loan is divided over the weeks from Tuesday 16 September 2008 until Monday 8 June 2009 (38 weeks).

	£
The weekly loan income taken into account is:	
Loan	4,625.00

Less disregards for books and equipment (£380) and travel (£295)	3,950.00
Divided by 38 weeks	103.95
Less £10 weekly loan disregard	93.95

£93.95 is taken into account as weekly income from his loan between 16 September 2008 and 8 June 2009.

For examples of calculations for 'old system' students, see the 2006/07 edition of this *Handbook*.

Courses not starting in the autumn term

Your student loan is divided over the number of weeks starting from the first day of the first benefit week on or after the beginning of a standard academic year and ending on the last day of the last benefit week on or before the last day of the academic year, but excluding benefit weeks that fall entirely within the quarter that is taken by the Department for Work and Pensions (DWP) to be the longest vacation.[25] '**Academic years**' in this case are 12 months beginning on 1 January, 1 April or 1 July for courses that begin in winter, spring or summer respectively.[26] '**Quarters**' are 1 January to 31 March, 1 April to 30 June, 1 July to 31 August, 1 September to 31 December.[27]

Example
Anya's course begins on Monday 5 January 2009. The main vacation is 12 June to 20 September 2009. She is claiming HB. Her loan is divided over the weeks from Monday 5 January 2009 to Sunday 28 June 2009 and from Monday 7 September 2009 until Sunday 27 December 2009. From 29 June 2009 to 6 September 2009 her student loan income will be nil for benefit purposes.

Courses lasting one year or less

Your loan is divided over the number of weeks from the first day of the first benefit week on or after the start of a standard academic year until the last day of the last benefit week on or before the last day of the final term. The academic year is taken to begin on 1 September, 1 January, 1 April or 1 July, depending on whether your course begins in the autumn, winter, spring or summer. The resulting weekly amount is then taken into account from the point you actually start attending or undertaking the course.

If you leave your course early

If you abandon your course early or are dismissed from it before you have had the final instalment of your student loan in that academic year, the loan continues to be taken into account up until the end of the term in which you leave. The end of term is taken to be the end of December if you leave in the autumn term, the end of March if you leave in the winter term, the end of June if you leave in the spring term and the end of August if you leave in the summer.

The amount of loan taken into account is that which remains from the loan that was paid from the start of the standard academic year (eg, 1 September for students whose courses begin in the autumn – see p232) to the end of the term in which you left, having subtracted that part of the loan (including disregards for books, equipment and travel) that would have been treated as your weekly income in a normal benefits calculation up until the day you left.[28] The examples below illustrate how this amount is calculated.[29]

Example

Nick abandons his course on 1 November 2008. He is in the second year of a three-year course and is claiming IS. His benefit week starts on a Monday.

Work out weekly amount of annual loan

	£
Loan	4,625.00
Less disregards (£675)	3,950.00
Divided by 43 weeks	91.86

Work out amount of loan prior to leaving the course

Multiply the weekly amount of annual loan by the number of benefit weeks from the week after the one that includes the start of the academic year until the end of the benefit week that includes the day Nick left the course.

Multiply weekly loan (£91.86) by
9 weeks (1 September to 2 November 2008) £826.74

Work out amount of loan since leaving the course

To do this, add the loan instalments paid for the terms up to the one in which Nick left, deduct disregards and deduct the loan worked out for the period prior to leaving.

	£
Loan up to end of term (£4,625 divided by 3)	1,541.67
Less disregards (£675)	866.67
Deduct amount of loan prior to leaving (£826.74)	= 39.93

Work out weekly amount of loan from leaving course to end of term

Divide the total amount of loan for the period since leaving the course by the number of weeks left in the term. Count from the benefit week that includes the day Nick left the course until the benefit week that includes the end of term (ie, end of December, March, June or August).

Divide £39.93 by eight weeks
(3 November 2008 to 28 December 2008) £4.99

£4.99 a week is taken into account from 3 November 2008 until 28 December 2008.

If you leave your course nearer to the end of term, this formula could result in there being no loan income taken into account for the remainder of the term. Note that if you repay the loan it is nevertheless taken into account as income until the end of term.[30] So you could be refused IS, JSA or ESA despite having no other money to live on. However, if the Student Loan Company asks you to repay the loan rather than you repaying voluntarily, guidance tells DWP decision makers to disregard the loan as income from the date of the request.[31]

Grants

Higher education grants

The higher education (HE) maintenance grant for full-time undergraduate students in the 'current system' who do not have a benefits claim in their own right, and the adult dependants' grant paid by the Department for Innovation, Universities and Skills (DIUS), the Welsh Assembly or the Department for Employment and Learning in Northern Ireland (DELNI), are taken into account over the duration of the course, whether it comprises 52 weeks or fewer. They are treated as income over the same period as the student loan, if you have one or are eligible for one.[32] This is the case even though DIUS guidance says that such grants cover 52 weeks.

Example

Fiona has a student loan (£4,625) and an adult dependants' grant (£2,575) totalling £7,200. She is claiming IS. She is in the second year of a three-year course and her first term starts in September. Her loan and grant are divided over 43 weeks from Monday 1 September 2008 until Monday 29 June 2009.

The weekly loan and grant income taken into account is:

	£
Total grants and loan	7,200.00
Less disregards for books and equipment (£380) and travel (£295)	6,525.00
Divided by 43 weeks	151.74
Less £10 weekly loan disregard	141.74

£141.74 is taken into account as weekly income from her loan and grants between 1 September 2008 and 29 June 2009. Her weekly income from her loan and grants between 30 June and 6 September 2009 is nil. If she is refused IS during the year because her income is too high, she should claim again on 30 June 2009.

Example

Dave receives a student loan of £6,475 and an HE maintenance grant of £2,835 to do his full-time undergraduate degree in London. This is his first year and his first term begins on Monday 6 October 2008. Dave lives with his partner, Kareen, and their two children. Kareen claims JSA and her benefit week starts on a Monday. Dave's student loan and maintenance grant will be taken into account when working out Kareen's JSA. His student loan and maintenance grant are divided over the 43 weeks from Monday 1 September 2008 to Sunday 28 June 2009. However, as he is a first year student, his loan and grant are not taken into account until he starts his course on Monday 6 October. So, from Monday 1 September until Sunday 5 October 2008, his student loan and grant income are not taken into account for Kareen's benefit purposes. From Monday 6 October 2008 to Sunday 28 June 2009 his student loan and grant income will be included in the calculation to determine the amount of JSA Kareen receives. From Monday 29 June until Sunday 6 September 2009 his student loan and grant income is nil again for benefit purposes.

Nursing and midwifery bursaries

There are two types of bursary available to allied health professionals. A non-means-tested bursary is available for students studying a diploma course. If you are studying for a degree, a means-tested bursary is available. In addition to the means-tested bursary you can receive a non-means-tested reduced rate loan from the DIUS or DELNI. In Northern Ireland, the basic element of the nursing bursary is not means tested, but the dependants' additions are means tested.

The income from both types of bursary, dependants' allowance and single parent addition are taken into account. As these are paid in monthly instalments, they are taken into account over 52 weeks. The reduced rate loan should be treated over the same period as other student loans. The NHS childcare grant is disregarded in full.

Social work bursaries

Social work bursaries should be taken into account for the period they are paid. In England, this is 52 weeks.

In England, the element paid for travelling expenses should be disregarded.[33] However, this is not usually specifically identified, so benefits offices may take the full bursary into account. Speak to an adviser for assistance.

Postgraduate grants

A postgraduate award that is assessed for study throughout the calendar year is taken into account for the number of benefit weeks within the full calendar year.[34]

Students on a Postgraduate Certificate of Education course may get the same student loan and grants as undergraduates and these are treated in the same way as undergraduate loans and grants.

If you leave your course early

For IS, income-based JSA and income-related ESA, if you abandon your course or are dismissed from it, your grant continues to be taken into account until the end of the term or vacation in which you stop being a full-time student or, if earlier, until you repay the grant or the period for which the grant is payable ends.[35]

For HB and CTB, your grant is taken into account until the grant provider asks you to repay it.[36]

---

4. Hardship funds and other payments

Hardship funds, and Access to Learning, Financial Contingency and Learner Support Funds

Hardship funds are treated differently from student grants and loans. Hardship funds include payments from the:[37]

- Access to Learning Fund;
- Welsh Financial Contingency Fund;
- Northern Irish hardship funds;
- further education (FE) Learner Support Fund.

In general, if the payment is for living costs, it is taken into account in full if it counts as capital, or with up to a £20 a week disregarded if it counts as income. If the payment is for other costs, it is disregarded. Ask your college for a letter saying what the payment is for and how it is paid.

Lump-sum payments count as capital. Regular payments count as income.

Grants from FE funds specifically for childcare are disregarded altogether.[38]

Lump-sum payments

Lump-sum payments are taken into account as capital if they are intended and used for food, ordinary clothing or footwear, household fuel, rent met by housing benefit (HB), housing costs met by income support (IS), jobseeker's allowance (JSA) or employment and support allowance (ESA), council tax or water charges.[39] Although taken into account as capital, they only affect your benefit if they bring your capital above the £6,000 lower limit (see p241 for details). Payments for school uniforms or sports clothes or sports shoes are ignored, as these do not count as 'ordinary clothing or footwear'.

Regular payments

Regular payments are taken into account as income if they are intended and used for food, ordinary clothing or footwear, household fuel, rent met by HB, housing costs met by IS, JSA or ESA, council tax or water charges.[40] But up to £20 a week is disregarded. You cannot get the £20 disregard in full as well as the full disregards available on a student loan, widowed parent's allowance or war pensions. If you get one of these other payments in addition to a hardship payment, your maximum weekly disregard is £20. For example, if you have a student loan and receive a war pension, £10 a week is disregarded from each. If you also receive regular payments from a hardship fund, these would count in full as you have already used up your £20 disregard.

Regular payments intended and used for anything else, such as childcare expenses, are completely disregarded.

Payments before a course starts or before a loan is paid

A payment from a hardship fund made before the course starts is always ignored as income even if it is for living costs. A payment made before you get the first instalment of your student loan is ignored as income, provided it is intended to tide you over until your loan is paid.

Institutional bursaries

Bursaries paid by institutions for living costs are treated as income over the period for which they are paid.

Voluntary or charitable payments

Regular voluntary or charitable paymentsare ignored for IS, JSA, HB and council tax benefit. For IS and JSA, if paid as a lump sum, the payment is taken into account as capital whatever it is intended for.

Career development loans

Career development loans are always treated as income rather than capital, no matter how they are paid.[41] The loan is taken into account if it is intended and used for food, ordinary clothing or footwear, household fuel, rent met by HB, housing costs met by IS, ESA, council tax or water charges. Once the period of education supported by the loan is completed, the loan is disregarded altogether, whatever it was originally intended for.

5. Earnings

Your earnings and the earnings of your partner, if you have one, are taken into account in the benefit assessment. It is your net weekly earnings that are taken into account – ie, after deducting:
- income tax;
- Class 1 national insurance contributions;
- half of any contribution you make towards a personal or occupational pension.

Some of your earnings are disregarded. The highest disregard that applies in your circumstances is deducted:
- £25 for lone parents claiming housing benefit (HB) or council tax benefit (CTB) who are not claiming income support (IS) or income-based jobseeker's allowance (JSA);
- £20 for lone parents claiming IS or JSA;

- £20 for someone who gets a disability premium;
- £20 for someone who gets a carer's premium;
- £20 for someone who gets a work-related activity or support component in her/his HB/CTB applicable amount;
- £20 for part-time firefighters and some other emergency auxiliaries;
- £20 for an employment and support allowance claimant (higher if doing permitted work);
- £10 for couples, whether one or both of you are working;
- £5 for single people.

For HB and CTB only, there is an additional disregard (£16.05) for some people working 16/30 hours a week.

For HB and CTB, childcare costs for registered childminders, nurseries and play schemes can be disregarded from earnings in some circumstances. Childcare costs of up to £175 a week for one child or £300 for two or more children are deducted from weekly earnings for:

- lone parents who are working;
- couples who are both working;
- couples, where one is working and one is incapacitated or in hospital or prison.

In each case, the work must be for 16 hours or more a week.

For full details of the way earnings are treated, see CPAG's *Welfare Benefits and Tax Credits Handbook*.

---

6. **Benefits and tax credits**

Some benefits are taken into account in the assessment of income support (IS), income-based jobseeker's allowance (JSA), income-related employment and support allowance (ESA), housing benefit (HB) and council tax benefit (CTB), and others are ignored or partially ignored.

Benefits and tax credits **taken into account in full** include:

- child benefit for HB and CTB;
- child tax credit (CTC) for HB and CTB;
- carer's allowance;
- contribution-based JSA;
- contributory ESA;
- incapacity benefit;
- most industrial injuries benefits;
- retirement pension;
- working tax credit.

Benefits and tax credits **completely disregarded** include:

- attendance allowance;

- child benefit;
- CTC for IS, JSA and ESA;
- disability living allowance;
- social fund payments.

Benefits and tax credits **partly disregarded** include:
- widowed mother's allowance and widowed parent's allowance, which have £10 a week disregarded for IS, JSA and income-related ESA, £15 a week for HB and CTB (but you do not get this disregard if you already have £10 disregarded from a student loan or £20 disregarded from hardship fund payments).

7. Maintenance

For housing benefit and council tax benefit, £15 a week is disregarded from maintenance paid to you by a former partner or your child's other parent. Regular payments count as income and lump sums or irregular payments count as capital.

However, it is expected that by the end of 2008 all payments of this kind will be disregarded.

8. Savings and capital

There are limits on the amount of savings or capital you can have and still claim benefit. These limits are described below. Some kinds of capital are not counted in the assessment. For details see CPAG's *Welfare Benefits and Tax Credits Handbook*.

You cannot get income support, income-based jobseeker's allowance, housing benefit (HB) or council tax benefit (CTB) if your savings or other capital are above £16,000.

If your capital is £6,000 or less it does not affect your benefit at all.

If your capital is between £6,000.01 and £16,000, you are treated as though you have income from this capital of £1 a week for every £250 or part of £250 between these limits. This is referred to as 'tariff income'. For example, if you have savings of £6,525, your tariff income is £3 a week.

These limits are different if you or your partner are aged 60 or over. All your capital is ignored if you or your partner get pension credit guarantee credit. Otherwise, tariff income of £1 for each £500 or part of £500 between the limits is taken into account in the assessment of HB and CTB.

Notes

2. Grants and loans
1 Memo DMG JSA/IS 130 para 4
2 **IS** Reg 66A(3) and (4) IS Regs
  HB Reg 64(3) and (4) HB Regs
3 **IS** Reg 66A(4)(a) IS Regs
  HB Reg 64(4) HB Regs
4 **IS** Reg 67A(5)b IS Regs
  JSA Reg 136(5) JSA Regs
  HB Reg 64(5) HB Regs
  CTB Reg 51(5) CTB Regs
5 **IS** Reg 41(6) IS Regs
  JSA Reg 104(5) JSA Regs
  HB Reg 41(4) HB Regs
  CTB Reg 31(4) CTB Regs
6 **IS** Reg 62(2) IS Regs
  JSA Reg 131(2) JSA Regs
  See also Memo DMG JSA/IS 130, para 7,
  July 2006
7 **IS** Reg 62(2)(a) IS Regs
  HB Reg 59(2)(a) HB Regs
8 **IS** Reg 62(2) IS Regs
  JSA Reg 131(2) JSA Regs
  See also Memo DMG JSA/IS 130, para 6,
  July 2006
9 **IS** Reg 62(2) IS Regs
  JSA Reg 131(2) JSA Regs
  See also Memo DMG JSA/IS 130, para 7,
  July 2006
10 **IS** Reg 62(2)(c) IS Regs
  HB Reg 59(2)(b) HB Regs
11 paras 5.246 – 5.249 GM
12 **IS** Reg 62(2)(h) IS Regs
  HB Reg 59(2)(g) HB Regs
13 **IS** Reg 62(2)(g) and (h) IS Regs
  JSA Reg 131(2) JSA Regs
  HB Reg 59(2) HB Regs
14 **IS** Reg 62(2)(a) IS Regs
  JSA Reg 131(2)(a) JSA Regs
  See also Memo DMG JSA/IS 130, para 8,
  July 2006
15 **HB** Reg 59(6) HB Regs
16 paras 5.361 – 5.364 GM
17 **IS** Sch 9 para 11(a) IS Regs
  HB Sch 5 para 11 HB Regs
18 ALG Guidance 2006/07 para 4.5
19 ALG guidance 2006/07 para 1.7
20 **IS** Reg 68 IS Regs
  JSA Reg 138 JSA Regs
  HB Reg 68 HB Regs
  CTB Reg 55 CTB Regs

21 **IS** Reg 66B IS Regs
  JSA Reg 136A JSA Regs
  HB Reg 65 HB Regs
  CTB Reg 52 CTB Regs

3. Dividing income throughout the year
22 **IS** Reg 66A(2)(c) IS Regs
  HB Reg 64(2)(d) HB Regs
23 **HB** Reg 2 HB Regs
  CTB Reg 2 CTB Regs
24 **IS** Reg 66A(2)(b) IS Regs
  HB Reg 64(2)(d) HB Regs
25 **IS** Reg 66A(2)(aa) IS Regs
  HB Reg 64(2)(b) HB Regs
26 **IS** Reg 61(1) IS Regs
  HB Reg 53(1) HB Regs
27 **IS** Reg 66A(2)(aa) IS Regs
  HB Reg 64(2)(b) HB Regs
28 **IS** Reg 40(3A) IS Regs
  HB Reg 40(7) HB Regs
29 See also HB/CTB Circular A31/2001 Part
  6 and Annex D for guidance and a
  sample calculation, together with HB/
  CTB Circular A39/2001, para 19
30 CJSA/549/2003
31 para 30305 Vol 6 DMG
32 **IS** Reg 62(3B) IS Regs
  HB Reg 59(7) HB Regs
33 **IS** Reg 62(2)(h) IS Regs
  HB Reg 59(2)(g) HB Regs
  CTB Reg 46(2)(g) CTB Regs
34 **IS** Regs 61 and 62(3)(a) IS Regs
  HB Regs 53 and 59(5)(a) HB Regs
35 **IS** Reg 29(2B) IS Regs
  JSA Reg 94(2B) JSA Regs
36 *Leeves v Chief Adjudication Officer,*
  reported as R(IS) 5/99

4. Hardship funds and other payments
37 **IS** Reg 61 IS Regs
  HB Reg 53 HB Regs
38 **IS** Reg 61(1) IS Regs
  JSA Reg 130 JSA Regs
  HB Reg 53(1) HB Regs
  CTB Reg 43(1) CTB Regs
39 **IS** Reg 68 IS Regs
  HB Reg 68 HB Regs
40 **IS** Reg 66B IS Regs
  HB Reg 65 HB Regs
41 **IS** Reg 41(6) IS Regs
  HB Reg 41(4) HB Regs

Chapter 21

How income affects tax credits

This chapter covers:
1. Working out your income (below)
2. Grants and loans (p244)
3. Earnings (p246)
4. Benefits (p246)
5. Other income (p247)

This chapter explains how HM Revenue and Customs treats your income when working out your entitlement to tax credits. It outlines the type of student income that is taken into account, as well as how other income, such as earnings, is treated. Most forms of student support are, however, disregarded for tax credits purposes. The rules apply to both part-time and full-time students.

For details of the rules of entitlement to tax credits, see Chapters 18 and 19.

1. Working out your income

Step 1 **Add together all taxable income from the previous full tax year.**
Add all of your taxable benefits and income from employment or self-employment from the previous full tax year. Use the current full tax year if your income is lower or more than £25,000 higher than the previous year's.

Step 2 **Add any relevant student income.**
Add any relevant student income – adult dependants' grant, lone parents' grant, or living costs elements of a career development loan (see p244) – from the same period.

Step 3 **Add any other relevant income.**
Add any other relevant forms of income from the same period.
This is the total income on which your claim will be assessed.

Step 4   **Calculate any excess.**

If your total income is less than £15,575 for child tax credit or £6,420 for working tax credit, you will receive the maximum to which you are entitled.

If it is more than £15,575 (or £6,420), subtract £15,575 (or £6,420) from the total amount. Divide the remainder by 100 and multiply by 39. This is the amount that should be subtracted from your total maximum entitlement (see Chapters 18 and 19 for details of how this is calculated) to give the amount you will receive.

2. Grants and loans

Most grants and loans are disregarded when calculating a student's income for tax credit purposes (see below).[1] The following are the exceptions.

- Adult dependants' grant. Any grant received for an adult dependant is included in the calculation.
- Career development loan. Any part of this paid for living costs for the period supported by the loan is taken into account in full.[2]

Grants and loans checklist

Student support	Treatment
Further education income	
Adult learning grant	Disregarded
Care to Learn grant	Disregarded
Childcare fund	Disregarded
Education maintenance allowance	Disregarded
Further education award (Northern Ireland)	Disregarded
Learner Support Fund grant	Disregarded
Sixth-form childcare allowance	Disregarded
Special educational needs allowance	Disregarded
Travel grant or expenses	Disregarded
Welsh Assembly learning grant	Disregarded
Undergraduate income	
Access to Learning Fund grant	Disregarded
Adult dependants' grant	Taken into account in full
Care leavers' vacation grant	Disregarded
Childcare grant	Disregarded
Disabled students' allowance	Disregarded
English Opportunity bursary	Disregarded
Financial Contingency Fund grant	Disregarded

Hardship funds	Disregarded
Higher education grant	Disregarded
Institutional bursaries or scholarships	Disregarded
Maintenance grant	Disregarded
NHS dependants' grant for children	Disregarded
NHS healthcare bursary	Disregarded
Northern Ireland higher education bursary	Disregarded
Nursing and midwifery bursary	Disregarded
Parents' learning allowance	Disregarded
Part-time students' grant for course costs	Disregarded
Part-time students' grant for fees	Disregarded
Social work bursary	Disregarded
Special support grant	Disregarded
Student loan for living costs (including any means-tested element where appropriate)	Disregarded
Travelling expenses	Disregarded
Tuition fee grant	Disregarded
Tuition fee loan	Disregarded
Welsh Assembly learning grant	Disregarded

Postgraduate income

Books and equipment expenses	Disregarded
British Academy grant	Disregarded
Research council studentship or scholarship	Disregarded
Residential study	Disregarded
Social work bursary	Disregarded
Supplementary grants	As for undergraduate income
Teacher training grant	Disregarded
Tuition fees grant or loan	Disregarded

Other income

Career development loan	Disregarded, except for any amount applied or paid for living expenses during the period supported by the loan, which is taken into account in full

3. Earnings

Your gross earnings from the last full tax year plus those of your partner (if any) are taken into account in the tax credit assessment. 'Gross earnings' means all income before any income tax or national insurance contributions are deducted. It also includes tips, overtime pay, taxable expenses and taxable payments related to the termination of employment such as redundancy pay and strike pay.[3] If you make any contributions to a personal or occupational pension approved by HM Revenue and Customs, these contributions should be disregarded.[4] The first £100 a week of statutory maternity, paternity and adoption pay is disregarded, but payments above this are included.[5] Statutory sick pay is included in full.[6] Any payments which are exempt from income tax should be ignored for the purposes of tax credits.

For full details of the way earnings are treated, see CPAG's *Welfare Benefits and Tax Credits Handbook.*

4. Benefits

Generally speaking, benefits that are not taxable are disregarded when calculating tax credits, and benefits that are taxable are included. For full details of the way social security benefits are treated, see CPAG's *Welfare Benefits and Tax Credits Handbook.*

Benefits **disregarded** include:[7]
- child benefit;
- disability living allowance;
- employment and support allowance (child tax credit only – cannot be claimed with working tax credit)
- guardian's allowance;
- housing benefit;
- lower rate of short-term incapacity benefit (IB);
- income support (except to strikers);
- income-based jobseeker's allowance (JSA);
- maternity allowance;
- social fund payments;
- most war pensions;[8]
- increases for a child or adult dependant paid with any of the above benefits.

Benefits **taken into account in full** include:
- bereavement allowance;
- carer's allowance;
- long-term IB;

- higher rate of short-term IB;
- contribution-based JSA (although amounts above the 'taxable maximum' are ignored. In practice, people are not paid above this amount so in the majority of cases all contribution-based JSA will be included);
- increases for a child or adult dependant paid with any of the above benefits.

Benefits **partly taken into account** include state retirement pension (and private and occupational pensions) and widows' pensions. These are included in tax credit calculations, although the first £300 of the total income from pensions, income from capital, and foreign or notional income is disregarded.

5. **Other income**

Savings and investments

Savings and investments are ignored as the tax credit assessment is based on income only. Any taxable income from your savings and investments is included, although the first £300 of the total income from pensions, income from capital, and foreign or notional income is disregarded.

Property

As with savings and investments, the capital value of any property is ignored, but any taxable rental income is included, although the first £300 of the total income from pensions, income from capital, and foreign or notional income is disregarded.[9]

Maintenance

Regular maintenance from an ex-partner is ignored, regardless of how the arrangement was made. Similarly, any support received from an ex-partner for your child(ren) is also ignored.[10]

For further details of how other income is treated, see CPAG's *Welfare Benefits and Tax Credits Handbook*.

Notes

2. Grants and loans
1 Reg 8 TC(DCI) Regs
Reg 19(c) table 8 para 2 TC(DCI) Regs

3. Earnings
2 Reg 4 TC(DCI) Regs
3 Reg 3(7)(c) TC(DCI) Regs
4 Reg 4(1)(h) TC(DCI) Regs
5 Reg 4(1)(g) TC(DCI) Regs

4. Benefits
6 Reg 7(3) TC(DCI) Regs
7 Reg 5 TC(DCI) Regs

5. Other income
8 Reg 11 TC(DCI) Regs
9 Reg 19 table 6 para 10 TC(DCI) Regs

Chapter 22

How income affects health benefits

This chapter covers:
1. Working out your income (below)
2. Grants and loans (p250)
3. Hardship funds and other payments (p254)
4. Earnings (p255)
5. Benefits and tax credits (p255)
6. Maintenance (p256)
7. Savings and capital (p256)

This chapter explains how your income is treated when your entitlement to health benefits under the NHS low income scheme is worked out. It outlines the type of student income that is taken into account and how much can be disregarded, as well as how other income, such as earnings, is treated. It applies to both part-time and full-time students.

If you are not otherwise exempt from healthcare costs (see Chapter 11) and have less than £16,000 (£17,250 in Wales), or £21,500 if you are in a care home (£22,000 in Wales) a year in property, savings, or other assessed income or capital, you are eligible to apply for at least some assistance.

The exact amount of help you receive depends on the amount of excess weekly income (if any) you are assessed as having, once it is offset against a personal allowance and your housing costs. The NHS Business Services Authority Patient Services calculates this from the information provided on Form HC1.

1. Working out your income

The way that student income is taken into account for health benefits is broadly the same as for means-tested benefits.

Step 1   **Apply annual disregard.**

From the student loan, deduct the disregarded amount of £675 for books, equipment and travel.

Step 2   **Divide income throughout the year.**

Divide the annual amount of loan by 52 weeks, unless you are in the final or only year of your course, in which case you should divide by the number of weeks between the start and finish of your course.

Step 3   **Weekly disregard.**

Unlike the means-tested benefits assessment, there is no weekly disregard of £10 on the student loan, unless you receive a premium in your applicable amount, an allowance because of deafness (separate to any disabled students' allowance), or you are not a student but your partner is. If you fall into any of these categories, disregard £10.

Step 4   **Add other income to weekly loan amount.**

Add together any other weekly income (except for 'mandatory' awards such as research council awards or non-means-tested NHS bursaries) – eg, from hardship funds or a career development loan (see p254), earnings (see p255), tariff income from capital (see p256), benefits and tax credits (see p255) – ignoring any amount that is disregarded.

Step 5   **Divide mandatory grant income over 52 weeks.**

Divide any mandatory grant or bursary over 52 weeks and add this to the weekly amounts where appropriate. Sums in excess of a maintenance grant are disregarded. This total, added to the weekly loan total calculated at Step 4, is the amount of income used in the health benefit assessment.

2. **Grants and loans**

Student loan

A student loan includes:
- the maximum loan for which you are eligible, including any means-tested element (where applicable). This is taken into account as your income whether or not you apply for it. The Government believes that it is the primary source of public support to students and, therefore, should be fully exhausted before further support is given;
- any payments for extra weeks' attendance.

The NHS Business Services Authority Patient Services disregards £675 for books, travel and equipment from the annual student loan.

Grants

In general, grants intended for living costs (such as the old maintenance grant, the NHS bursary and the social work bursary) are taken into account and grants for other costs are disregarded. For details of how Access to Learning Fund and other hardship grants are treated, see p254.

In England and Wales, the first £1,260 of any maintenance grant or Welsh Assembly learning grant for new students paid to 'current system' students subject to variable or flexible tuition fees is taken into account, but amounts above this are ignored. In Northern Ireland, the first £1,760 of the higher education bursary is taken into account, but amounts above this are ignored.[1] Institutional bursaries and scholarships are taken into account if they are paid for living costs.

If you are *not* eligible for a student loan, £675 for books, travel and equipment is deducted from your grant.

Social work bursaries are usually divided over the number of weeks of study, except where classroom weeks exceed 45, in which case they are divided by 52.

Teacher training bursaries are divided over the number of days they are paid, then multiplied by seven to give a weekly amount. The £675 disregard is not applied.

Grants in further education

The following further education grants are **disregarded**:
- education maintenance allowance;
- adult learning grant;
- Care to Learn grant;
- travel expenses allowance.

Grants in higher education

The following higher education (HE) grants are completely **disregarded**:
- HE grant for 'old system' students;
- Welsh Assembly learning grant for 'old system' students;
- part-time course costs grant;
- childcare grant;
- parents' learning allowance;
- disabled students' allowance;
- travel expenses;
- tuition fees grants and loans.

The following grants are **taken into account**:
- care leavers' vacation grant (Northern Ireland);
- adult dependants' grant;
- teacher training bursary;
- nursing and midwifery bursary;
- social work bursary.

Postgraduate grants

Any research council or other maintenance grant and dependants' allowances are taken into account. Supplementary grants are treated in the same way as those for undergraduates (see p251). Ignore:

- grants for tuition fees;
- grants for residential study away from your normal home;
- grants intended to meet the costs of books and equipment.

Grants and loans checklist

Student support	Treatment
Further education income	
Adult learning grant	Disregarded
Care to Learn grant	Disregarded
Childcare fund	Disregarded
Education maintenance allowance	Disregarded
Learner Support Fund grant	Taken into account if paid for basic living
Financial Contingency Fund grant	costs, disregarded if paid for other items
Sixth-form childcare grant	Disregarded
Special educational needs allowance	Disregarded
Travel expenses allowance	Disregarded
Welsh Assembly learning grant	Disregarded
Undergraduate income	
Access to Learning Fund grant,	Taken into account if paid for basic living
Financial Contingency Fund grant and	costs (as capital if not regular payments),
Northern Irish hardship funds	disregarded if paid for other items
Adult dependants' grant	Taken into account in full
Care leavers' vacation grant	Taken into account in full
Childcare grant	Disregarded
Disabled students' allowance	Disregarded
Higher education grant	Disregarded
Institutional bursaries or scholarships	Taken into account if paid for living costs
Loan (including any means-tested element	Taken into account
where appropriate)	Disregarded:
	– £675 a year for books, travel and equipment; *and*
	– £10 a week in certain circumstances (see above)
Maintenance grants (including Welsh Assembly learning grant for 'new system' students)	Any sum in excess of £1,260 (£1,760 in Northern Ireland, see above)

NHS healthcare bursary Nursing and midwifery bursary	Means-tested: taken into account in full Non-means-tested: taken into account, except for £675 a year disregard for books, travel and equipment
Parents' learning allowance	Disregarded
Part-time grant for course costs	Disregarded
Part-time grant for tuition fees	Disregarded
Social work bursary	Taken into account, with £675 a year disregard if you are not entitled to a student loan
Special support grant	Disregarded
Teacher training bursary	Taken into account
Travelling expenses	Disregarded
Tuition fee grant	Disregarded
Tuition fee loan	Disregarded
Welsh Assembly learning grant for 'old system' students	Disregarded

Postgraduate income

Books and equipment	Disregarded
Research council studentship or scholarship	Taken into account, except for an annual £675 books, travel and equipment disregard
Residential study	Disregarded
Social work bursary	Taken into account
Supplementary grants	As for undergraduate income
Teacher training salary	Taken into account
Tuition fees grant or loan	Disregarded

Example

Oliver is a third-year full-time undergraduate in Wales. He receives the maximum away-from-home student loan (£3,020), the maximum Assembly learning grant for 'new system' students (£2,835) and £20 a week from his parents for food and bills.

When calculating his income for health benefits purposes, subtract £675 from his student loan, to give £2,345 and include the first £1,260 of his Welsh Assembly learning grant. This gives £3,605. Divide this by 52 weeks (to give £69.32). The £20 a week he gets from his parents is added to this figure and his income is, therefore, assessed to be £89.32 a week.

This income would then be set against the appropriate income support personal allowances, housing and other costs to determine whether or not it exceeds or falls short of Oliver's requirements. If it does fall short he would receive full support. If his income exceeds this amount, he may receive partial support, depending on the level of excess.

3. **Hardship funds and other payments**

Access to Learning Fund and other hardship funds

Discretionary support provided when you are in financial difficulty is treated differently from other student grants and loans. This support can include:
- higher education (HE) Financial Contingency Fund, Northern Irish hardship funds or Access to Learning Fund;
- further education (FE) Learner Support Fund or Financial Contingency Fund.

In general, if the payment is for living costs it is taken into account in full if it counts as capital, or with up to a £20 a week disregard if it counts as income. If the payment is for other costs, it is disregarded. For example, an FE Learner Support Fund grant solely for childcare costs is disregarded. Ask your college for a letter saying what the payment is for and how it is paid.

Lump-sum payments count as capital. Regular payments count as income.

Lump-sum payments

Lump-sum payments are taken into account as capital if they are intended and used for living costs such as food, ordinary clothing or footwear, household fuel, rent, council tax or water charges. Payments for anything else are disregarded. Although taken into account as capital, this only affects your entitlement if it brings your capital above the £16,000 lower limit (or £17,250 in Wales). See p256 for details.

Regular payments

Regular payments are taken into account as income if they are intended and used for food, ordinary clothing or footwear, household fuel, rent, council tax or water charges. Up to £20 a week is disregarded. You cannot get the £20 disregard in full as well as the full disregards available on a student loan or voluntary and charitable payments (or on widowed parent's allowance or war pensions). If you get one of these other payments as well as a payment from the Access to Learning Fund (or equivalent), your maximum weekly disregard is £20.

For example, if you have a student loan and regular payments from the Access to Learning Fund, £10 a week is disregarded from each. If you also receive regular payments from a charity, these would count in full as you have already used up your £20 disregard on the loan and the hardship fund payment.

Regular payments intended and used for anything else, such as childcare expenses, are completely disregarded.

Voluntary or charitable payments

These are treated in the same way as hardship fund payments.

Career development loans

Career development loans are always treated as income, not capital, no matter how they are paid. The loan is taken into account if it is intended and used for living costs – eg, food, ordinary clothing or footwear, household fuel, rent, council tax or water charges. Once the period of education supported by the loan is completed, the loan is disregarded altogether, whatever it was originally intended for.

4. Earnings

Your earnings and the earnings of your partner, if you have one, are taken into account in the health benefits assessment. It is your net weekly earnings that are taken into account – ie, deducting:

- income tax;
- Class 1 national insurance contributions;
- half of any contribution you make towards a personal or occupational pension.

5. Benefits and tax credits

If you receive income support (IS), income-based jobseeker's allowance (JSA), income-related employment and support allowance or child tax credit, you automatically get free health benefits (see Chapter 11).

Housing benefit and council tax benefit are effectively disregarded, as the NHS Business Services Authority Patient Services only takes into account the rent and council tax paid directly by the applicant when determining need.

Benefits and tax credits **taken into account** in full include:

- carer's allowance;
- contribution-based JSA;
- incapacity benefit;
- most industrial injuries benefits;
- retirement pension;
- working tax credit.

Benefits and tax credits **completely disregarded** include:

- attendance allowance;
- child benefit for IS and JSA once your IS or JSA no longer includes allowances for children;

- disability living allowance;
- social fund payments.

Benefits and tax credits **partly disregarded** include:
- widowed mother's allowance and widowed parent's allowance, which have £10 a week disregarded. **Note:** you do not receive this disregard if you already have £10 disregarded from a student loan or £20 disregarded from hardship fund payments.

6. **Maintenance**

Regular maintenance payments (eg, child support and parental or spousal contributions towards maintenance) count as income. As a general rule, income will normally be taken into account in the week in which it is paid, subject to a weekly disregard of £5, £10 or £20 depending on circumstances. Irregular payments are averaged over the 13 weeks prior to your claim and lump sums are treated as capital.

7. **Savings and capital**

There are limits on the amount of savings or capital you can have and still claim health benefits.

You cannot get health benefits if your savings or other capital is above £16,000 (£17,250 in Wales).

If your capital is £6,000 or less it does not affect your benefits at all. If your capital is between £6,000.01 and £16,000 (a higher limit if you are in a care home), you are treated as though you have an income from this capital of £1 a week for every £250 (or part of £250) between these amounts. This is referred to as 'tariff income'. For example, if you have savings of £6,525, your tariff income is £3 a week.

Notes

1 The National Health Service (Travel Expenses and Remission of Charges) Amendment (No.2) Regulations 2006, No.2171

Part 4

Other issues

Chapter 23

Council tax

This chapter covers:

Basic facts

– Council tax is a local tax on residential dwellings.
– You do not pay council tax if you are under 18.
– Council tax does not apply in Northern Ireland.
– Students sharing accommodation solely with other full-time students do not pay council tax.
– Students sharing accommodation with non-students do not pay, although they may be liable for periods before 1 April 2004.
– Students who own the home in which they live are liable, but may be exempt or get a discount.
– Full-time students liable to pay council tax can claim council tax benefit if they get income support or income-based jobseeker's allowance, or if they have children, are disabled or are over 60. Part-time students are eligible for benefit whatever their circumstances.
– From April 2006, a full-time student sharing with others who all get income support, jobseeker's allowance or pension credit and do not pay rent to the student qualifies for a second adult rebate of 100 per cent.

1. **What is council tax**

Council tax is a tax on residential dwellings and is paid to the local authority. There is one amount to pay and one bill for each dwelling unless it is exempt from council tax. A 'dwelling' includes a self-contained flat.

Each dwelling is allocated a valuation band from A to H based on property values in 1991 (2005 in Wales). Council tax is lowest for those in Band A.

Some dwellings are exempt from council tax. If the dwelling is exempt, there is no council tax to pay for anyone who lives there or for a non-resident owner. There are also exemptions specifically for students (see p263).

Properties occupied solely by students are usually exempt. Students who share with non-students are also exempt from payment of council tax, although the property itself is not exempt. However, the law in the latter case was changed in 2004 and students who shared with non-students may be held to be jointly liable to pay council tax for periods before 1 April 2004 (see p263). If you are a student and you are liable, the amount to pay may be reduced if you are eligible for council tax benefit or second adult rebate (see p266 or p267).

2. Who pays council tax

As a student, you may be exempt from paying council tax if:
- the accommodation in which you live is exempt (see p262); *or*
- you are not liable to pay (see p263).

If neither of these applies, it may be possible to reduce the council tax bill if:
- the liable person can get a discount (see p265); *or*
- the liable person can get council tax benefit (CTB – see p266) or second adult rebate (see p267).

Who counts as a student

If you are aged 19 or under, whether you count as a student for council tax purposes depends on whether you are on an advanced or non-advanced course. For older students, one rule applies whatever level of course you do.

19 or under in non-advanced education

You are regarded as a 'student' for council tax purposes if you are aged 19 or under and on a non-advanced course of more than 12 hours a week.[1]

A **'non-advanced course'** is one below the level of a foundation degree, honours degree, HNC, HND or NVQ Level 4. It includes A levels, AVCEs, National Diplomas and National Certificates. The course must last more than three months.[2] It does not include:
- evening classes;[3]
- correspondence courses;[4]
- courses taken as a result of your office or occupation.[5]

The hours that count are those required by the course rather than those you actually do, if they are different.

To work out your hours, average out over term times the hours required under the course for tuition, supervised study, exams, and supervised exercise, experiment, project and practical work.[6]

You are treated as a student for each day from the day you start the course until the day you complete it, abandon it or are dismissed from it.[7] So you count as a student during term times, during short vacations at Christmas and Easter and during the summer if your course continues after the summer. If your course ends in the summer and you begin a different one in the autumn, you do not count as a student in the summer between courses.[8] However, you might still have a 'status discount' (see p265).

> ### Example
> Drew is 18 and taking three A levels at college. Including his classes, exams and supervised study, his course hours are 18 a week. He is a student for council tax purposes.

19 or under in higher education

The rules are the same as they are for those aged 20 or over (see below).

20 or over in non-advanced or higher education

You are regarded as a 'student' for council tax purposes if the course requires attendance for at least 21 hours a week in at least 24 weeks each academic year.[9]

Hours include periods of study as well as tuition. If you are on a sandwich course, include required periods of work experience.

To count as a student you must be enrolled on a course with an educational institution. You are a student from the day you begin the course until the day you complete it, abandon it or are no longer permitted by the educational institution to attend it.[10] So if you take time out and are not enrolled on the course during that period, you do not count as a student for council tax purposes and you may become liable for council tax (check whether you can get CTB). On the other hand, if you take time out but are still enrolled on the course, you continue to count as a student so long as you have not abandoned it completely and the institution has not said you can no longer attend the course. Because the law says you are not a student if you are 'no longer permitted by the institution to attend', it suggests that your dismissal from the course must be final. So you could argue that if you are temporarily suspended from the course but still registered, you do still count as a student. In an informal letter, written in 1996, the former Department of the Environment (then responsible for the council tax) stated:

> In our view a period of intercalation will remain within the period of a course. . . and therefore, provided that the person remains enrolled at the education establishment, they will continue to fall within the definition of a full-time student.[11]

Your college or university determines the number of hours. You may need evidence from it to prove to the local authority that you count as a student. Colleges and universities are required by law to provide you with a certificate if you ask for one while you are a student or up to a year after you leave the course.[12] After that, they may still give you a certificate, but are not legally required to do so. The certificate must contain:[13]

- the name and address of the institution;
- your full name;
- your term-time address and home address (if known by the institution);
- a statement that you are (or were) a student – ie, that you are enrolled on a course requiring attendance of at least 21 hours a week over at least 24 weeks a year; *and*
- the date you became a student and the date your course ends.

Postgraduate students

Full-time postgraduate students are regarded as 'students' for council tax purposes in the same way as other full-time higher education students.

In the past, some postgraduate research students have had difficulty in securing council tax exemption because local authorities have considered that their periods of 'study, tuition or work experience' do not meet the requirements of the regulations, and that, in particular, research does not count as 'study'. This has been successfully challenged in an appeal in Kent and, although it does not set a legal precedent, local authorities are obliged to take such decisions into account when making their own decisions.

Other postgraduate students have had difficulty in securing exemption during the thesis 'writing up' period after the formal end of the course. Whilst some local authorities are sympathetic and will extend student status after the end of the course, others have been known to regard such students as liable as they are no longer 'within the period of their course'. If this affects you, seek advice from your students' union or institution's advice centre.

Note: students who have completed their undergraduate course and intend to start a postgraduate course in the following academic year are not exempt as they are not within the period of either course. Depending on your circumstances, however, you may be able to claim council tax benefit (see p266) or a discount on the bill (see p265).

Exempt dwellings

A dwelling is exempt if everyone who occupies it is:[14]
- a student; *or*
- a student's overseas partner if s/he entered the UK on a visa that denies the right to work or claim benefits. If the partner has the right to work but not to claim benefits, s/he should come under this exemption; *or*
- under age 18; *or*

- under age 20 and left non-advanced education at school or college after 30 April – this only applies between 1 May and 31 October of the year they left school or college; *or*
- 'severely mentally impaired'.

An unoccupied dwelling is exempt for up to four months if it is the main residence of a student (and not of anyone else who is not a student) and it was last occupied by one or more students. This allows an exemption to continue, for example, to the student's term-time accommodation through the summer vacation. Dwellings left unoccupied by a student owner are exempt indefinitely as long as the owner has been a student since s/he last occupied the dwelling or within six weeks of leaving it. Unoccupied dwellings which are substantially unfurnished are exempt for up to six months. If you are liable for council tax and anyone who is jointly liable with you is also a student, and the dwelling is no one's main residence, the dwelling is exempt without time limit.

If the dwelling is exempt, there is no council tax to pay.

There are a number of other exemptions that are not specifically aimed at students. For details see CPAG's *Council Tax Handbook*.

Who is liable for council tax

Most full-time students are not liable to pay council tax. This is because either the dwelling is exempt because everyone who lives there is a full-time student or, if a student lives with non-students, s/he is deemed exempt from liability for council tax due on the property.

If the dwelling is not exempt from council tax, at least one person is liable for the bill. Who that is depends on her/his position in a liability hierarchy. The person who comes first (highest up) in the hierarchy is the one who is liable to pay. If there are two or more people at the same level in the hierarchy, they are usually jointly liable.

Council tax liability hierarchy
Resident with a freehold interest in the property
Resident with a leasehold on the property, or the superior leaseholder if there is more than one
Resident tenant
Resident statutory or secure tenant
Resident who is a licensee
Other resident, including a squatter

If students share accommodation with non-students who are at the same level in the hierarchy, the non-students are liable but the students are not.[15] However, this has only been the case since 1 April 2004 and, therefore, if you were a student and shared accommodation before this date with one or more non-students who were at the same level in the hierarchy, you may be jointly and severally liable for council tax due during that time (see below).

There remains one situation where a student may still be liable for the council tax. If you live with one or more non-students, but you are higher on the hierarchy of liability than the non-students – eg, you are the owner of the property or the only person named on the tenancy agreement, the property ceases to be exempt from council tax. However, because you are higher up on the hierarchy of liability you, and not the non-students in the property, would be liable for the council tax. In this case you may, nevertheless, be entitled to a discount on the bill or to CTB, depending on your circumstances.

Example: joint tenants

Three students, Pooja, Joey and Zarah, share a flat as joint tenants. While they are all students the flat is exempt and there is no council tax to pay. Joey drops out of his course. The flat is no longer exempt and Joey is solely liable for the whole council tax bill (although there is a discount). Pooja and Zarah are not liable for any council tax. Joey should apply for CTB if his income is low.

Examples: students who remain liable

Antonia is studying full time and owns the flat in which she lives. She rents out a room to a friend who is not a student. Antonia is liable for the council tax. As there is only one non-student at the property, there is a 25 per cent discount on the bill. Her friend is not liable for any council tax.

Raj is studying full time and rents the flat in which he lives. He sub-lets a room to a friend who is also a student. Raj is higher up on the hierarchy of liability, but, as both of them are students, the flat is exempt and the bill is nil.

Joint and several liability

Joint and several liability means that, in legal terms, you can be held liable for all or part of a bill, even thought here may be more than one person named. This gives the local authority the right to pursue as many or as few people for payment of the bill as it likes, regardless of how many liable residents are, or were, in the property.[16]

Example: joint and several liability

In the 2003/04 academic year Amy was a full-time student and shared a house with two other students, Binda and Caroline. Initially, the property was exempt. However, Amy decided to leave her course in January 2004 and started full-time employment. The house then ceased to be exempt from council tax liability and, as joint residents, all three women became jointly and severally liable until 1 April 2004. After this date, because of changes to the law, only Amy was liable and, as the only eligible person, she received a 25 per cent discount. No tax for either period was paid.

One year later, when all three have moved to other residences, the local authority pursued payment of the outstanding council tax for the period between January and April 2004 and also for tax due after this date. It had no contact details for Amy or Binda, so sent the full bill for the earlier period to Caroline. Legally, Caroline is required to pay the total amount. She is not, however, required to pay any tax due on the property after 1 April 2004; the local authority can only pursue Amy for this.

In practice, local authorities will try to bill as many liable people as possible. If they cannot contact all of the liable people, those who they can contact can be required to take on the total debt between them.

Couples

Normally couples (of the same or opposite sex, and whether married, in a civil partnership or cohabiting) who live together are jointly liable for the council tax. Students, however, are exempt from this rule. If you have a non-student partner who is liable for council tax, you are not jointly liable while you are a student.[17]

Discounts

The full council tax bill assumes that there are two adults living in the dwelling. You get a discount of 25 per cent if there is only one person living there. You get a discount of 50 per cent if there is no one living there. Full-time students who are liable can get a 100 per cent discount if the people they share with do not pay them rent and all receive income support, jobseeker's allowance or pension credit (see below). You also get a discount if there is no one or just one adult living there, other than people in certain specified circumstances. These people are sometimes described as 'invisible' (because they are disregarded when counting how many live in the dwelling) or as having a 'status discount'.

The following people are disregarded in this way:
- anyone under 18 years old;
- anyone aged 18 or over for whom child benefit is payable;
- full-time students;
- partners of students who are not British citizens and whose immigration status prevents them from taking up paid employment or accessing social security benefits (though not necessarily both);
- someone under age 20 who was on a non-advanced course of education and who left school or college after 1 May – the status discount lasts from 1 May until 31 October;

- student nurses (ie, those studying for registration);
- apprentices training for an NVQ and on low pay;
- others – eg, carers, hospital patients and trainees (see CPAG's *Council Tax Handbook*).

Disability reduction

The council tax bill is reduced to the valuation band below your own band if you or anyone else (adult or child) who is resident in the dwelling is substantially and permanently disabled and uses a wheelchair indoors or needs an extra room.

3. **Council tax benefit**

Council tax benefit (CTB) is administered by local authorities and helps pay the council tax. To get CTB you must meet all of the following conditions.

- You are liable for council tax. Most full-time students are not liable for council tax and have no need to claim benefit.
- You do not count as a student, or you do count as a student but are still eligible for CTB (see below).
- You are 'habitually resident' in the UK, Ireland, Channel Islands or the Isle of Man and not a 'person subject to immigration control'. These terms are explained in CPAG's *Welfare Benefits and Tax Credits Handbook*.
- You have no more than £16,000 capital.[18] There is no capital limit if you are aged 60 or over and getting the pension credit guarantee credit.
- Your income is sufficiently low. CTB is means tested so the amount you get depends on how much income you have.

Students eligible for council tax benefit

Part-time students can claim CTB. If you are a full-time student you cannot claim CTB unless:[19]

- you are under 19, or aged 19 and you started your course when you were under 19 and not in higher education;
- you are a full-time student aged 20 or over or aged 19 when you started your course, or aged under 19 if you are in higher education, and:
  - you get income support (IS) or income-based jobseeker's allowance (JSA); *or*
  - you are a lone parent or part of a full-time student couple with a child; *or*
  - you are a disabled student.

The way 'full-time student' is defined is the same as for housing benefit (HB – see p131). **Note:** it is not the same as the council tax definition described in this chapter. The groups of students eligible for CTB are the same as those eligible for HB (see p130).

You can get a claim form for CTB from the local authority. There is usually one form for claiming both CTB and HB. If you are claiming IS or income-based JSA, you claim CTB at the same time. You can claim backdated CTB if you receive a council tax bill for a past period on the grounds that the local authority has only just notified you of liability.

4. **Second adult rebate**

All students who are liable for council tax can claim second adult rebate. The law refers to this rebate as 'alternative maximum council tax benefit'. It is intended for people whose bill is higher because they live with others who cannot get a status discount and who cannot make a full contribution towards a share of the bill. You can only get a second adult rebate if you live with someone else who is not a full-time student.

Whether you get a rebate or not depends on the income of the people who share with you. Your own income or capital is ignored.

You can get a second adult rebate if:

- you are liable for council tax; *and*
- you have a 'second adult' (see below) living with you; *and*
- the second adult is on income support (IS) or income-based jobseeker's allowance (JSA), or has a low income; *and*
- you do not get rent from a tenant or sub-tenant (arguably rent from students or others who have a status discount should not disbar you from getting second adult rebate);[20] *and*
- if you are in a couple, one or both of you must be students or have a status discount for some other reason; *and*
- if you are jointly liable for the council tax, all of those jointly liable must, or all but one must, be students or have a status discount for some other reason.

A **'second adult'** is someone aged 18 or over who is a non-dependant – ie, someone who lives with you on a non-commercial basis, and is not a student and does not have a status discount for any other reason.

If you are eligible for second adult rebate and for council tax benefit, the local authority will decide which is worth the most to you. You cannot get both at the same time. If you get a second adult rebate, you get a reduction of 25 per cent, 15 per cent or 7.5 per cent depending on the income of the second adult.

Where a full-time student shares with others who all get either IS, JSA or pension credit and do not pay rent to the student, the discount can be 100 per cent. As the rules around second adult rebate are complex, you should get advice from your students' union, institution or local Citizens Advice Bureau.

Examples

Terry and his wife, June, live with their daughter, Minnie, aged 22. June is a student. Minnie is claiming JSA. Terry rents their house from a housing association. Terry can claim second adult rebate. Minnie is the second adult.

Dean is a student and he owns the flat he shares with his brother, Steve. Steve is aged 19 and works for the minimum wage. Dean can claim second adult rebate. Steve is the second adult.

Notes

2. Who pays council tax
1   Sch 1 para 5(1) CT(DD)O
2   Sch 1 para 6(1)(a) CT(DD)O
3   Sch 1 para 6(1)(e) CT(DD)O
4   Sch 1 para 6(1)(c) CT(DD)O
5   Sch 1 para 6(1)(d) CT(DD)O
6   Sch 1 paras 5(3) and 6(2) CT(DD)O
7   Sch 1 para 3 CT(DD)O
8   Sch 1 para 5(2) CT(DD)O
9   Sch 1 para 4(1) CT(DD)O
10 Sch 1 para 3 CT(DD)O
11 Council tax information letter 5, 29 April 1996
12 Sch 1 para 5 LGFA 1992
13 art 5 CT(DD)O
14 Reg 3 CT(ED)O
15 s74 LGA 2003
16 s6 LGFA 1992
17 ss9 and 77 LGFA 1992

3. Council tax benefit
18 Reg 33 CTB Regs
19 Reg 45(2) CTB Regs

4. Second adult rebate
20 s131(6)(a) and (7) SSCBA 1992

Chapter 24

....

Tax and national insurance

This chapter covers:
1. Income tax (below)
2. National insurance (p273)
3. Further information (p276)

This chapter provides a brief introduction to income tax and national insurance (NI) as they affect full-time students. For more detailed advice, contact your local HM Revenue and Customs office. More information can also be found at www.hmrc.gov.uk.

In principle, students are not in any special position with regard to income tax. However, local authority grants, most other educational grants and scholarships, most research awards, student loans, and grants from the Access to Learning Fund do not normally count as taxable income. This means that most full-time students do not have to pay income tax or NI contributions on their student support.

1. Income tax

Rates and allowances

Income tax is charged on assessable income (income from all sources not subject to tax exemption) received during a financial year (6 April to the following 5 April). The rates for the tax year 2008/09 are listed below.[1]

....

Income tax rates 2008/09
20 per cent basic rate on taxable income up to £34,800.
40 per cent higher rate on your taxable income above £34,800.

....

Every person resident in the UK has a personal allowance. This is an amount of yearly income on which you do not have to pay tax. It is deducted from total taxable income before the rate bands are applied. There may also be other tax allowances that you could claim, depending on your personal circumstances.

Income tax allowances 2008/09

Personal allowance[2]	£6,035
Blind person's allowance (additional)[3]	£1,800

Example

Alice earns £10,000 in her placement year. She pays no tax on the first £6,035 of this and 20 per cent on the remaining £3,965. This means her total income tax for the year is £793. If she were registered blind, she would not pay tax on the first £7,835 (the combination of her personal and blind person's allowances).

Non-domiciles

Most students coming from overseas will be regarded as non-domiciled (generally if you and/or your father were born outside the UK). This means different rules apply in some cases, but much will depend on your own circumstances. If you have any income or gains arising from any source outside the UK then you should contact HM Revenue and Customs (the Revenue) for advice.

Married students

The incomes of a husband and wife are taxed separately; each of them is responsible for his or her own tax returns.

Sponsorships and scholarships

Sponsorships and scholarships are not usually taxable, provided they do 'no more than support a student during a period of study'.[4] If you are required to work in a company or organisation and its sponsorship is part-payment for this, you should contact the Revenue for guidance.

Bank and building society interest

Banks and building societies have to deduct income tax from interest payments before they are credited to your savings account. However, if you believe your income will not exceed your personal allowance over the year, you can fill out Form R85 to allow your bank or building society to pay the interest without deducting tax. If tax is deducted from your interest and you are not due to pay any, or if the tax deducted is more than you are due to pay, you can claim the tax back by completing Form R40.

Rates of tax on savings income (above your personal allowance – see above) are 10 per cent (the starting rate), then 20 per cent (the basic rate) and finally 40 per cent (the higher rate).[5]

Taxable bands for savings income 2008/09

10 per cent starting rate	£0 – £2,320
20 per cent basic rate	£2,321 – £34,800
40 per cent higher rate	above £34,800

Dividends on shares are also taxed, at 10 per cent up to the basic rate limit of £34,800 and then at 32.5 per cent for any amount above that. If you have shares in a company, when you get your dividend it should be accompanied by a tax credit voucher which shows the amount of the dividend payable and the amount of the tax credit that goes with that dividend. '**Dividend income**' for tax purposes is the dividend plus the tax credit.[6]

The tax credit is not tax deducted on your behalf; rather, it represents the fact that the company paying the dividend has paid tax on the profits used to pay the dividend. The tax credit, which is 10 per cent of the dividend income, can therefore be set against your tax liability on the dividend. Put another way, as some tax has already been paid on these earnings the amount you have to pay is reduced accordingly.

For more information on receiving your interest without tax being deducted and about claiming tax back, see www.hmrc.gov.uk/taxback. There are links to Forms R40 and R85 (www.hmrc.gov.uk/menus/otherforms.htm), as well as to the leaflet *Bank and Building Society Interest: are you paying tax when you don't need to?* If you want to contact a Revenue office, go to www.hmrc.gov.uk/menus/contactus.shtml or telephone 020 7667 4001.

Paying tax on your earnings

Vacation and part-time earnings

Students who are employed during vacations would normally expect to have tax deducted at source under the pay-as-you-earn (PAYE) system. However, if you will not earn more than the balance of your personal allowance over the whole tax year (see p270) you should ask your employer to complete the Form P38(S), which enables the employer to pay your wages without deducting any tax. This does not apply to evening or part-time work outside normal holiday times, or to summer work where you expect to earn more than the personal allowance. In these instances, you are required to complete Form P46, unless you have a P45 from a previous employer. You may have to complete a tax return at the end of every tax year to prove to the Revenue that your total taxable income has not exceeded your personal allowance.

Example

Jamie takes a job during the summer vacation. He will work 24 hours a week and earn £7 an hour. The job is for eight weeks. Jamie will not work during term time so his annual income for income tax purposes is £1,344. This is below his personal allowance of £6,035 so he can ask his employer to complete Form P38(S).

Placement students

Wages or salaries paid to placement students during periods of practical experience (including sandwich courses) are taxable as earned income under PAYE, subject to the usual tax-free allowances. However, if you are a placement student, any wages/salary paid for periods spent at college, while normally taxable, can be paid tax free if:

- you are enrolled in college for at least one academic year; *and*
- attendance at college amounts to at least 20 weeks' full-time instruction within that academic year; *and*
- your earnings, including lodging or subsistence allowances, do not exceed £15,000 (excluding any fees paid by the employer).

These rules also apply if you are being released by your employer to study a course but continue to be paid as a full-time employee. If the qualifying period is less than one year, the above amounts should be reduced on a *pro rata* basis.

Further guidance is available at www.hmrc.gov.uk/students/wf27_1.htm.

How income tax is paid

Employed earners

Under the PAYE system, tax is deducted by your employer from each wage payment.

Self-employed earners

If you are self-employed, you pay tax directly to the Revenue. You have to pay assessed tax in two instalments (31 January and 31 July). Self-employed students may be required to complete a self-assessment return, which may require assistance to complete. Contact your local Revenue office for information and help. There is a specific helpline for self-assessment earners: 0845 900 0444.

Tax and benefits

Income support and housing benefit are not normally taxable. Jobseeker's allowance (JSA) (both contribution-based and income-based) is taxable. However, tax is not deducted while benefit is paid but instead reduces the refund you might otherwise receive through the PAYE system when you return to work.[7] Further information on taxation of JSA for students is available at www.hmrc.gov.uk/students/.

2. National insurance

National insurance (NI) is the government scheme to ensure that all those who earn above a certain amount contribute to the social security system. Paying into the scheme entitles you to a range of benefits later in life, including the state pension. The National Insurance Contributions Office keeps records of everyone's contributions and should issue you an NI number on your 16th birthday.

Employers need an NI number for each employee in order to comply with taxation law. If you do not have an NI number you will find it difficult to secure employment. If you lose your number, or do not have one – eg, if you are an international student who is permitted to work in the UK, you must contact your local Jobcentre Plus office or, in Northern Ireland, the Department for Social Development.

If a new number must be issued, the process can take several weeks to be completed. However, if you have lost your number, your employer can send the appropriate tax forms to HM Revenue and Customs (the Revenue) without one, and attempts will automatically be made to trace your number and inform your employer when it is found. If the Revenue cannot trace the number it will instruct your employer to use a temporary, randomly generated reference until a permanent number is issued or found.

Who must pay national insurance contributions

Vacation or part-time work

Students are not required to pay NI contributions on any forms of student support. However, if you take up employment and your pay exceeds the earnings threshold of £105 a week (or £455 a month) you must pay Class 1 (earnings-related) contributions. Your employer deducts these from your wages. The rate of contribution for 2008/09 is 11 per cent of all earnings above the £105 a week threshold but below £770. All earnings above £770 a week incur a 1 per cent rate of contribution.[8]

> *Example*
> Bob earns £800 a week. He pays no NI contributions on the first £105. He pays 11 per cent on the next £665 (£73.15) and 1 per cent on the remaining £30 (£0.30). His weekly NI contribution is, therefore, £73.45.

If you are self-employed, you have to pay flat-rate Class 2 contributions of £2.30 for each week of self-employment if your income exceeds £4,825 in the 2008/09 tax year. If you have a lower income you must apply for an exception.[9] You also have to pay Class 4 contributions of 8 per cent on profits or gains between £5,435 and £40,040 and 1 per cent on any amount above this, but only if you are resident in the UK for income tax purposes.[10] Contact the Revenue for more details.

Postgraduate students

If you are a research student you should check if you are liable for Class 1 or Class 2 contributions if you are paid for teaching or demonstrating.

Placement students

Placement students are liable to pay Class 1 contributions while receiving wages/salaries for periods of work experience, although this income can be classed as exempt scholarship income for periods spent attending college.

Note: if you have been released from work to take a course but continue to be paid by your employer, some of this income can qualify as scholarship income and is exempt from contributions. However, insufficient NI contributions can affect your entitlement to certain social security benefits. For more information, see www.hmrc.gov.uk/students/wf27_2.htm.

Age limits

No NI contributions are payable if you are under the age of 16 or over pension age, although you may have to apply for an exemption if your earnings would otherwise attract contributions.

Voluntary contributions

Your entitlement to the state retirement pension depends on you having paid NI contributions at a set level for a set number of years during your 'working life'. For anyone retiring after 6 April 2010, enough contributions for 30 years must have been paid to receive a full pension.

Reduced rates of the basic state pension are possible but NI contributions must still have been made at the correct rate for at least 25 per cent of the required time.

However, if you have not, or believe you may not have, paid this amount of contributions you can pay voluntary contributions to make up the 'missing' years. These contributions are paid at a flat rate under Class 3; the rate for 2008/09 is £8.10 a week.[11]

You can only preserve your entitlement to the state pension and to widows' and bereavement benefits in this way. If you do not have a recent record of employment you cannot gain access to short-term benefits (eg, income-based jobseeker's allowance (JSA), incapacity benefit (IB) and maternity benefit) by paying Class 3 contributions.

Deciding whether to pay voluntary contributions

Before committing yourself to paying voluntary Class 3 contributions, you should consult your local National Insurance Contributions Office (NICO) or contact the State Pension Forecasting Team on 0845 300 1068 or online at www.thepensionservice.gov.uk to establish your likely pension at retirement age and, therefore, whether it is necessary to make voluntary contributions in the light of your personal circumstances and overall contribution record. This is especially relevant if you are a mature or postgraduate student, have taken time out of work for children or caring duties, or have lived abroad for long periods of time during your working life. Under the current rules, most younger students will not have a reduction to any pension entitlement by not paying contributions during their studies, as they will have sufficient time after completing full-time education in which to qualify for full pension rights.

Voluntary contributions may generally only be paid up to the end of the sixth tax year after they were 'due' other than in exceptional circumstances. Again, contact the NICO for further information.

If you are thinking of replacing the additional state pension (previously the state earnings-related pension) with a personal or occupational pension, always check which would be the most advantageous for your personal circumstances. It is advisable to belong to the additional state pension scheme if you are within 20 years of retirement. Pension Service leaflets are available from Jobcentre Plus offices and Citizens Advice Bureaux or from www.thepensionservice.gov.uk.

Contribution rates

Contribution rates 6 April 2008 to 5 April 2009

Contribution type	Weekly earnings	Employee's contribution
Class 1	Below £105 (earnings threshold)	Nil
	£105.01–£770	11% (in additional state pension) 9.4% (contracted out of additional state pension)
	£770.01 and over	1%
Class 2 (self-employed)		£2.30 flat rate a week of self-employment
Class 3 (voluntary)		£8.10 a week flat rate
Class 4 (self-employed)	On profits between £5,435–£40,040	8%
	On profits above £40,040	1%

National insurance contributions and benefits

- **Class 1 contributions** may later entitle you to IB, employment and support allowance (ESA), income-based JSA, basic state pension, bereavement allowance and widowed parent's allowance.
- **Class 2 contributions** may later entitle you to IB, ESA, basic state pension, bereavement allowance and maternity allowance.

- **Class 3 contributions** allow you to top up your benefit entitlement to ensure a higher state pension, and widows' and bereavement benefits.
- **Class 4 contributions** do not lead to any social security benefit entitlements but they do attract some tax relief.

The exact level of necessary NI contributions varies depending on the benefit. Paying NI contributions does not entitle you to benefits you would not otherwise be able to claim as a student.

3. Further information

- HM Revenue and Customs website: www.hmrc.gov.uk.
- Information for students: www.hmrc.gov.uk/students/.
- Leaflet RD171 *Shortfall in Your Pension Contributions?*
- Information on claiming tax back: www.hmrc.gov.uk/taxback.
- Address of your nearest HM Revenue and Customs Office: www.hmrc.gov.uk/menus/contactus.shtml.
- Information on tax issues for students: www.litrg.org.uk

Notes

1. Income tax
  1 ss1 and 4 FA 2008
  2 s2 FA 2008
  3 s3 IT(I)O 2008
  4 s331(2) ICTA 1988
  5 s4 and Sch 1 FA 2008
  6 s8 ITA 2007
  7 ss671–75 IT(EP)A 2003

2. National insurance
  8 s1 NICA 2002
  9 s11 SSCBA 1992
  10 s15 SSCBA 1992
  11 s13 SSCBA 1992

Chapter 25

....

Time out from studies

This chapter covers:
1. Time out because of ill health (below)
2. Time out because of pregnancy or children (p281)
3. Time out to be a carer (p283)
4. Re-sits (p283)

This chapter provides a checklist of student support and benefits that you may be eligible for if you have to take time out from your studies. You must meet the usual rules of entitlement. For more details about a specific benefit, including how to claim, see the relevant chapter.

---

1. Time out because of ill health

Full-time students

If you are a full-time student, your entitlement to benefits depends on how long you have been ill, whether you have paid any national insurance (NI) contributions and whether you need personal care or have mobility difficulties. Most students are not eligible for benefits until they have been ill for 28 weeks. Once you have recovered from your illness, you may be able to 'sign on' for certain benefits until you can return to your course.

From the start of your ill health

You are eligible for incapacity benefit (IB) or employment and support allowance (ESA) after three days of incapacity for work if you have paid sufficient NI contributions in recent years.

If your claim started before 27 October 2008, you are eligible for IB. If your claim starts on or after that date, you are eligible for contributory ESA (a new benefit which replaces IB – see Chapter 10).

After three months

You can claim disability living allowance (DLA) if you need personal care or have mobility difficulties. You are eligible for this after three months if your disability is likely to last at least another six months.

If you get DLA you can also claim income-related ESA if you are claiming on or after ESA was introduced on 27 October 2008. Before this date, you could claim income support (IS) if you got DLA.

After 28 weeks

Claims before 27 October 2008
You can claim:
- IS for basic financial support and help with a mortgage if you have one;
- IB, if you were aged 19 or younger when your incapacity started and you claim before the end of a continuous period of 196 days (28 weeks) of incapacity that began before your 20th birthday (see Chapter 13);
- housing benefit (HB) to help with your rent (and rates in Northern Ireland if you are liable);
- council tax benefit (CTB) to help with your council tax if you are liable.

The 28-week period runs from the day your incapacity for work begins, not from the day you leave your course. You do not need to have been working to count as incapable of work. **Note:** you can be incapable of work but still be able to study, so IB can continue when you return to college or university.

Claims on or after 27 October 2008
You can claim:
- contributory ESA in youth from your 19th birthday. Ask your doctor for a backdated medical certificate for 28 weeks of limited capability for work. If you are already 20 by the time you have had 28 weeks of limited capability for work, you can still claim as long as you do so straight away, and as long as your limited capability for work started before your 20th birthday. Otherwise, if you are over 20 but under 25, you can claim contributory ESA in youth only if you leave the course;
- HB to help with your rent (and rates in Northern Ireland if you are liable);
- CTB to help with your council tax if you are liable.

The 28-week period runs from the day your limited capability for work begins, not from the day you leave your course. See p108 for how your limited capability for work is assessed. You do not need to have been working to count as having limited capability for work. **Note:** you can have limited capability for work but still able to study, so contributory ESA can continue when you return to college or university.

Once you have recovered
Once you have recovered, you may need to wait some time before you are re-admitted to your course. During this time you can claim:[1]
- jobseeker's allowance (JSA). You need to 'sign on' at your Jobcentre Plus office;

- HB;
- CTB.

You can claim from the day you recover until the day before the college or university agrees you can return to your course – up to a maximum of one year. You cannot claim the above benefits if you get a grant or loan during this period. Once the student support stops, you can claim.

Student support

Full-time undergraduate students under the 'old' or 'current' system of support (see Chapters 2, 3 and 4) receiving a student loan paid for living costs, higher education grants and supplementary grants may have their student support suspended after 60 days' absence because of ill health.[2] However, local authorities, Student Finance England (SFE) and education and library boards (ELBs) have the discretion to continue making student loan payments for living costs for the rest of the academic year.[3]

Your college or university should write to your local authority/SFE/ELB explaining why it has suspended you from your course. You should also contact your local authority/SFE/ELB in writing and request that it continues to pay you while you are ill.

Any student who is personally eligible can also apply to the college or university for discretionary help from the hardship fund, Access to Learning Fund or Financial Contingency Fund.

If you receive a bursary from your college or university and want to take time out from your studies, you should check with the institution to see if it will continue to be paid while you take the time out and what will happen when you return to your studies.

Example

Kerry is 23. She is studying for a degree in engineering at Manchester University.

She completes her first year on a full-time basis from September 2008 to July 2009, for which she receives a full student loan for tuition fees, a full student loan for living costs, a full maintenance grant and a £310 institutional bursary. She begins her second year in September 2009 and receives the same support. In February 2010 she has to suspend her studies because of illness. She will not be paid any further fee loan until she returns to her studies. She continues to receive her student loan for living costs and maintenance grant for 60 days. She applies to her local authority to have her student loan and grant payments extended while she is ill. The local authority agrees to continue her loan payments, but not her grant payments until she recovers from her illness, which is in June 2010. She applies to her institution for her bursary to continue to be paid. The institution agrees to this. Kerry agrees with her institution to return to her studies in January 2011. She can claim JSA from June 2010 until she returns to her studies in January 2011.

If you are receiving an adult learning grant and need to interrupt your studies for any reason, the guidance states:[4]

> Some ALG [adult learning grant] learners may require long-term absence and it is possible that this may interrupt their studies (for example maternity leave, broken limbs, jury service or terms of imprisonment). In such cases, we must balance the need to treat people as individuals with the overall rationale for ALG, which is to test the effect of a **weekly** allowance on participation, retention and achievement. There must be no unlawful discrimination against individuals, pregnant women must not be treated less favourably than a person sentenced to a term of imprisonment which interrupts their studies.

Therefore, your circumstances should be assessed on a weekly basis and consideration given to how the payment will affect your ability to continue your studies and achieve your qualification.

Part-time students

If you are a part-time student you can claim IS (before 27 October 2008) or income-related ESA (on or after 27 October 2008) as soon as you are ill and incapable of work. You do not need to wait 28 weeks and you can claim whether or not you get DLA.

From the start of your ill health

Claims before 27 October 2008
From the start of your ill health you can claim:
- IS;
- IB, if you have paid sufficient NI contributions in recent years;
- HB;
- CTB.

You should claim IS and IB at the same time. Use Form SC1 for IB and Form A1 for IS. Depending on the claimant's age, IB is often paid at lower levels than IS, at least to start with, so you may get IB topped up with a small amount of IS.

If you are already getting JSA, you continue to receive it for two weeks. After two weeks, you need to claim IS and/or IB instead.

Claims on or after 27 October 2008
From this date ESA replaces IB and IS on the grounds of incapacity or disability. You can claim:
- ESA if your income is low or you have not paid enough NI contributions;
- HB;
- CTB.

After three months

You can claim DLA if you need personal care or have mobility difficulties. You are eligible for this after three months if your disability is likely to last for at least another six months.

After 28 weeks

Claims before 27 October 2008

You can claim IB if you were aged 19 when your incapacity started and you claim before the end of a continuous period of 196 days (28 weeks) of incapacity that began before your 20th birthday.

The 28-week period runs from the day your incapacity for work begins, not from the day you leave your course.

Claims on or after 27 October 2008

Although you can claim ESA from the start of your ill health, if you have not paid enough NI contributions you will not get contributory ESA and you will only get income-related ESA if your income is low. If you are turned down for these reasons, you can claim contributory ESA again after 28 weeks if your ill health began before your 20th birthday. This is called contributory ESA in youth (see p105).

Once you have recovered

You can claim JSA if you are available for work.

2. **Time out because of pregnancy or children**

Student support

If you are a full-time undergraduate student receiving a student loan paid for living costs and any grants for living costs, your local authority, Student Finance England (SFE) or education and library board (ELB) has the discretion to continue making these payments for the rest of that academic year.[5]

Your college or university should write to your local authority/SFE/ELB explaining why it has suspended you from your course. You should also contact your local authority/SFE/ELB in writing and request that it continues to pay you while you are taking time out.

If you are an NHS-funded healthcare student in England or Wales you can continue to receive your bursary whilst on maternity leave. Contact the Student Grants Unit in England or Wales for details.

You could also apply to your college or university for support from the hardship fund, Access to Learning Fund or Financial Contingency Fund.

If you receive a bursary from your college or university and want to take time out from your studies, you should check with the institution to see if this will continue to be paid while you take the time out and what will happen when you return to your studies.

If you receive an adult learning grant, see p280.

Benefits

There is no provision for pregnant full-time students to claim income support (IS) or housing benefit (HB).

As a part-time student, you can claim IS once you reach the 11th week before your 'expected week of childbirth', or earlier if your pregnancy has made you ill and incapable of work.

If you have an employer you may be able to get statutory maternity pay. If you are not working now but have worked recently, you may be able to get maternity allowance.

Once the baby is born there are various benefits you can claim.

See Chapter 16 for more details.

Lone parents

Once the baby is born, a lone parent can claim the following while studying full time:
- child benefit;
- child tax credit (CTC);
- IS if your youngest child is 16 (12 from 26 November 2008;
- jobseeker's allowance in the summer vacation (for those who are not eligible for IS, or those who are eligible but would prefer to claim JSA instead);
- HB;
- council tax benefit (CTB) (if liable for council tax).

Fathers and partners

If your partner has had a baby and you have an employer, you may be able to claim statutory paternity pay. You can claim if you are the child's father or the mother's partner (married, unmarried or of the same sex) and you will be caring for the baby or the mother.

Couples

A full-time student couple (ie, both of you are students) with a child can claim the following throughout the course:
- child benefit;
- CTC;

- HB;
- CTB (if liable for council tax).

A full-time student couple with a child can claim the following in the long vacation:
- IS (if eligible under the usual non-student rules); *or*
- JSA.

Couples can also claim a Sure Start maternity grant if one of them gets a qualifying benefit (see p201).

If you are a full-time student and a parent and you have a partner who is not a student, they can claim benefits for you under the usual benefit rules.

3. **Time out to be a carer**

If you are a full-time student, you may have stopped doing your course to care for someone. If you suspend your studies, your local authority, Student Finance England or education and library board has the discretion to keep paying your student loan and grant for living costs, if you have been receiving one.[6] You could also apply to your college or university for support from the hardship fund, Access to Learning Fund or Financial Contingency Fund.

If, once your caring responsibilities come to an end, you have to wait before you can return to the course, you can 'sign on' for jobseeker's allowance, and claim housing benefit and council tax benefit. You can claim for up to a year until the day from which the university or college agrees you can return to your course.[7] You are not eligible, however, if you get a grant or loan during this time.

If you receive a bursary from your college or university and want to take time out from your studies, you should check with the institution to see if this will continue to be paid while you take the time out and what will happen when you return to your studies.

If you receive an adult learning grant, see p280.

See Chapter 7 for information on claiming carer's allowance.

4. **Re-sits**

If you are a full-time student taking time out to re-sit exams, you are still treated as a student during your absence from the course. You cannot claim income support (IS) or jobseeker's allowance (JSA) during this time, unless you would be eligible anyway as a student (eg, as a lone parent or disabled student).

One exception applies to students taking professional qualifications set by a professional institute or some other body unconnected with their own college or university – eg, chartered accountants. They may be able to claim IS or JSA while taking time out for re-sits. If you are in this situation, you may need to be prepared to appeal and argue that caselaw supports you getting benefit.[8]

If you receive a bursary from your college or university and want to take time out from your studies, you should check with the institution to see if this will continue to be paid while you take the time out and what will happen when you return to your studies.

Notes

1. **Time out because of ill health**
   1 **JSA** Reg 1(3D) JSA Regs; para 30121 DMG
     HB Reg 56(6) HB Regs
     CTB Reg 45(7) CTB Regs
     HB/CTB Circular A32/2000 para 6
   2 Reg 110(12) E(SS) Regs
   3 Reg 110 (10)-(11) E(SS) Regs
   4 ALG guidance, section 7.1.6

2. **Time because of pregnancy or children**
   5 Reg 110(10)-(11) E(SS) Regs

3. **Time out to be a carer**
   6 Reg 110(10)-(11) E(SS) Regs
   7 **JSA** Reg 1 JSA Regs
     HB Reg 56(6) HB Regs
     CTB Reg 45(7) CTB Regs
     HB/CTB Circular A32/2000 para 6

4. **Re-sits**
   8 CJSA/1457/1999

Appendices

Appendix 1

Information and advice

Student support

Official guidance

The Department for Innovation, Universities and Skills (DIUS) issues guidance on existing higher education (HE) student support legislation and forthcoming provision. The guidance has no legal standing, but may be quoted in an appeal. It is available at www.dius.gov.uk. Guidance includes:

- notes for local authorities on the student support regulations;
- *Student Support Update* – a monthly newsletter;
- student support information notes containing announcements of forthcoming student support provision;
- Access to Learning Fund guidance for colleges.

The DIUS also issues guidance to local authorities on implementing education maintenance allowances. This is available at ema.direct.gov.uk/. There is also guidance issued for adult learning grants, available at the Learning and Skills Council (LSC) website at www.alg.lsc.gov.uk. The LSC also provides guidance on implementing the Learner Support Fund. This is available at lsf.lsc.gov.uk. Information and guidance on funding in Wales is available from the Welsh Assembly at www.wales.gov.uk. Information and support fund guidance for HE institutes in Northern Ireland is available on the Department for Employment and Learning website at www.delni.gov.uk.

Advice

Contact student advisers within institutions and students' unions for advice on student support. A list of advisory services is available at the website of the National Association of Student Money Advisers at www.nasma.org.uk.

Social security benefits and tax credits

Publications

The following guide books are available from CPAG at 94 White Lion Street, London N1 9PF. An order form is available at www.cpag.org.uk/publications, or telephone CPAG on 020 7837 7979.

- *Benefits for Students in Scotland* 2008/09, £12.50

- *Welfare Benefits and Tax Credits Handbook* 2008/09, £35. Also available online – visit http://onlineservices.cpag.org.uk for more information.
- *Council Tax Handbook* 7th edition (November 2007) £16
- *Guide to Housing Benefit and Council Tax Benefit* 2008/09, £24
- *The Young Person's Handbook*, 8th edition (September 2007) £15.95

Official guidance

The following guidance, used by decision makers in the Department for Work and Pensions (DWP) and local authorities, is available at www.dwp.gov.uk. Select 'resource centre/other specialist information/for professionals and advisers'. This guidance has no legal standing so you cannot quote it in an appeal, but it can be useful if you are seeking to have a decision overturned by an internal revision or supersession.

In Northern Ireland, the equivalent guidance is provided by the Department of Social Development (DSD), available at www.dsdni.gov.uk.

- *Decision Makers Guide*
- *A Guide to Housing Benefit and Council Tax Benefit*
- *A Guide to Income Support*
- *A Guide to Incapacity Benefit*

Legislation

- *The Law Relating to Social Security*
  - Volume 6 deals with income support
  - Volume 8 deals with housing benefit and council tax benefit
  - Volume 11 deals with jobseeker's allowance

  This is available at www.dwp.gov.uk. These volumes are officially produced and contain updated Acts and Regulations relating to social security.
- *Social Security Legislation*, Volumes 1 to 4. Published by Sweet and Maxwell, these volumes contain updated Acts and Regulations covering social security and tax credits with explanatory commentary. Available from CPAG.
- CPAG's *Housing Benefit and Council Tax Benefit Legislation*. Published by CPAG, this contains updated Acts and Regulations and a detailed commentary. Also available online – visit http://onlineservices.cpag.org.uk for more information.
- *Decisions of the social security commissioners*. Reported decisions are available from the DWP website at www.dwp.gov.uk. Unreported decisions are available from the website of the commissioners' office at www.osscsc.gov.uk.

Advice

Contact your student services department or students' union for advice.

Appendix 2

Useful addresses

General sources of information

Child Poverty Action Group

94 White Lion Street
London N1 9FP
Tel: 020 7837 7979
Advice line: 020 7833 4627
(2–4pm Monday to Friday)
advice@cpag.org.uk
www.cpag.org.uk

CPAG provides an advice,
information and training service to
advisers.

Educational Grants Advisory Service

501–505 Kingsland Road
London E8 4AU
www.egas-online.org/

EGAS gives information on
alternative sources of student
funding. Complete a questionnaire
on its website or send a SAE.

National Union of Students

Second Floor
Centro 3
19 Mandela Street
London NW1 0DU
Tel: 0871 221 8221
www.nus.org.uk

NUS provides information on
entitlement to student support,
benefits and tax credits, along with
other student welfare issues.

National Union of Students-Union of Students in Ireland

42 Dublin Road
Belfast BT2 7HN
Tel: 028 90 244641
www.nistudents.org/

NUS-USI represents students in
Northern Ireland and can provide
advice and information on student
support and benefits.

Skill: National Bureau for Students with Disabilities

Chapter House
18–20 Crucifix Lane
London SE1 3JW
Tel/minicom: 020 7450 0620
Information service: 0800 328 5050
Information service minicom: 0800
068 2422
info@skill.org.uk
www.skill.org.uk

Skill produces a number of booklets
and information sheets.

UKCISA (UK Council for International Student Affairs)
9–17 St Albans Place
London N1 0NX
Tel: 020 7288 4330
Helpline: 020 7107 9922 1–4pm,
Monday to Friday
www.ukcisa.org.uk

UKCISA provides advice and information for overseas students.

Support for learning

Arts and Humanities Research Council
Whitefriars
Lewins Mead
Bristol BS1 2AE
Tel: 0117 987 6500
www.ahrc.ac.uk

Biotechnology and Biological Sciences Research Council
Polaris House
North Star Avenue
Swindon SN2 1UH
Tel: 01793 413 200
www.bbsrc.ac.uk

Care Council for Wales
Sixth Floor, West Wing
South Gate House
Wood Street
Cardiff CF10 1EW
Tel: 029 2022 6257
Fax: 029 2038 4764
info@ccwales.org.uk
www.ccwales.org.uk

The CCW provides bursary support to undergraduate social work students in Wales.

Career development loans
Tel: 0800 585 505
www.direct.gov.uk/cdl

Dance and drama awards
www.direct.gov.uk/danceanddrama

Department for Children, Schools and Families
Sanctuary Buildings
Great Smith Street
London SW1P 3BT
Tel: 0870 000 2288
Info@dcsf.gsi.gov.uk
www.dcsf.gov.uk

Responsible for learner support for 16–19-year-olds in England.

Department of Education, Lifelong Learning and Skills
Tel: 08456 088 066
www.wales.gov.uk

Responsible for education funding in Wales.

Department for Employment and Learning
Student Support Branch
4th Floor
Adelaide House
39–49 Adelaide Street
Belfast BT2 8FD
Tel: 028 9025 7777
Fax: 028 9025 7778
studentsupport@delni.gov.uk
www.delni.gov.uk

Responsible for student support in Northern Ireland.

Department of Health
PO Box 77
London SE1 6XH
Tel: 08701 555 455
Fax: 01623 724524
doh@prolog.uk.com
www.dh.gov.uk

Responsible for NHS-funded
students in England.

**Department of Health, Social Services
and Public Safety**
Bursary Administration Unit
Central Services Agency
25 Adelaide Street
Belfast BT2 8FH
Tel: 028 9055 3661
Fax: 028 9055 3689
www.dhsspsni.gov.uk

Provides financial support for
nursing and midwifery students in
Northern Ireland. It also provides
bursaries for social work students in
Northern Ireland.

Social Work Student Incentive Scheme
Castle Buildings
Stormont
Belfast BT4 3SQ
Tel: 028 9052 0517

**Department for Innovation,
Universities and Skills**
Tel: 0870 0010 336
info@dius.gsi.gov.uk
www.dius.gov.uk
www.studentfinanceengland.co.uk

Responsible for student support for
higher education in England and for
adult learners in further education in
England. DIUS booklets and leaflets
are available from the above number

or the student finance direct website.
They include:
- *Bridging the Gap: a guide for the
  disabled students' allowance (DSA)
  in higher education in 2008/09*
- *Childcare Grant and Other Financial
  Help for Student Parents in Higher
  Education 2008/09*
- *Financial Support for Higher Educa-
  tion Students in 2008/09*
- *Financial Help for Part-time Higher
  Education Students 2008/09*
- *Money to Learn: financial help for
  adults in further education and
  training*

**Department for Innovation,
Universities and Skills European Team**
Student Finance Services European
Team
PO Box 89
Darlington DL1 9AZ
Tel: 0141 243 3570
euteam@slc.co.uk

Provides information about
applications by European Union
students for fee payment support in
England.

Economic and Social Research Council
Polaris House
North Star Avenue
Swindon SN2 1UJ
Tel: 01793 413 000
www.esrc.ac.uk

Educational Guidance Service for Adults
4th Floor
40 Linenhall Street
Belfast BT2 8BA
Tel: 028 9024 4274
info@egsa.org.uk
www.money2learn.com

Engineering and Physical Sciences Research Council
Polaris House
North Star Avenue
Swindon SN2 1ET
Tel: 01793 444 000
www.epsrc.ac.uk

Learning and Skills Council
Tel: 0870 900 6800
info@lsc.gov.uk
www.lsc.gov.uk

Allocates funding to colleges in England for post-16 education.

Medical Research Council
20 Park Crescent
London W1B 1AL
Tel: 020 7636 5422
www.mrc.ac.uk

Natural Environment Research Council
Polaris House
North Star Avenue
Swindon SN2 1EU
Tel: 01793 411 500
www.nerc.ac.uk

NHS Business Services Authority
Social Work Bursary
Sandyford House
Archbold Terrace
Newcastle Upon Tyne NE2 1DB
Tel: 0845 610 1122
www.ppa.org.uk/swb

Administers social work bursaries for all social work students in England.

NHS Careers Helpline
Tel: 0845 6060 655

The English National Board for Nursing, Midwifery and Health Visiting no longer deals with enquiries, but information on entry into these professions can be obtained from the NHS Careers Helpline.

NHS Student Grants Unit
Hesketh House
200-220 Broadway
Fleetwood
Lancashire FY7 8SS
Tel: 0845 358 6655
bursary@nhspa.gov.uk
www.nhsstudentgrants.co.uk

Provides information on funding and assessments for students undertaking allied health professions courses in England.

NHS (Wales) Student Awards Unit
3rd Floor
14 Cathedral Road
Cardiff CF11 9LJ
Tel: 029 2019 6167
www.nliah.wales.nhs.uk

Provides information and assessments for students undertaking allied health professions courses in Wales.

Science and Technology Facilities Council
Polaris House
North Star Avenue
Swindon SN2 1SZ
Tel: 01793 442 000
www.scitech.ac.uk

Student Loans Company Ltd

100 Bothwell Street
Glasgow G2 7JD
Tel: 0800 405 010
Minicom: 0800 085 3950
Fax: 0141 306 2005
www.slc.co.uk

Training and Development Agency for Schools

Tel: 0845 6000 991 (for English speakers)
Tel: 0845 6000 992 (for Welsh speakers)
Minicom: 0117 915 8161
www.tda.gov.uk

Responsible for teacher training in England.

Universities and Colleges Admissions Service

Rose Hill
New Barn Lane
Cheltenham GL52 3LZ
Tel: 0870 1122 211
Minicom: 01242 544 942
enquiries@ucas.ac.uk
www.ucas.com

Contact UCAS for information on applying to higher education, or to obtain copies of two useful booklets:
* *A Parent's Guide to Higher Education*
* *A Mature Student's Guide to Higher Education*

Benefits and tax credits

Benefit Enquiry Line

Victoria House
9th Floor
Ormskirk Raod
Preston PR1 2QR
Tel: 0800 88 22 00

Child Tax Credit and Working Tax Credit Helpline

England and Wales:
Tel: 0845 300 3900
Textphone: 0845 300 3909

Northern Ireland:
Tel: 0845 603 2000
Textphone: 0845 607 6078

Department for Social Development

www.dsdni.gov.uk

Responsible for social security in Northern Ireland.

Department for Work and Pensions

Caxton House
Tothill Street
London SW1H 9DA
www.dwp.gov.uk

Responsible for social security in England, Wales and Scotland. The website has information on entitlement to benefits and provides advisers with the decision makers' guidance.

HM Revenue and Customs

Tax Credits Office
Preston PR1 0SB
Tel/textphone: 0845 300 3900 (England and Wales)
Tel/textphone: 0845 603 2000 (Northern Ireland)
www.hmrc.gov.uk

Local Government Ombudsman

Tel: 0845 602 1983
www.lgo.org.uk

Investigates claims of maladministration by local authorities in England in respect of benefit claims or student support applications.

Public Services Ombudsman for Wales

1 Ffordd yr Hen Gae
Pencoed CF35 5LJ
Tel: 01656 641 150
www.ombudsman-wales.org.uk

Investigates claims of maladministration by local authorities in Wales in respect of benefit claims or student support applications.

Northern Ireland Ombudsman's Office

Freepost BEL 1478
Belfast BT1 6BR
Tel: 0800 34 34 24
www.ni-ombudsman.org.uk/

Investigates claims of maladministration by local authorities in Northern Ireland in respect of benefit claims or student support applications.

HM Revenue and Customs

www.hmrc.gov.uk/students

For information on claiming tax back: www.hmrc.gov.uk/taxback
For the address of your nearest HMRC office: www.hmrc.gov.uk/menus/contactus.shtml

NHS Business Services Authority Patient Services

Tel: 0845 850 1166
www.ppa.org.uk

Advises students on low-income scheme claims.

Other issues

Department of Health

PO Box 777
London SE1 6XH
Tel: 08701 555 455
Fax: 01623 724 524
dh@prolog.uk.com

For bulk orders of HC1 forms (eg, for students' union advice centres).

Appendix 3

Abbreviations used in the notes

General abbreviations

Art(s)   Article(s)
EWHC   England and Wales High Court
para(s)   paragraph(s)
reg(s)   regulation(s)
s(s)   Section(s)
Sch(s)   Schedule(s)

Acts of Parliament

Acts of Parliament can be ordered from The Stationery Office, PO Box 276, London SW8 5DR (tel: 0870 600 5522; fax: 0870 600 5533). Recent Acts are available at www.hmso.gov.uk.

CA 1989   Children Act 1989
C(LC)A 2000   Children (Leaving Care) Act 2000
CPA 2004   Civil Partnership Act 2004
EA 1988   Employment Act 1988
EA 1989   Employment Act 1989
ETA 1973   Employment and Training Act 1973
FA 2005   Finance Act 2005
HEA 2004   Higher Education Act 2004
ICTA 1988   Income and Corporation Tax Act 1988
IT(EP)A 2003   Income Tax (Earnings and Pensions) Act 2003
JSA 1995   Jobseeker's Act 1995
LGA 2003   Local Government Act 2003
LGFA 1992   Local Government Finance Act 1992
LSA 2000   Learning and Skills Act 2000
NHSA 1977   National Health Service Act 1977
NICA 2002   National Insurance Contributions Act 2002
PA 1995   Pensions Act 1995
SSAA 1992   Social Security Administration Act 1992

SSCBA 1992	Social Security Contributions and Benefits Act 1992
TCA 2002	Tax Credit Act 2002
THEA 1998	Teaching and Higher Education Act 1998

Regulations

Regulations can be ordered from The Stationery Office, PO Box 276, London SW8 5DR (tel: 0870 600 5522; fax: 0870 600 5533). Recent Regulations are available at www.hmso.gov.uk. Each set of Regulations has a statutory instrument (SI) number and a date. You ask for them by giving their date and number.

ALGL(HE)(W) Regs	The Assembly Learning Grants and Loans (Higher Education)(Wales) Regulations 2008 No.1273
CB Regs	The Child Benefit (General) Regulations 2006 No.223
C(LC)(E) Regs	The Children (Leaving Care) (England) Regulations 2001 No.2874
C(LC)(W) Regs	The Children (Leaving Care) (Wales) Regulations 2001 No.1855
CT(DD)O	The Council Tax (Discount Disregards) Order 1992 No.548
CT(ED)O	The Council Tax (Exempt Dwellings) Order 1992 No.558
CTB Regs	The Council Tax Benefit (General) Regulations 2006 No.215
CTB(SPC) Regs	The Council Tax Benefit (Persons who have Attained the Qualifying Age for State Pension Credit) Regulations 2006 No.216
CTC Regs	The Child Tax Credit Regulations 2002 No.2007
E(ALGS)(W) Regs	The Education (Assembly Learning Grant Scheme) (Wales) Regulations 2002 No.1857
E(G)(DD)(E) Regs	The Education (Grants, etc.) (Dance and Drama) (England) Regulations 2001 No.2857
E(GDPS) Regs	The Education (Grants for Disabled Postgraduate Students) Regulations 2000 No.2330
E(MA) Regs	The Education (Mandatory Awards) Regulations 2003 No.1994
EMA(PA) Regs	The Education Maintenance Allowance (Pilot Areas) Regulations 2001 No.2750
E(SS) Regs	The Education (Student Support) Regulations 2008 No.529
E(SS) No.2 Regs	The Education (Student Support) (No.2) Regulations 2008 No.1582
E(SS)(NI) Regs	The Education (Student Support) (Northern Ireland) Regulations 2008 No.250
E(WMTTIS) Regs	The Education (Welsh Medium Teacher Training Incentive Supplement) Regulations 1990 No.1208

HB Regs	The Housing Benefit (General) Regulations 2006 No.213
HB(SPC) Regs	The Housing Benefit (persons who have attained the qualifying age for state pension credit) Regulations 2006 No.214
HSS&WF(A) Regs	The Healthy Start Scheme and Welfare Food (Amendment) Regulations 2005 No.3262
IS Regs	The Income Support (General) Regulations 1987 No.1967
IT(I)O	The Income Tax (Indexation) Order 2005
IT(I)(No.2) O	The Income Tax (Indexation) (No.2) Order 2004 No.3161
JSA Regs	The Jobseeker's Allowance Regulations 1996 No.207
NA(AR) Regs	The National Assistance (Assessment of Resources) Regulations 1992 No. 2977
NHS(CDA) Regs	The National Health Service (Charges for Drugs and Appliances) Regulations 2000 No.620
NHS(DC) Regs	The National Health Service (Dental Charges) Regulations 1989 No.394
NHS(DC) Regs	The National Health Service (Dental Charges) (Wales) Regulations 2006 No.491
NHS(FP&CDA)(W) Regs	The National Health Service (Free Prescriptions and Charges for Drugs and Appliances) (Wales) Regulations 2007 No.121
NHS(GOS) Regs	The National Health Service (General Ophthalmic Services) Regulations 1986 No.975
NHS(OCP) Regs	The National Health Service (Optical Charges and Payments) Regulations 1997 No.818
NHS(TERC) Regs	The National Health Service (Travelling Expenses and Remission of Charges) Regulations 2003 No.2382
NHS(TERC)(W) Regs	The National Health Service (Travelling Expenses and Remission of Charges) (Wales) Regulations 2007 No.1104
SFCWP Regs	The Social Fund Cold Weather Payments (General) Regulations 1988 No.1724
SFM&FE Regs	The Social Fund Maternity and Funeral Expenses (General) Regulations 2005 No.3061
SPPSAP(G) Regs	The Statutory Paternity and Statutory Adoption Pay (General) Regulations 2002 No.2822
SS(C&P) Regs	The Social Security (Claims and Payments) Regulations 1987 No.1968
SS(C)(RNIFP)O	The Social Security (Contributions) (Re-rating and National Insurance Funds Payments) Order 2005 No.878
SS(DLA) Regs	The Social Security (Disability Living Allowance) Regulations 1991 No.2890
SS(ICA) Regs	The Social Security (Invalid Care Allowance) Regulations 1976 No.409

TC(DCI) Regs	The Tax Credits (Definition and Calculation of Income) Regulations 2002 No.2006
TC(ITDR) Regs	The Tax Credits (Income Thresholds and Determination of Rates) Regulations 2002 No.2008
WTC (EMR) Regs	The Working Tax Credit (Entitlement and Maximum Rate) Regulations 2002 No.2005

Other abbreviations

ALG Guidance	Adult Learning Grant Guidance
DMG	Decision Makers Guide
EMA Guidance	Education Maintenance Allowance Guidance
GM	The Housing Benefit and Council Tax Benefit Guidance Manual
IR	Inland Revenue leaflets
LEA Guidance	Local Education Authority Guidance on the E(SS) Regs and E(MA) Regs
SF Dir	Social fund directive
SFG	The Social Fund Guide

See Appendix 1 for more details.

References like CIS/142/1990 and R(SB) 3/89 are references to commissioners' decisions.

Index

How to use this Index

Entries against the bold headings direct you to the general information on the subject, or where the subject is covered most fully. Sub-entries are listed alphabetically and direct you to specific aspects of the subject.

The following abbreviations are used in the index to refer to welfare benefits:

CA	carer's allowance	HB	housing benefit
CTB	council tax benefit	IB	incapacity benefit
CTC	child tax credit	IS	income support
DLA	disability living allowance	JSA	jobseeker's allowance
ESA	employment and support allowance	WTC	working tax credit

ORDER FORM

for more copies of this or other CPAG Handbooks

BENEFITS FOR STUDENTS IN SCOTLAND HANDBOOK, 2008/09 edition

6th annual edition – fully updated to cover the latest changes.

September 2008   978 1 906076 19 1   £12.50

CHILDREN'S HANDBOOK SCOTLAND: A benefits guide for children living away from their parents, 1st edition: 2008/09

A brand new Handbook funded by the Scottish Government as part of its Getting It Right for Every Child programme.

November 2008   978 1 906076 17 7   £12.00

WELFARE BENEFITS AND TAX CREDITS HANDBOOK, 2008/09 edition

The definitive comprehensive guide to all benefits and tax credits. See next page for details of how to access this *Handbook* online. Like the other titles listed below, this Handbook has full coverage of the position in Scotland.

April 2008   978 1 906076 12 2   £36.00

(£8.50 post free for individual benefit claimants – direct from CPAG)

FUEL RIGHTS HANDBOOK, 14th edition

The standard practical guide to coping with fuel bills, debt and related problems with fuel supply. Fully updated with all major changes since the previous (2005) edition.

March 2008   978 1 906076 05 4   £17.00

COUNCIL TAX HANDBOOK, 7th edition

This authoritative guide to all aspects of the tax is fully updated with all changes since the previous (2005) edition.

November 2007   978 1 906076 06 1   £16.00

PERSONAL FINANCE HANDBOOK, 2nd edition

Fully updated for general advisers, teachers, consumers and anyone involved in financial literacy work, this Handbook is an accessible guide to everyday financial products and services.

October 2007   978 1 906076 01 6   £15.00

Payment with order

_____ Benefits for Students in Scotland Handbook @ £12.50 each   £_____
_____ Children's Handbook Scotland @ £12.00 each   £_____
_____ Welfare Benefits & Tax Credits Handbook @ £36.00 each   £_____
_____ Fuel Rights Handbook @ £17.00 each   £_____
_____ Council Tax Handbook @ £16.00 each   £_____
_____ Personal Finance Handbook @ £15.00 each   £_____

Postage & packing: For orders up to £100 in value, add £3.99 flat fee;
                   £100.01–£400, add £5.99;
                   over £400, add £9.99.   P&P: £_____
                                                 Total: £_____

I enclose a cheque/PO for £_____ payable to Child Poverty Action Group

Title _____ First Name _____ Last Name _____

Organisation _____ Dept _____

Address _____

_____ Postcode _____

Return form with payment to: CPAG, Dept SSHBK, 94 White Lion Street, London N1 9PF
For details of ordering by credit/debit card or for other information see www.cpag.org.uk

CPAG Online Information Services

CPAG's online services contain the web's most comprehensive in-depth information on welfare benefits, tax credits and child support. Accessed with a simple username and password, they make it easy for subscribers to find the information they need. There is full coverage of the position in Scotland. Annual subscriptions can include any or all of the four packages.

- **CPAG's Welfare Benefits and Tax Credits Online** (basic version)
  The main *Handbook* text, updated throughout the year. For users who want an updated, searchable online *Handbook* but don't need access to legislation/caselaw. Price per concurrent user for annual subscription: £36 + VAT (£42.30 inc)

- **CPAG's Welfare Benefits and Tax Credits Law Online**
  Includes the *Handbook* text updated throughout the year, with consolidated social security and tax credit legislation plus commissioners' decisions and caselaw. Footnotes in the *Handbook* link directly to the relevant law. Price per concurrent user for annual subscription: £48 + VAT (£56.40 inc)

- **CPAG's Child Support Law Online**
  Consists of the *Child Support Handbook* text linked to legislation and caselaw. The *Handbook* text is updated once a year in line with the print edition, but the legislation and caselaw are updated throughout the year. Price per concurrent user for annual subscription: £29 + VAT (£34.08 inc)

- **CPAG's Housing Benefit and Council Tax Benefit Law Online**
  This has the commentary from *CPAG's HB/CTB Legislation* (Findlay), updated twice a year in line with the print edition, linked to legislation, commissioners' decisions/ caselaw updated throughout the year. Price per concurrent user for annual subscription: £100 + VAT (£117.50 inc)

Visit the online services homepage (http://onlineservices.cpag.org.uk) to get more information on the packages, see the latest updates and sign up for a free 7-day trial.

Bulk discounts: 10% off for 10 or more users and 20% off for 25 or more users. Please contact Ldawson@cpag.org.uk if you have 50 or more users.

Payment with order

No. users

_____ CPAG's Welfare Benefits and Tax Credits Online (basic) @ £36.00 + VAT
(£42.30 inc) each   £_____

_____ CPAG's Welfare Benefits and Tax Credits Law Online @ £48.00 + VAT
(£56.40 inc) each   £_____

_____ CPAG's Child Support Law Online @ £29.00 + VAT (£34.08 inc) each   £_____

_____ CPAG's Housing Benefit and Council Tax Benefit Law Online @ £100.00 + VAT
(£117.50 inc) each   £_____

Total: £_____

I enclose a cheque/PO for £_____ payable to Child Poverty Action Group

Title _____ First Name _____ Last Name _____

Organisation _____ Dept _____

Address _____

_____Postcode _____

Email (to receive your online password): _____

Return this form to: CPAG, Dept SSHBK, 94 White Lion Street, London N1 9PF